Contents

	Introduction	4
1	Stages in the design process	6
2	Aesthetics	20
3	Ergonomics	38
4	Structures	46
5	Mechanisms	70
6	Control electrics and electronics	108
7	Pneumatics	168
8	Materials	196
9	Energy	273
	Numerical answers	309
	List of suppliers	310
	Project index	311
	Index	314
	Acknowledgements	319

Introduction

We live in a **high technology society**. In simple terms this means that our way of life, our standard of living and the wealth of our country is dependent upon the manufacture of sophisticated products and, of course, all of these have to be **designed**. Indeed, everything which has ever been made was designed by someone. I wonder how many different things *you* have designed without actually realising it? The layout of a room perhaps, a flower bed in the garden, the cover for a school book and so on. But what 'makes' someone design something? It happens because human beings like to be creative and when a person 'sees a problem' or 'identifies a need' the reaction is to try to 'do something about it'. Look at the photographs here and see if you can 'work out' the needs which inspired the designs.

To a stone-age family standing in the rain, the need for shelter might appear obvious. It is not always so easy, however, to **identify needs** in today's world – but this is one of the skills *you* will be expected to develop whilst studying design and technology at school.

To our early ancestors, with only limited materials and skills, design was probably a very 'hit and miss' affair. Today we have numerous different materials and access to an enormous range of information, knowledge and skills. Further, we have the facilities for using these resources to their best advantage to ensure that our designs **work well**, **look good**, are **safe to use** and so on. Even so, it is important to realise that the manufacture, use and disposal of any product will have both beneficial and detrimental effects upon people, wildlife and the environment. Look at the photographs again and think for a moment about how the various technologies identified are beneficial and in what ways they can cause harm. For example, chemical technology has provided farmers with insecticides and artificial fertilizers. The benefits include increased crop yields and cheaper food in the shops. Among the negative effects, however, is the pollution of rivers and lakes.

Chemical technology: crop spraying

Materials technology: product packaging

Vehicle technology: heavy transport

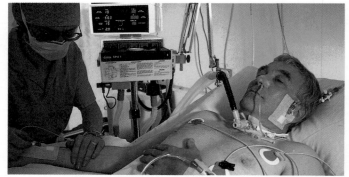
Medical technology: intensive care unit

Design and Technology

JAMES GARRATT

The right of the
University of Cambridge
to print and sell
all manner of books
was granted by
Henry VIII in 1534.
The University has printed
and published continuously
since 1584.

CAMBRIDGE UNIVERSITY PRESS

Cambridge   New York   Port Chester   Melbourne   Sydney

Published by the Press Syndicate of the University of Cambridge
The Pitt Building, Trumpington Street, Cambridge CB2 1RP
40 West 20th Street, New York, NY 10011
10 Stamford Road, Oakleigh, Melbourne 3166, Australia

© Cambridge University Press 1991

First published 1991

Printed and bound in Great Britain by Scotprint, Musselburgh

British Library cataloguing in publication data

Garratt, James
 Design and technology
 1. Technology. For schools
 I. Title
 600

ISBN 0 521 36969 X

Typeset by Oxprint Ltd, Oxford

Acknowledgements

The author wishes to thank the former Principal, Christopher Evans, and the former Deputy Head, Peter Green, of Countesthorpe Community College, for their support and cooperation during the writing and production of this book, and all the pupils whose work is photographed or illustrated in the book. The help of colleagues within the Design and Technology department is also gratefully acknowledged. Finally, he wishes to thank his wife Jenny for her invaluable help and support over the past three years.

To the student

Design and Technology has been written for you to use for GCSE and at Key Stage 4 in the National Curriculum. You should use this book to look up information when you require it rather than trying to read it from cover to cover. For this reason it has a very simple layout designed to make the information contained easy to understand and locate. Sometimes you may need to read a whole chapter, in which case you should refer to the contents list on page 3. Alternatively use the index at the end of the book to locate more specific information. For project briefs and ideas use the project index. Chapter 1 describes the **stages in the design process** which embody the National Curriculum attainment targets. It is suggested, therefore, that you read the introduction and chapter 1 first.

Control technology: automated production

Power technology: electricity generation

Aircraft technology: intercontinental flight

Information technology: police records department

Clearly, designers and technologists have an enormous responsibility for the well-being of people in our society, of all the peoples of the world, and of the very future of planet Earth. When studying design and technology at school, *you* will be expected to act as a responsible designer whilst **generating designs** to solve problems or satisfy needs.

Whenever anything is made, of course, from the simplest to the most complex product, **materials**, **components** and **tools** will be used, and **skills** and **knowledge** will be required. A thorough understanding and application of these resources, therefore, is necessary to ensure a high quality product. When studying design and technology at school, *you* will be expected to use these resources to their best advantage whilst **planning** and **making** products yourself.

For **economic** reasons, designers try to make sure that their products appeal to a large number of people. Imagine for a moment going into a shop yourself to buy a new pair of 'trainers' – you wouldn't buy 'just any pair'. You would try them on to see if they were comfortable, examine them to see if you liked the style and appearance, think about the quality of the materials and whether they were good value for money, and so on. In other words, you would **evaluate** them. Whilst studying design and technology at school you will be expected to evaluate the products *you* make. This is an important process for designers and technologists, not only because they need to assess the product's sales potential, but also because their **products** (as we have seen) **have the potential to affect all of our lives**.

Studying design and technology, therefore, will help you to: identify needs and opportunities, generate designs, plan and make products (artefacts, systems and environment) and to evaluate your own work and that of others. In the next few pages, two pupils, Pauline and Nick, help to illustrate the **stages in the design process** through which these skills can be developed.

CHAPTER ONE

Stages in the design process

Situation

Designers and technologists are men and women who set out to solve **practical** problems which arise out of life's **situations.** Here is an example of a situation in which Pauline and Nick became involved.

On reaching old age, some people find it very difficult, and often frightening, to climb up and down stairs. The solution might be to live downstairs, to move house, or maybe to go into an old people's home. Mrs Brown didn't want to do any of these things. She wanted to continue to live as she had always lived.

Analyse the situation

Before attempting to solve a problem, it is important to **analyse** the situation to sort out exactly what the problem is. (For further details see p.10).

Write a brief

Once the problem is fully understood, the next step is to write a design **brief.** A brief is a short statement giving the general outline of the problem to be solved. (For further details see p.10).

Carry out research

Sometimes a problem can be solved 'straight out of your head' using your own knowledge and imagination. However, to obtain the best possible solution you will almost certainly need to gain some new knowledge and information, and this will require **research.** (For further details see p.11).

Write a specification

Having researched the problem you should have a good understanding of what is required and a clearer understanding of the design limits which will affect what can ultimately be achieved. A **specification** can now be prepared. This must outline specific details of the design which must be satisfied, and identify the design limits. (For further details see p.12).

Work out possible solutions

Possible solutions to the design brief should now be considered. Draw some ideas on paper. Your first idea will not necessarily be the best, so try several different designs (at least three). By combining your own ideas and information obtained from research, you should begin to move towards a good solution. (For further details see p.13).

Select preferred solution

A decision must now be made. You must decide which solution to develop. Ideally, the chosen solution will be the one which best satisfies the specification – but this is not always possible. (For further details see p.13).

Prepare working drawings and plan ahead

At this stage, working drawings of the chosen design should be prepared. They should contain all the **details** of the design which are important to its construction.

Planning for the work ahead is also important at this stage to ensure that you complete the work on time. (For further details see p.14).

Construct a prototype

You are now ready to **make** the product – this is sometimes called realisation. In industry a prototype is usually built first, and the final product is a development of this. In school, the prototype is often all you have time to make (or sometimes just a model), but this is probably the most interesting part of the work. It involves building, testing and modifying the design to try to satisfy the specification. (For further details see p.15).

Test and evaluate the design

The prototype, or final product must now be **tested** to see if it solves the problem outlined in the specification. Very few designs are perfect. To discover how successful your project has been, you must ask questions like: How well does it function? Does it work reliably? Can it be used safely? And so on. (For further details see p.17).

Write a report

Finally, a report must be written on the project. In school your report provides **evidence** of your ability to analyse, plan, design, carry out practical work, evaluate and communicate. In industry the report has other uses. (For further details see p.18).

Note you can see photographs of this project on page 163.

The design process flow chart

The design process can be illustrated using a 'flow chart'.

The large arrows show how you normally progress from one stage to the next. However, you will soon discover that problem solving is not always this straightforward. Often you will have an idea, or discover something which will make you re-think an earlier stage. This process is sometimes called **feedback**. The side arrows show how feedback may occur.

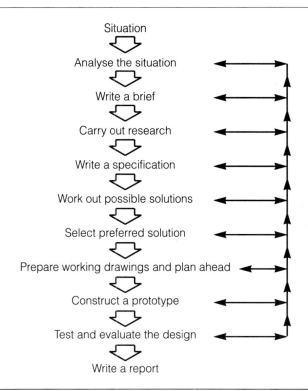

Situation

Analyse the situation

Write a brief

Carry out research

Write a specification

Work out possible solutions

Select preferred solution

Prepare working drawings and plan ahead

Construct a prototype

Test and evaluate the design

Write a report

Further details of the design process

Analysis of the situation

The process of analysing a situation will help you to sort out in your mind exactly what the problem is. Asking questions about the situation is one way of sorting out the problem.

Pauline and Nick talked to Mrs Brown in her home to learn more about the problems which old people face in getting up and down stairs.

Sometimes it can help you to sort out a problem if you actually 'put yourself in the situation'.

Putting someone else in the situation and observing their actions and reactions is another useful approach.

Because different people respond in different ways to a situation, a questionnaire can be another useful means of analysing a problem.

All your observations and thoughts should be recorded. Use a notepad, sketchbook, camera, tape recorder or even a video camera, for this purpose.

The brief

Once a problem has been analysed, it should be possible to write a short statement describing the problem to be solved. This is called a **brief**.

It may be a very short statement, such as 'Design a burglar alarm for use in the home', or be more precise 'Design a burglar alarm for use in the home which warns of false entry through windows and doors by sounding an alarm'. It is important that the brief is not so vague that the designer is unclear about what is needed, e.g. 'Design a burglar alarm'. Alternatively, it must not be so detailed that the designer doesn't have the freedom to be creative.

An example of a project brief is shown here. It is the brief which Pauline and Nick wrote after analysing the problem illustrated on page 6.

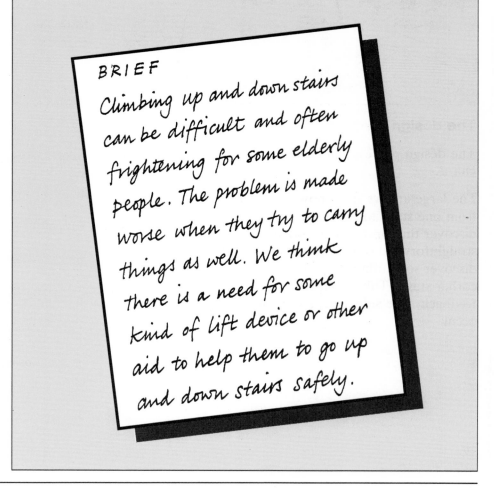

Research

Having written a brief, you are now ready to seek out information which will help you to produce a successful design. This is called **research**.

First you must decide what information you require. This of course will vary from project to project, and will depend upon the knowledge you already have.

A useful step towards making this decision is to use the chart shown. Start by asking yourself the questions 1 to 5. Then read the column headed **Areas of research**. This will suggest areas of research which are relevant to the questions. Some of the terms used will be familiar to you – others will not. Part of your research should include reading about unfamiliar concepts.

Areas of research

1

What is the practical **function** (or functions) of the design? (What must it do?)

A design's practical functions can include:

structural support, protection, containment,
mechanical movement and control,
electrical operations and control,
energy transfer etc. etc.

2

What part does **appearance** (shape and form, surface texture, colour, etc.) play in the design's function?

Shape and form is important to a design's:

aesthetic qualities, ergonomics, strength, stability, rigidity, safety, aerodynamics etc.

Surface texture, finish and colour can be appropriate to a design's:

aesthetic qualities, mechanical, optical and **thermal properties, durability** etc.

3

What **materials** are suitable for the design?

The **properties** of a material will determine its suitability for a design. These will include the physical properties of:

strength, hardness, toughness, density, thermal conductivity, durability etc. etc.,

and the aesthetic qualities determined by **colour, surface texture, pattern** etc.

A materials **cost** and availability are also important factors.

4

What **construction** methods are appropriate to the design?

Construction techniques fall into the categories of:

cutting and shaping – by sawing, filling, drilling etc.
fabrication – the assembly of parts using screws, bolts, glues, solder etc.
moulding – by the application of a force on the material.
casting – using a mould to form the shape of a solidifying material.

A particular material can only be worked in a limited number of ways. The method of construction therefore will be determined by the chosen **material**, the availability of manufacturing facilities, the skills of the work force and the production costs.

5

What are the likely **social** and **environmental effects** of the design?

The **manufacture, use** and **disposal** of any product will have both beneficial and detrimental effects upon people, wildlife and the environment. (See page 4.) The designer therefore, has an enormous responsibility to consider very carefully the potential effects of any new design. These will include:

Health and safety factors, noise, smell, aesthetic qualities, pollution etc.

Where to obtain the information

Research can involve reading, listening, talking, and of course observing.

General background information can be obtained from **reading** magazines, data sheets and other written material. Your teacher will be able to suggest suitable books etc., and of course you can ask at your school and local libraries.

If more detailed information is required you may need to **write a letter** to a particular industry, government department or research establishment, for example.

Looking at similar products is a useful form of research. You can quickly learn about the different methods and techniques used. You will then be in a good position to start thinking about your own product, and ways of improving on current designs. However, it is important not to allow other people's solutions to become a barrier to your own creativity.

A valuable area of research is often within your own community. Sources of information can include industries, museums, shops and of course parents and friends.

Factors which affect peoples' lives are sometimes described as the **social implications of technology**. School subjects like Humanities and Politics for example, can often provide information and ideas related to this area of your research.

Conclusion

Having carefully researched the topic, you should identify the information which is most likely to be of use to you. At this stage you should also be able to identify the **design limits** which will affect what can ultimately be produced. These will vary between school and industry but can include for example, costs. In industry the costs will include research, design, materials and processing costs, wages etc. In school, material costs are probably the most limiting factor. Time imposes limits too. It is no use developing a solution if the time is not available to produce it. In school, the time allocated to project work can significantly affect what can be achieved. Your personal skills and your school's facilities will also limit what you can achieve, and so on. It is important therefore, to consider these factors before writing the specification.

Specification

A **specification** is a detailed description of the problem to be solved. It should 'spell out' exactly what the design must achieve, whilst taking into account the design limits which will affect the final solution. It can be in the form of a list or a written statement.

The specification written by Pauline and Nick is shown here.

Note   A specification should only state that which is required to solve the problem – not how to solve it, this comes later.

SPECIFICATION.
a) The device must either carry, or assist the person, up and down the stairs
b) It must be very easy to use, and not have any complicated controls.
c) It must be completely safe for the user, and any persons or animals standing nearby.
d) It must not obstruct the normal use of the stairs.
e) It must be neat and attractive.
f) It must be cheap to operate.
g) The cost of the equipment should not exceed £350.

Possible solutions

This is the stage in the design process when you need to be really **imaginative** – to think up, and draw, lots of really good ideas for solving the problem set out in the brief.

However, it is easy to become engrossed in the first idea which comes into your mind. This can lead to a lot of frustration, especially if you get 'bogged down' with a problem and see no way to solve it.

It is so important not to let this happen. One way to avoid it is to only spend 10 to 15 minutes working on one idea before you move on to the next.

You should ideally think of at least three different ways of solving the problem before you concentrate on any one in particular. Quick sketches and notes are all that is really needed at this stage.

'I'm stuck'

Don't spend too long on one idea

The chosen solution

When you feel ready to make a choice from your range of possible solutions, the first step should be to **look back at the specification**.

Then, by comparing what the specification '**asks for**', to what each of your designs **can provide**, you should be able to choose the one which will '**do the job best**'. Alternatively, you might decide that a combination of your ideas will provide the best solution. Before a final decision is made it may be necessary to make some simple models to test and compare the different designs.

Note   It is important to realise that you may **not** actually be able to use the best solution. You must ask the questions: Do I have the **time** to complete the work? Can I, or the school **afford** the materials and components required? And, do I have, or can I acquire, the necessary **skills** to complete the project?

'Which one shall I choose?'

Working drawings

Once you have decided which design to develop, the next stage is to produce some working drawings. It is from these drawings that the prototype, or final product, will be made.

The type of drawings you produce will depend upon your own particular skills. You might choose to produce a **detailed** freehand drawing. Alternatively, you may prefer to make a 'technical drawing', using a drawing board and instruments. If you enjoy using a computer, you could produce a 'print out' from diagrams developed on the VDU.

Whichever method you use, the aim is to produce a detailed drawing containing all the information needed to allow the design to be made. This will include: dimensions, angles, technical data (component values etc.), materials and so on.

Prepare working drawings

Planning

Before any practical work can begin, it is very important to **plan out** the work ahead. It is important for a number of reasons:

a) Planning should help you to get the work finished on time.

Your teacher will tell you how much time is available. With this information you should draw up a **timetable** showing how much time you expect to spend on each part of the design. As the work progresses, changes may have to be made to this timetable if jobs take less time, or longer than expected.

b) Planning should also ensure that you have the necessary materials, components and equipment available when you need them.

Make a **list** of these requirements and check with your teacher that they are available. If something needs ordering, for example, you may need to rearrange your work timetable to fit in with these changes. Your work plan will also help you to decide 'what to do next' if, for example, equipment, materials or components are not available when you need them.

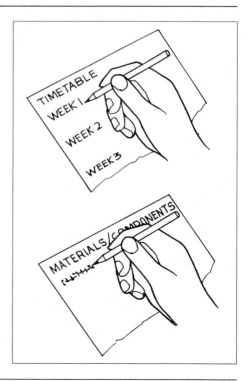

Construction work

Having worked out a timetable, and collected some of the materials and components you need, construction work can begin. The construction of a prototype, or final product, can involve a great deal of skilful activity. This can include. taking measurements and marking out, cutting, moulding, casting and fabricating. Fabricating can include: brazing, welding, pinning and jointing, the use of adhesives, and not least, the use of nuts and bolts. In addition, projects which have electrical circuitry can involve circuit construction techniques such as etching,

soldering and wiring. All these activities are potentially dangerous.

It is important therefore:

- **never to use tools, equipment or machinery without your teacher's permission,**
- **always to wear protective clothing and goggles where appropriate,**
- **to observe the safety regulations in your school.**

The pictures and captions which follow also give some guidance on how to work safely.

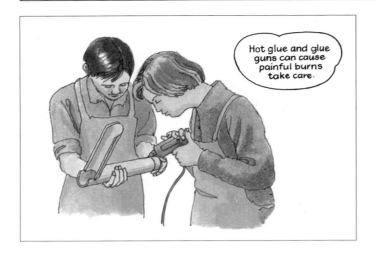

The pillar drill

Construction work – continued

Tests and modifications

As construction work progresses, and the design begins to 'take shape', you will automatically carry out **tests** on the design. You might test the strength of a joint, the operation of a mechanism, the working of an electrical circuit etc. In addition to these 'ongoing' tests, **complete systems** will need to be tested at various stages. It is important to make these tests to check that the product satisfies the specification. If as a result of testing you feel that the design does not perform as required, you might have to change part of the design. Whenever you make a change to the original design, you have made what designers call a **modification**. Sometimes however, a problem cannot be overcome with a modification. In such cases an alternative solution would have to be considered. Where part of a project has to be re-designed, a number of alternative solutions should be considered in the normal way.

If you were designing in industry, it would be necessary to consider how a proposed modification, or change of design, would affect the design's production. This would depend, for example, on the staff, materials, equipment and resources available to the industry. In addition, it would be necessary to consider how any increased costs would be met. For these reasons, a **written report** would have to be prepared.

Reporting on tests and modifications in school technology projects

Because of the importance of carrying out tests, making modifications, or re-designing, most examination boards will expect you to write about these in your final **project report**. (See page 18.) It is therefore important to keep a note of these activities to ensure that you do not forget about them.

Final test and evaluation

When construction work is complete, the entire project must be **tested** *to see if it does the job for which it was designed.* It will be necessary to look back at the specification and check each requirement carefully.

An **evaluation** can then be written. This should be a statement outlining the strengths and weaknesses in your design. It should describe where you have succeeded and where you have failed to achieve the aims set out in the specification.

Here is a list of questions which will help you to prepare this statement.

1 How well does the design function?
2 Does the design look good?
3 Is the product safe to use?
4 Did I plan my work adequately?
5 Did I find the construction straightforward or difficult? (Did I use the most appropriate method of construction?)
6 Were the most suitable materials used?
7 Did it cost more or less than expected?
8 How could I have improved on my design?

Answer these questions carefully. Be honest in your evaluation.

The report

The purpose of a school project report is to provide your teacher and the examiner with **evidence** of your ability to analyse, design, plan, carry out practical work, evaluate and communicate.

What should a project report contain?

This will depend upon the type of course you are following, and the examination board which your school is using. Your teacher will tell you exactly what is required. As a general rule however, you can assume that the **evidence** listed above will be required in almost all types of reports. A guide to help you present this information is given below.

How to present your report

Your report should begin with a 'title page' upon which is written your **name**, **school**, **date** and the **project title**.

The second page should list the **contents** of your report giving page numbers. (All pages in your report should be numbered.)

Situation – Begin your report with an explanation of how you identified the need or opportunity for your design and technological activities (your project). This should include notes on the investigations you carried out and how you planned them. Include here any questionnaires, notes from interviews etc., which you made use of. Next, show why you considered your project a worthwhile thing to do. You should 'back up' this **evaluation** with evidence gathered during your investigations. This should include your own opinions and observations and those of others, including potential users. Show also that you considered relevant social, economic, environmental and technological factors before proceeding with your project.

Brief – Your project **brief** (which states the need or opportunity which you have identified) should be written next.

Research – Give a brief account of how you began to tackle the problem. This should include details of **research** carried out to help you develop your ideas. Next describe *how* this information helped you. Include here reference to function, appearance, materials, methods of construction and social and environmental factors and so on.

Specification – The **specification** should be given next. The quality of this specification will demonstrate your ability to analyse a problem in detail and show your understanding of the limitations imposed on the design.

Possible solutions – The next step is to describe the range of **possible solutions** you considered. The **sketches** and **notes** which you made at this stage are the ones which should be included here. If you explored ideas used in existing products, explain this, and show how you used them to develop your own ideas. Describe any models you made, and any tests you carried out, and explain how this work helped you to improve and refine your ideas and to recognise the restrictions imposed on the design by materials, methods of manufacture, costs etc.

Chosen solution – Next you should outline how you arrived at the **chosen solution**. This will have required you to **evaluate** each of the possible solutions with regard to the specification. In other words, you will have considered the strengths and weaknesses in each design, and have chosen the one design (or combination of designs) which best satisfied the specification. Include this evaluation here and show that you also considered your own skills, your school's facilities and the availability and cost of materials and components.

Working drawings – Here you should include the **working drawings** which you prepared. They should be neat and clear. They should be easy for the teacher, the examiner and indeed anyone who sees them, to understand.

Realisation – Planning is essential for successful project work. Show that you planned the stages in the manufacture of your project, and considered the constraints of time, materials and labour by including your **timetable** and **materials list** here.

Details of the **construction work** can now be given. The kind of information required here will include: notes on **how the work progressed**, the **test** you carried out, the kind of **problems** you faced with materials, tools, processes, methods of manufacture etc., and the **decisions** you had to make to overcome these problems. Include here any sketches, notes and plans you produced to assist you during the making of the product. If you had to review the original design proposal in the light of problems encountered, explain this. Any **modifications** made as a result should be fully explained using sketches, diagrams and notes. If part of the project was **re-designed**, rather than modified, the possible solutions you considered must be described and the reasons for the chosen solution given.

Final tests and evaluation – Now you must describe how successful your project has been – that is, you must **evaluate** it. Your evaluation should outline the **strengths** and **weaknesses** in (1) the product itself, (2) the materials and processes used to realise the product and (3) the way *you* tackled the task.

Product – Begin by describing the **tests** made on the completed product and outline the results of these tests. Use these results to show where you have **succeeded** and where you have **failed** to satisfy the specification. For example, if you designed a drinks dispenser and it failed to dispense the required quantity of liquid, then you would have failed to achieve one of the design's **functions**. This must be reported and explained. But equally, of course, your successes must be reported too. *All of the design's functions* must be evaluated in this way. Similarly, a detailed evaluation of the product's **aesthetic** qualities must be made. Where possible, the evaluation should take into account the views and reactions of potential users of the product and show the extent to which you have met the needs of others.

An often difficult, but important, area for evaluation is **economics**. Where appropriate, you should comment on your product's sales potential, production costs, profitability and so on.

Because people's lives can be affected by the things we make, the possible **social** and **environmental** effects of the product must be evaluated.

Finally, you should mention **how you could improve your design**. This might include a description of further modifications or developments you considered, but did not have time to carry out. Alternatively, you might conclude that further development of the product would not be worthwhile, and you should say why.

Materials and processes – This part of the evaluation concerns **production** matters. If you feel that you made the right choices of materials and components for your product, say so and explain why. Alternatively, if you think that the product could have functioned better, looked better, been cheaper to make, safer to use and so on, using different materials or components, explain this too. Similarly, you should evaluate the techniques and processes used to make the product, either justifying those used or suggesting alternative approaches.

The task – The final part of the report should be an evaluation of 'how *you* tackle the task'. Include here a review of your initial investigations, research, design work, and your planning and making activities. In each case, comment on the way you went about the tasks and the decisions you made. Describe what you think you did well, and what you did less well, and suggest how you might do better in the future.

NOTE – The relationship between the National Curriculum attainment targets for design and technology and the project report, is indicated using coloured tints as illustrated below.

AT1	Identifying needs and opportunities
AT2	Generating a design
AT3	Planning and making
AT4	Evaluating

CHAPTER TWO

Aesthetics

Chapter 1 described the *stages in the design process*. This, and the following chapters contain information and ideas to help you progress through those stages.

Function

The most important reason for designing something is to solve a problem to satisfy a need. A successful design therefore must **function** properly – that is, it must do the job for which it was designed. A lot of information which may help you with the **functional** aspects of your designs can be found in chapters 3–9 in this book.

Appearance and aesthetics

Whilst it is essential that a design functions properly, because we have feelings and emotions and are surrounded by the things we make, it is important that it also 'looks good'. The qualities which make a design attractive to look at or pleasing to experience, determine its **aesthetic** appeal. It is through the senses of sight, touch, hearing, smell and taste that these qualities can be appreciated.

However, one person's ideas about what 'looks good' can be very different from another's. This is because our aesthetic judgement is conditioned by so many different factors – not least the many **influences** upon us in our everyday lives. Some of these influences can be identified in the photographs shown here, and are discussed further at the end of this chapter.

For economic reasons, designers try to make sure that their designs appeal to a large number of people. As a consumer, you have to decide if they look good to you and will function properly. As a designer and maker, you have to make the same decisions. This chapter will help you to make decisions about a design's **appearance**.

Elements of visual design

When thinking about the appearance of a design, it is useful to 'break down' the visual form into elements which can be easily examined. This will help you to understand and develop your own feelings about **appearance**.

Line

Lines are the basic elements used to organise a visual form. They can exist in their own right, but are usually joined together to create shapes and forms and to organise space and structure.

Lines can also be used to apply decoration, provide information, evoke feeling, etc.

Shape and form

A **shape** is an area enclosed by lines. As you can imagine, numerous different shapes are possible. Shapes are two dimensional – they have length and width, but no depth.

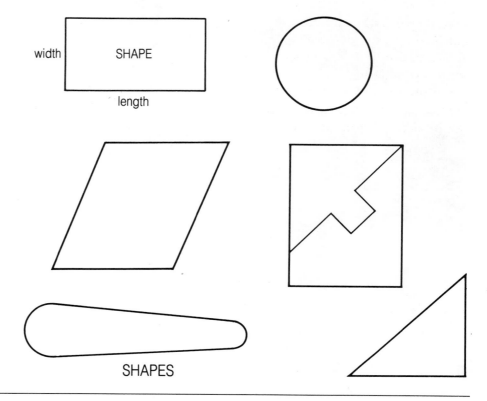

SHAPES

Forms have depth as well as length and width and are described as three dimensional. Many designs are 'built up' from a number of different component parts which make up the whole. The combination, arrangement and proportion of these parts creates the **form** of the overall design.

Geometric shapes and forms are regular and precise and usually arise out of the purpose for which the design is being made. They are fundamental to the appearance of most manufactured products and structures and indeed are often dictated by the choice of manufacturing process.

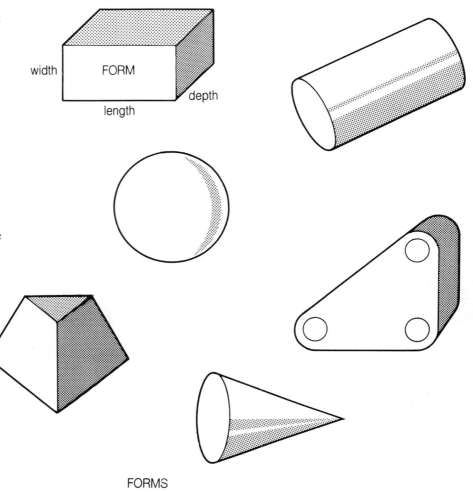

FORMS

Free shapes and forms are very much less precise and have greater application in the 'decorative' aspects of a design and in craft based products. Their variety is limitless and numerous variations can be derived from natural objects.

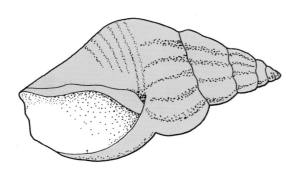

Look at the products and structures pictured here. Try to visualise their 'make up' in terms of line, shape and form. Think about how the particular materials used, and the method of manufacture, have determined or dictated certain aspects of the design's appearance. Think also about your own 'feelings' related to the design's shape and form. Some of the words which can be used to describe the **aesthetic** qualities associated with shape and form include: 'stylish', 'functional', 'elegant', 'strong', 'tasteful', 'interesting', 'beautiful', 'sleek', – but can also include words such as 'repulsive', 'yuk', 'weak', 'boring'. Can you think of any more?

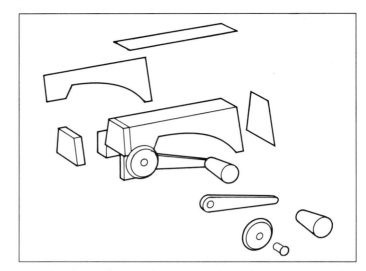

Lead guitar

Vacuum cleaner

Clock/radio

Patio furniture

Concorde

Greenhouse

Trolley jack

Texture

In addition to variations of shape and form, a designer can alter the design's appearance through the use of texture.

Texture is the 'surface finish' on a material. It is both **visual** and **tactile** – that is, we can both **see** and **feel** texture.

All materials have their own particular texture, and it is this which helps us to identify them. Even so, a material's texture will vary depending upon the way it was worked, or the manufacturing process used. For example, carved wood and planed wood have very different textures. Similarly, die cast aluminium can have a very different texture from sand cast aluminium. In the case of plastics, numerous different textures are possible depending on the nature of the polymer and the surface of the mould, and so on. Some examples of both natural and 'manufactured' textures are illustrated in the photographs.

We see texture when light strikes, and is reflected from, a material's surface. On a material which has surface relief, little shadows are cast which help to produce the particular visual effect. The brighter the light, the 'rougher' the surface appears.

Rough, smooth, hard, soft, warm, cold – these are just some of the **tactile** qualities associated with texture which we experience by touching and handling products. These qualities can be important to a design's function. For example, whilst a kitchen work surface should be smooth for reasons of hygiene (it must be easy to clean), paving slabs should ideally be rough for reasons of safety (they should prevent us from slipping in the wet).

Some of the words which can be used to describe the **aesthetic** qualities associated with texture include: 'functional', 'warm', 'pretty', 'attractive', 'hygienic', 'cold', 'clinical'. Can you think of any more?

Multi-textured baby's star toy

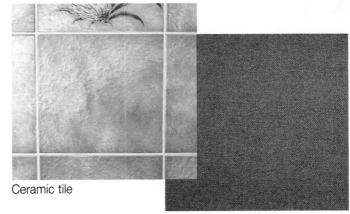

Ceramic tile

Hessian fabric

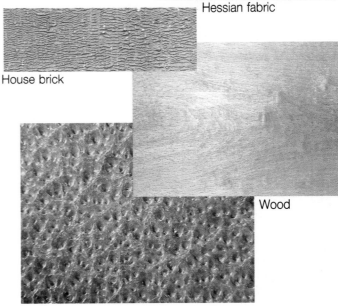

House brick

Wood

Leather

Colour

Just for a moment look around and study some of the things which surround you (or even just the objects in the picture shown here). Notice how your attention switches from one part of an object to another, and how certain details 'stand out' or attract you. Imagine how dreadfully dull and uninteresting the same objects would be if you saw them in just one colour and against the same coloured background.

Whilst shape, form and texture provide the basic characteristics of an object's appearance, it is through **colour** that we see *detail* and *variation* in these features, as our attention is drawn from one part of the design to another. But this is not all, as you will see later.

The colour wheel

When thinking about colour and how to use it to change or affect a design's appearance, a useful aid is the 'colour wheel'.

In the mixing of inks, dyes and paints, there are three basic colours from which all the other colours (on the colour wheel) can be made – red, yellow and blue. These are called **primary colours** and are shown on diagram 1.

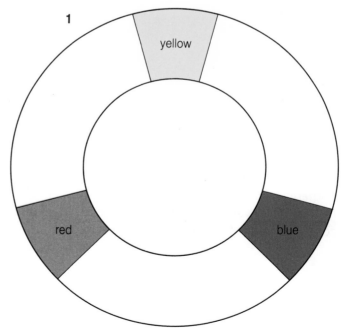

Primary colours

When two primary colours are mixed in equal amounts, a **secondary colour** is produced. There are three secondary colours – green, violet and orange. Diagram 2 shows that mixing yellow and blue produces green, blue and red produces violet and red and yellow produces orange.

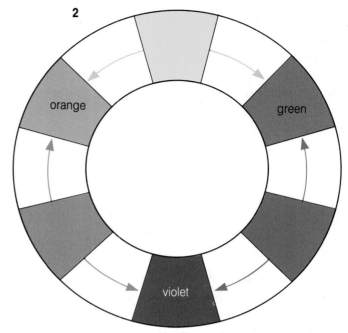

Secondary colours

Finally, when a primary and secondary colour are mixed a **tertiary colour** is produced, as shown in diagram 3. There are six tertiary colours, as shown in the complete colour wheel in diagram 4.

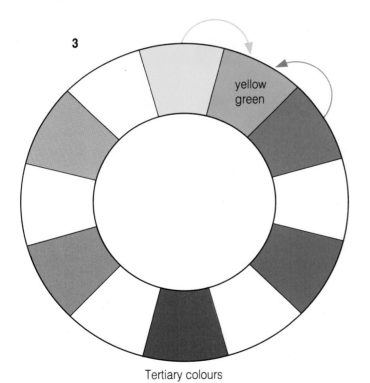

Tertiary colours

Full colour wheel
(Tertiary colours labelled)

Note The colours produced when mixing coloured **light** are different to the above. For an explanation of this you should refer to a good physics or science book.

Colour tone

By adding either **black** or **white** to a colour, we can change its **tone**. The addition of white makes the colour lighter (or paler), black makes it darker. The tonal range of red is shown here as an example.

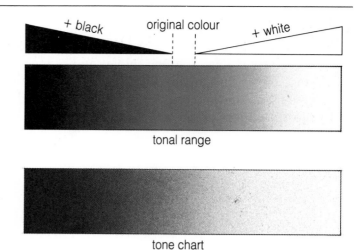

tonal range

Although black and white are not actually colours, they can of course be used in their own right in our designs, as we use real colours. A tone chart between black and white is shown opposite.

tone chart

Harmony and contrast

Colours can be used to create a sense of harmony or contrast in a design. Colours which are closest together on the colour wheel relate **harmoniously**. Diagram 1 shows a colour wheel (containing only the primary and secondary colours) divided into semi-circular arcs. Each arc shows a family of colours which are harmonious. Three other families could have been shown. If yellow, green and blue is one of them, what are the other two?

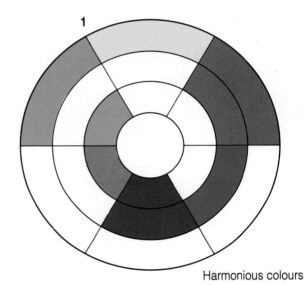

Harmonious colours

Colours which are opposite on the colour wheel (diagram 2) are those which have the greatest **contrast** and are known as complementary colours.

Choosing colours for a design which harmonise can make parts of the design look closely related. Alternatively, contrasting colours can be used to emphasise the difference between parts of a design or make something stand out, for example.

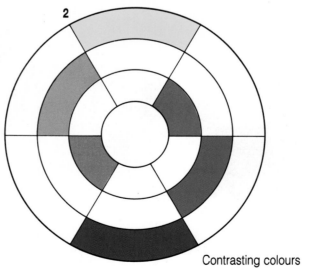

Contrasting colours

To help you understand the use of colour harmony and contrast in designs, look at the things which surround you at school, in the home, outdoors, in shops, etc. Look at them carefully and think about how colour harmony and contrast has been used in each design and for what *purpose*. You can begin by looking at the products pictured here. You might like to note down some of your ideas.

Lawn edger

Time teacher watch

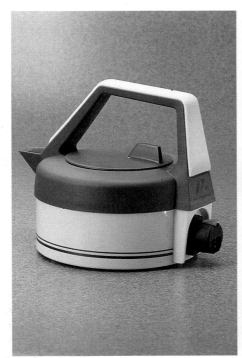

Automatic kettle

Bathroom

Size and weight

Colour can be used to create all sorts of different illusions which can affect our feelings about a design. For example, an object (or part of an object) can be made to look smaller by the use of a dark colour, or larger using a lighter colour.

Similarly, dark colours can be used to make things look heavier (or stronger) whilst lighter colours can make them look lighter in weight.

See if you can identify some designs in which light or dark colours have been used for the purposes described.

Colour and emotions

The way a design makes us feel has a lot to do with its aesthetic appeal, and through the use of colour our very moods can be affected. For example, yellow is supposed to have a soothing effect upon us, whilst red (in large areas) can be oppressive. Colours also can give a sense of **warmth** or **coldness**. The warm colours include red, orange and yellow, while the cool colours include violet, blue and green. Not least of course, colour can make things look bright or dull, exciting or boring.

With the above in mind, write down some of your feelings and thoughts about the room in the picture.

Colour association

Through our experiences as we grow up we come to associate different colours with particular situations, products or designs. Red for danger and green for safety is an obvious example. White for cleanliness is another. Do you think that people would buy brown nappies or black washing powder, for example?

See if you can think of any other colour associations and examples of how they are exploited in product design, packaging, advertising, etc.

Finally, remember to take colour association into account in your own designs.

Pelican crossing lights

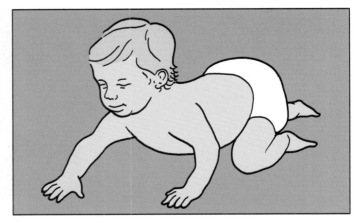

Principles of visual design

There are certain ways of arranging and combining the *visual elements* of a design which most people accept and feel comfortable with. As a consumer you make decisions all the time about whether things 'look right'. As a designer and maker you have to make the same decisions.

Some of the ways of *arranging* the visual elements are discussed below.

Proportion

Most of the things we design and make are made up of a number of different parts. When a design is in **proportion**, the relative size and arrangement of these parts, and the dimensions of the design as a whole, will 'look right', but of course this is a matter of personal taste.

Which of the cups and saucers shown here do *you* think has good proportions?

As well as being in proportion 'themselves', designs should also be in proportion to the environment in which they will be used and the people who will use them (see 'Ergonomics' chapter 3). If a design is suited to its purpose, and functions well, its dimensions will be right and its proportions should look good.

Maclaren buggy – a well proportioned design

Nature is very good at producing good proportions and can be a rich source of reference for designers. Take flowers and plants for example, they always seem to be 'just the right size' for their particular growing environment.

People through the ages have also striven to produce 'pleasing' proportions in their designs, and therefore the built environment is a valuable reference source. The ancient Greeks felt that the dimensions of a *rectangle* with the most pleasing proportions, had sides in a ratio of 1 to 1.6 (1 : 1.6) and they exploited this in the construction of the famous Parthenon. Many designers have since exploited this so called 'golden mean proportion' in their designs.

Balance

When the elements of visual design (shape, form, texture, colour, etc), are the 'same' on either side of an imaginary central line (one side being a mirror image of the other), the design is said to be **symmetrical**. Symmetry is one way of creating **balance** in a design, giving it a sense of stability.

Taj Mahal, India

Visual balance can also be created **asymmetrically**. This means that the visual elements on either side of the 'central line' may be different, but because of their differing proportions balance is maintained. It is not uncommon for a design to be symmetrical in one plane, and asymmetrical in another. The kettle shown here is an example.

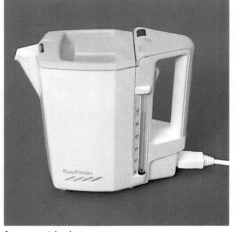

Asymmetrical

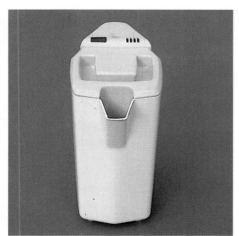

Symmetrical

33

Nature provides many examples of another kind of balance – **radial balance**, where elements of the design radiate in a uniform manner from a central point.

Radial balance in a light fitting

As a designer, an awareness of visual balance is very important, since a sense of stability in a design is more readily 'accepted' by the human mind than instability.

Radial balance

Harmony and contrast

The elements of visual design can be arranged to create either a sense of harmony or contrast within a design. The way in which colour can be used for this purpose was discussed on page 28.

When elements are in **harmony**, they make parts of the design look closely related and generally give a feeling of uniformity.

Table lamp with harmonising hexagonal features

Contrast is often used when you wish to attract attention, or emphasise some aspect of a design, or create a feeling of 'liveliness' for example. Interestingly, contrast can actually be used to enhance harmony. This can be achieved for example by contrasting some aspects of a design's appearance – colour or texture perhaps – to emphasise the harmonising features.

Table with contrasting geometrical forms

Pattern

An artistic decoration made up of repeated shapes, is probably the first thing you think of when you hear the word **pattern**. But patterns can be both two and three dimensional. They may be designed for a purpose, or occur naturally within the design's structure.

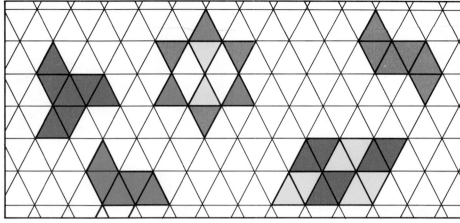

Triangular grid-patterns

Pattern is formed by the repeated use of lines, shapes, forms, texture, colour etc. The 'element' which is repeated to form the pattern is called a **motif**. Two dimensional patterns can be worked out on a grid, or drawn using a stencil, for example.

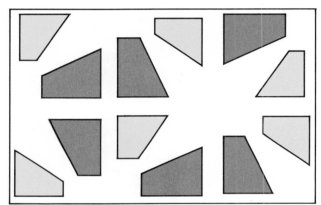

Pattern drawn with stencil

Stencil

The idea of repetition can be developed into **tessellations**, which are shapes or forms which 'interlock' within the design.

Patterns are usually designed to make something look more attractive or to disguise an unwanted feature. They are often applied to surfaces which have little decorative character of their own.

Tesselated pattern

Patterns which occur naturally within a design often arise out of **function**. The familiar pattern created by bricks in a wall arises out of the need to make the bricks 'key' together for strength. Even the pattern of holes in a pair of training shoes arises partly from the need to keep the feet cool.

An example of pattern in three dimensional design is in the repeated use of **standardised units**. This can be seen in designs ranging from kitchen equipment to buildings.

As a designer, an understanding of pattern is very important – not only as a decorative feature, but because the human eye is more comfortable with pattern than irregularity.

Vegetable rack

Conclusions

Some of the factors which can affect a design's **appearance** and its **aesthetic** appeal have been discussed in this chapter. However, aesthetics is a complex subject. In addition to our personal psychological 'make up' there are many different **influences** in our lives which can affect our aesthetic judgement. The photographs on pages 20 and 21 and those shown here illustrate some of these influences, and some are described below.

Environmental influences – the effects upon us resulting from how and where we have grown up.
Personal experiences – what we have done, seen and felt in our lives, including our physical and psychological interactions with objects, systems and environments.
Peer group influences – what our friends like or dislike.
Media influences – the effects of radio, television, magazines, etc, upon us.
Fashion – 'accepted' styles influenced by some peoples' ideas of what is 'good design'.
Travel – visiting other countries and experiencing different cultures.
Education – thinking about design and gaining experience of materials through their use in designing and making.

If you think about the above factors you will probably agree that most of them (if not all) will have some effect upon our thoughts, feelings, expectations and actions during our lives. It is not surprising therefore, that they can affect our **aesthetic** judgement.

With the above in mind, you might agree that as designers, makers and consumers, we should take every opportunity to observe, analyse and discuss designs both old and contemporary, and within nature, in the hope of 'broadening our minds' and developing our design skills.

CHAPTER THREE

Ergonomics

Most of the things we design and make are used by people. We may **touch** or **hold** them, **lift** or **carry** them, **manipulate**, **operate** or **control** them, **stand**, **sit** or **lie** on (or in) them, **wear** them, **look** at them and so on. Our **health** and **safety** and **comfort** therefore depend on them being **well designed and constructed**.

The study of the design of objects, systems and environments for their safe and efficient use by people is called **ergonomics**.

When designing for people, three main factors will require investigating:

the **size** of the people who will use the designs,
the **movements** they will make, and
the reactions of the body to the design through the **senses**.

People of course vary considerably in **size**. Some are tall, others short, some are plump, some thin. Some have large hands, some small, some can reach further than others and so on. Of course, these 'sizes' change throughout our lives. The skeleton is largely responsible for a person's size, although muscle and other body tissue plays an important part in a person's physical make up.

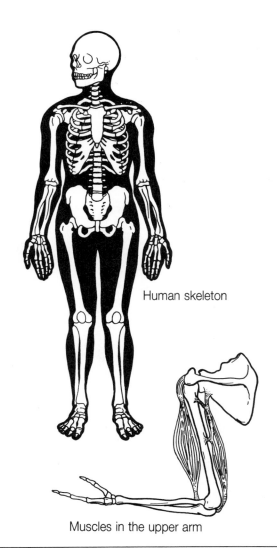

Human skeleton

Muscles in the upper arm

The structure of the skeleton, and the way in which the bones connect and articulate, enables human beings to perform a wide range of complex and intricate **movements**. The movements are produced by the contraction and relaxation of muscles (attached to the skeleton) under the control of the brain.

All human activity relies on the feedback of information from the **senses** to the brain (via the nervous system) to allow us to control our bodily movements and functions. In addition to these 'control messages', the senses of touch, sight, hearing, taste and smell also transmit 'sensation messages' (pain, irritation etc) and communicate information, and hence protect us from harm or warn us of danger.

When designing for people, therefore, all of these factors must be taken into account as we strive to mould the design to provide the greatest safety, comfort and advantage to the user.

Designing for people

Introduction

All design must begin with an understanding of the product's **functions** which should be listed in the specification (see page 12).

For example, the specification for a personal alarm might be as shown here, but in this case a vital piece of information is missing. It is essential to know **who** will use the design – their **age** and **sex** and whether they are **able-bodied** or **handicapped** and so on. Only then can the **ergonomic** factors be fully investigated.

PERSONAL ALARM SPECIFICATION
1. Must be easy to carry
2. Must be easy to activate in an emergency
3. Should produce a loud 'piercing' sound
4. Must be small enough to store in a handbag or pocket
5. Should be available in a range of colours
6. Maximum cost – £10

Total design

Some of a design's functions will relate directly to the *use of the product by the person*. Others will concern aspects of the design which have no direct 'contact' with the user. However, a designer must be concerned with the **total design**. For example, it would be of no use to design a powerful audio system for the personal alarm, if the components were too big to fit into a case of the appropriate size and shape.

Size

When designing for people you must take into account all the '**measurements**' which are important for the *safe and comfortable use* of the design. However, the shape and size of human beings vary greatly. Designing for an individual therefore, is very different from designing for a group of people. In the case of a group, the average measurements may have to be calculated, but this is not always a satisfactory solution. The science of measuring people is called **anthropometrics**.

Some measurements which might need investigating include:

hand (and other limb) dimensions – these will be important if the design is to be pushed, lifted, held, carried, operated, controlled, manipulated, etc.

body proportions – these are important to ensure that a design is appropriate to the 'size and shape' of the user.

design's overall dimensions – these are important to the convenience and safety of the design in relation to the user, other people and the environment in which the design will be used.

Movements

The human body is capable of a wide range of complex and intricate movements which enable us to carry out numerous different tasks and activities. If in normal use a design causes discomfort, pain or injury, it is a poor design.

Some of the factors to address when designing for movement include:

natural body movements – avoid designs which cause the body to make unnatural movements. *Observe and measure* the limits of the bodily movements in relation to your proposed design, to ensure that the body is protected from having to turn, reach, stretch, bend, lean, stoop, etc. too far.

restricted movements – some movements can prove difficult or painful for some elderly people. These should be taken into account in your designs as should the restricted movements of handicapped users.

body fatigue – human beings work most efficiently when the body feels warm and comfortable. Designs should therefore ensure that all movements and operations can be carried out in comfort and without causing excessive muscle strain. The age and sex of the user must of course be taken into account, since these factors affect a person's strength, stamina, agility, etc.

Dashboard and controls – Ford

balance – the body must remain in balance when moving (otherwise we would fall over). All designs should therefore satisfy or allow for this requirement.

A surfboard's design allows for the continuous adjustment of balance

space – it is important that the space in, on, under, and around a design is sufficient to allow the body to function normally, without limiting the natural movements or causing discomfort.

A tight squeeze – or just enough space?

Senses

Designs can 'come into contact' with the body in a number of ways. They can make physical contact, which we experience through the sense of touch, or 'contact' via the senses of sight, hearing, smell or taste. All of these forms of contact can cause irritation, discomfort or pain (as well as pleasurable sensations of course – see chapter 2).

Some important design factors therefore include:

size, shape and form – make sure that the design fits the part of the body which will come into contact with it, the hand, posterior, back, etc. and avoids uncomfortable or painful pressure points.

surface finishes – avoid sharp edges, dangerous corners and rough surfaces, but remember that texture can be important to good 'grip' in some designs.

supporting surfaces – whilst providing adequate support, these should be soft enough to be comfortable.

For maximum comfort, surfaces should also be designed to minimise sweating. This can be achieved through the appropriate use of materials and good ventilation, for example.

heat and cold – where necessary insulate against heat or cold for the protection and comfort of the user.

noise and vibration – in excess these can be very distressing and damaging to health, therefore observe British Standards.

visual elements – designs which communicate information through sight, using letters, words, symbols etc, should be of an appropriate size, be correctly positioned, use the most effective colour schemes, be well illuminated, display good contrast in colour, shape and form, and so on.

weight – designs which have to be lifted or carried should be designed for minimum weight and ease of use.

Terminal 4 check-in, Heathrow Airport

Design exercise

· Pick up your own **pen** and *look at it carefully* as you hold it in the normal writing position. Now write something with it.

Does it write well? Is it easy to use? Does it feel comfortable? Could you use it for a long period without discomfort? If you can answer '**yes**' to these questions, it would appear that your pen has been well designed for its main function.

Now put your pen down on the table. Does it 'stay' where you put it? Now put it in your pocket, pencil case or bag. Is it convenient to store there, and carry? Does it stay where you put it? Does it stay clean? These are just a few more questions to which you should ideally be able to answer '**yes**'.

Exercise

1 List and *describe in detail* all the **ergonomic** factors which you feel are important to the safe, comfortable and efficient use of a pen.

2 Outline the **anthropometric** data which you feel would be required to produce a successful design and describe how you might obtain some of this data in the classroom.

3 Write a specification for a pen for a particular market, and on paper, produce a range of possible designs.

The diagram opposite will remind you of the areas which need to be addressed. If necessary read this chapter again before you begin, or just scan the **bold headings**.

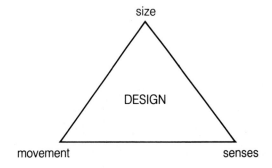

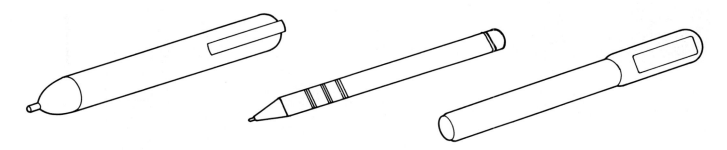

Note   With regard to the **safe** use of a pen, there has been a recent case of a boy who tragically died at school when a pen **top** became stuck in his throat.

CHAPTER FOUR

Structures

The Potteries shopping centre

The Forth bridges, Port Edgar, Scotland

BAe 748

A circus tent

A house under construction

Wherever you look you see examples of **structures**. They occur in nature, and in the things which people make to solve problems to satisfy needs.

What do structures do?

There are many different kinds of structures, each designed to perform a particular job. A few examples are given here. To be successful, all structures however, must:

1 Be capable of carrying the load for which they were designed without toppling over or collapsing, and,
2 Support the various parts of the object in the correct relative position.

Types of structures

The crane and the electricity pylon are examples of **frame structures**. Frames are made from bars joined together to form a 'framework'. This is one of the most economical ways of building structures. Some modern buildings have a frame structure which can only be seen during construction. Others are designed to make the 'frame' a feature of the design. How many different frame structures can you see in these pictures?

Other structures are formed in quite a different way. The body of a motor car, for example, is assembled from shaped panels and is called a **shell** structure.

Structural failure

From time to time something goes wrong with a design and a structure collapses or fails to do its job. There are many causes of structural failure and these can include: poor design, fatigue, and the failure of a material or joint.

Failure occurs because of **forces** acting on the structure. These can be **static** forces (stationary forces) due to the structure's own weight or the load being carried, OR **dynamic** forces (moving forces) produced by the wind, sea, vehicles, people etc.

This chapter looks at the design of structures through an understanding of the forces which act upon them.

A tower crane

An electricity pylon

Car body shells

The Lloyd's building, London

The design of frame structures

If you examine some pictures of familiar frame structures, you may notice a similarity between the structures, as well as obvious differences. In the illustration, Carmel has noticed a very important similarity.

Making structures rigid

Andrew is correct. A 'criss-cross' structure does make a framework rigid.

When **forces** are applied to a simple four-sided structure as shown here, it can be forced out of shape. A structure which behaves in this way is said to be **non-rigid**.

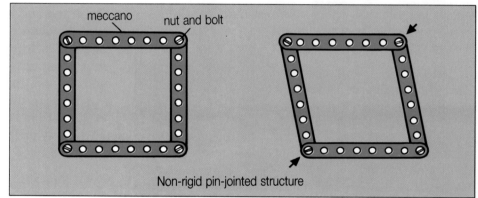

Non-rigid pin-jointed structure

By adding an extra bar (or member) however, corners **A** and **B** are prevented from moving apart. The structure therefore can no longer be forced out of shape, and is said to be **rigid**. Notice that the additional member has formed **triangles** in the structure. The effect is known as **triangulation**. The triangle is the most rigid frame structure.

Alternatively, a frame structure can be made rigid by the use of **gusset** plates. A gusset is simply a piece of material used to brace and join the members in a structure. Triangular gusset plates have been used in this structure.

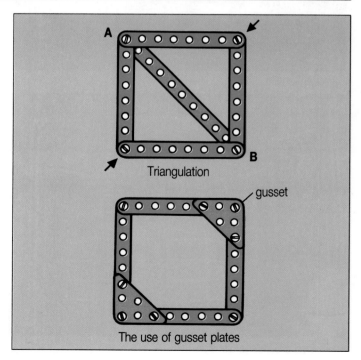

Triangulation

The use of gusset plates

Question

1 Some simple meccano structures are shown. Draw them on a piece of paper and label them R for rigid, and NR for non-rigid.

 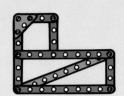 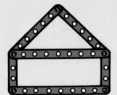 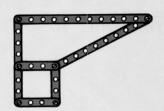 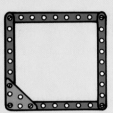

Stability

A structure which will not topple over easily when acted upon by a force is said to be **stable**.

Carmel has applied a force to her model tower by pulling on it with a piece of thread.

When the force is removed, the tower will fall back to its original position. This is the behaviour of a **stable** structure.

When a similar force is applied to this structure however, it tilts and topples over. This is the behaviour of an **unstable** structure.

To gain a better understanding of stability, it is necessary to understand **centre of gravity**.

Stability and centre of gravity

If you try to balance a ruler on your finger – as shown – the ruler topples and falls off.

It does this because the pull of gravity on the material to the right and to the left of your finger is not equal. It is the 'pull of gravity' acting on a substance which gives it its **weight**. (Weight is a **force** which we measure in newtons.)

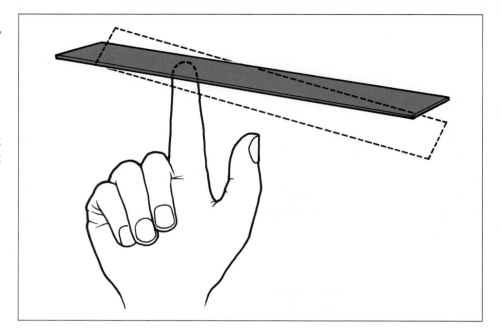

To balance the ruler you must find the point at which the pull of gravity (or weight) acting to the right and to the left of your finger is equal. When you have done this you have found the **centre of gravity**.

You can use this principle to find the centre of gravity of an irregular shaped object, too.

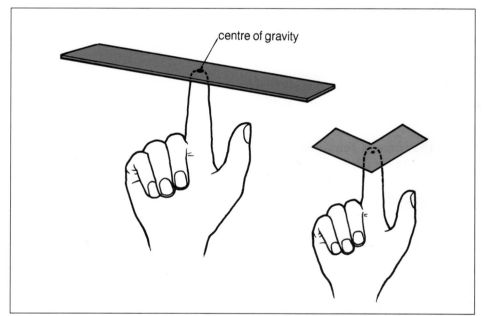

centre of gravity

Question

2 Where do you think the centres of gravity of these shapes are?

Draw the shapes on a piece of paper and mark the C of G with a dot.

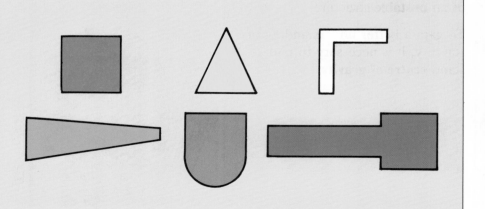

Finding the centre of gravity by experiment

You can check your answers to the above question by doing a simple experiment.

Using thick cardboard, cut out one of the shapes shown above. Hang the 'shape' and a **plumb line** from a nail or large pin. Then draw a pencil line directly underneath the plumb line.

Now hang the 'shape' and the plumb line from a different position. Again draw a pencil line underneath the plumb line. Where the two lines cross is the centre of gravity of the 'shape'.

Try this experiment with other shapes from Question 2.

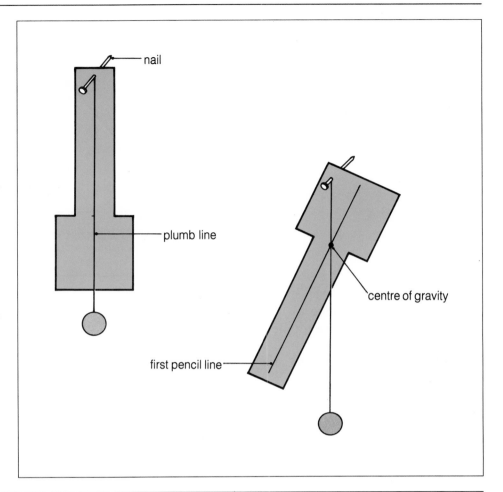

Stable and unstable structures

The **position** of a structure's centre of gravity has a lot to do with its stability.

When an stable structure is tilted, its centre of gravity **rises**. This is important because when the tilting force is removed, gravity pulls the structure back to its original position.

When an unstable structure is tilted however, its centre of gravity moves downwards.

If the centre of gravity moves outside the base area, gravity will make the structure topple over.

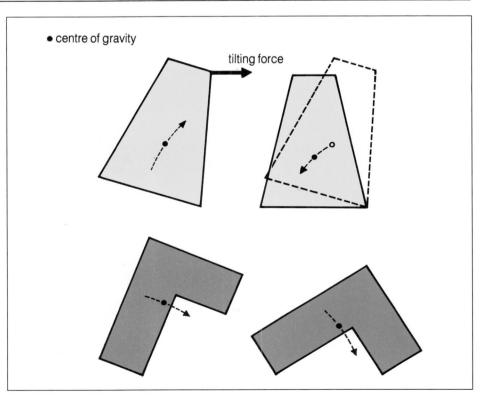

Some general rules about structural stability

The **lower** the centre of gravity of a structure, the more difficult it is to make it topple over. The lower the centre of gravity therefore, the more stable the structure.

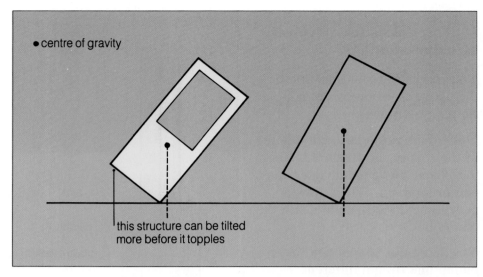

● centre of gravity

this structure can be tilted more before it topples

It is more difficult to make a structure with a **wide base** topple over. The wider the base therefore, the more stable the structure.

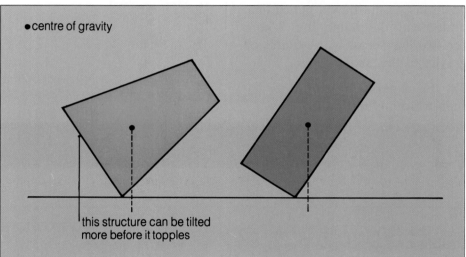

● centre of gravity

this structure can be tilted more before it topples

Question

3 Draw the structures shown on a piece of paper. Label them S for stable, and US for unstable.

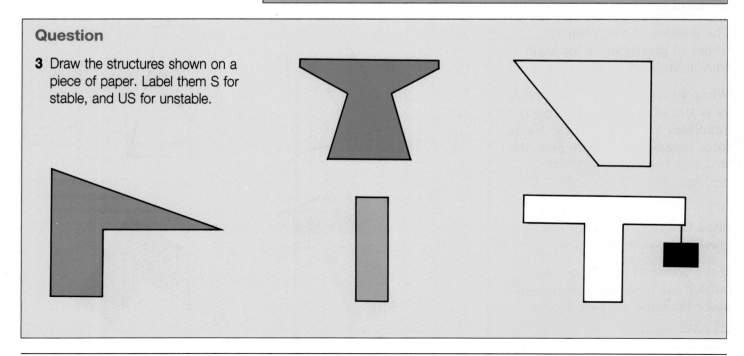

Forces in frame structures

A 'successful' structure must be able to withstand all the forces it will experience without toppling over or collapsing. An understanding of the kinds of forces which can act **on** and **within** a structure is therefore important to a designer. Five different kinds of forces are described below.

Tension forces

Forces which can cause a member to 'stretch' are called **tension** forces.

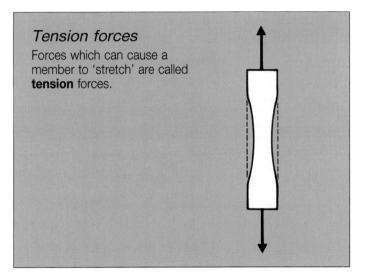

Compression forces

Forces which can cause a member to be 'squashed' or buckled are called **compression** forces.

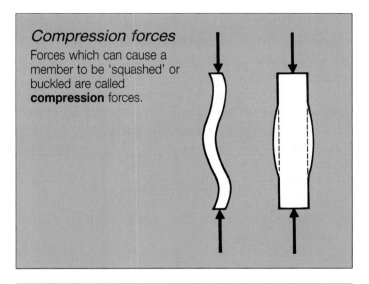

Shear forces

Shear forces act 'across' a material in such a way that one part of the structure can be forced to slide over another.

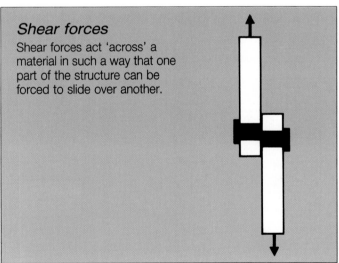

Torsional forces

When a turning force (or **torque**) is applied to a member, the member may twist. The member shown below is said to be in a state of **torsion**.

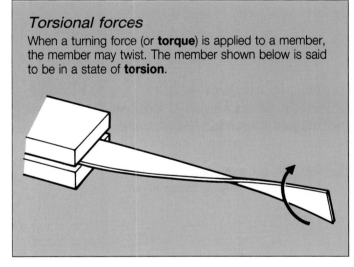

Bending forces

Forces which act at an angle to a member, tend to make it bend. These are called **bending** forces.

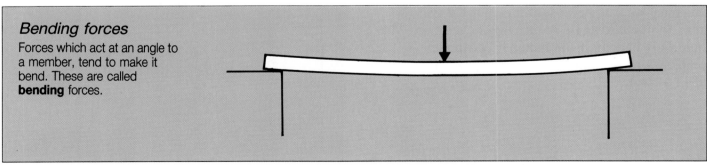

Structural analysis

When designing your first frame structure you may be uncertain about the types of forces acting in each member.

After designing and building this bridge, Carmel asked her teacher to explain how she could work out which forces were acting. The teacher began the explanation like this:

A structure always changes shape when a force is applied to it. In a straw model like this, you can actually watch this happening. The members may be stretched, compressed, bent etc, and in this way internal forces are set up which push back against the external forces produced by the load.

Analysing for tension and compression

In a simple structure it is easy to work out what kind of forces are acting.

In this structure for example, member **AB**, is being stretched by the load and therefore it feels a **tension** force.

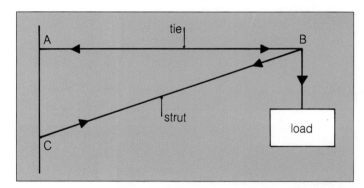

This must be true because if **AB** were to break (as shown), the points **x x** would **move apart**. This could only happen if the member was under tension. A member under tension is called a **tie**.

Member **CB** however, is being squashed. It therefore feels a **compression** force.

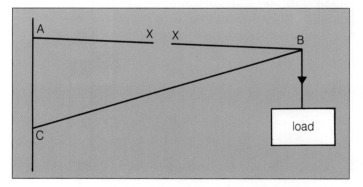

This must be true because if member **CB** were to break, points **x x** would **cross over** one another. This could only happen if the member was under compression. A member under compression is called a **strut**.

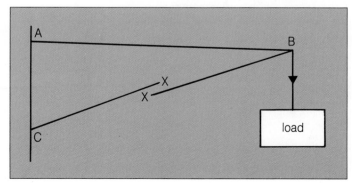

When designing a frame structure therefore, you can check for tension or compression by simply asking yourself this question: 'What would happen to the member if it broke – would the two ends move apart, or would they cross over one another?'

The identification of shear and torsion forces is usually fairly easy, and bending is likely to occur if a force is seen to be acting at an angle to a member.

Pupils building and testing a straw bridge

Questions

4 a Using the above ideas, analyse these structures for tension, compression and bending.

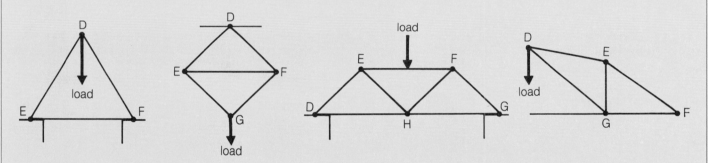

b Now analyse Carmel's bridge structure (shown here). Copy the diagram onto a piece of paper and label the forces acting either C compression, or T tension.

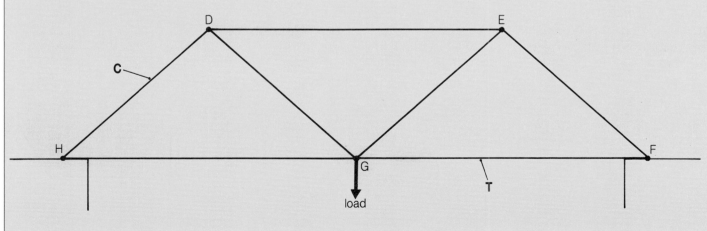

Types of members and their uses

As you have seen above, different members within a structure have to resist different kinds of forces. It is important therefore to choose the most suitable member for the job. In addition to its ability to resist forces however, weight, cost and appearance can be important factors in the choice of a member.

Structural sections

When a member is required to resist **tension forces**, flat strip, cable, or wire can be used successfully. However, all of these 'shapes' or **sections** are poor in compression.

When **compression forces** are present, angle girder, **I** girder and other similar sections must be used.

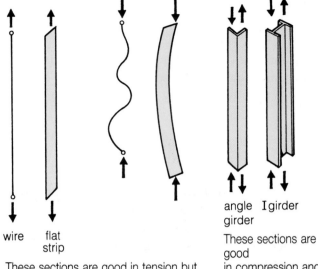

wire   flat strip

These sections are good in tension but poor in compression

angle girder   I girder

These sections are good in compression and tension

Beams

Any member which has to resist **bending** is called a **beam**. Beams are used a great deal in bridge construction and in buildings where we need to span a gap and carry a load.

The **stiffness** of a beam – its ability to resist bending – depends upon the material from which the beam is made, and the **section** of the beam.

For a given material, the stiffness of a simple beam is proportional to its breadth × depth^3 (b × d^3).

Question

5 Which is the stiffest beam section here?

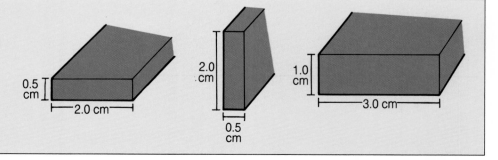

0.5 cm   2.0 cm

2.0 cm   0.5 cm

1.0 cm   3.0 cm

The design of beams

When a beam is loaded as shown, the upper surface 'feels' compression and the lower surface 'feels' tension. However, along an imaginary centre line called the neutral axis, the tension and compression forces cancel out, and the 'resultant' force is zero.

Originally, all beams were made of solid material which made them heavy and expensive. Today, however, many different beam sections are available which can be just as strong as a solid beam, but much lighter, thus giving them a better **strength to weight ratio**.

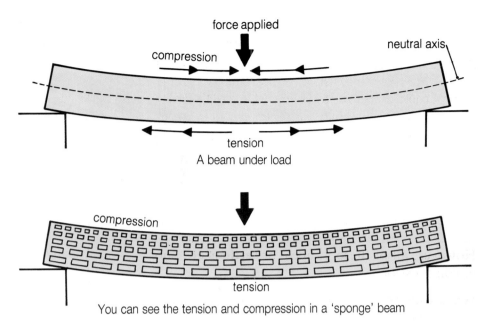

A beam under load

You can see the tension and compression in a 'sponge' beam

Questions

Designers aim to produce beams that are strong enough to do the required job, but at minimum cost and weight. Some good examples are shown here.

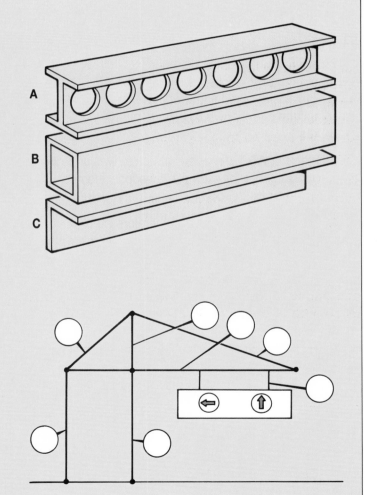

6 Use your understanding of structural sections, and a beam under load, to explain why beam **A** is a particularly good design.

7 The diagram shows the plans for a model road sign gantry (shown in two dimensions). It will be constructed from meccano flat strip and angle. Angle is almost twice the cost of flat strip.
   a Choose the most suitable members to make the structure rigid and strong, but at the same time, as light as possible and at minimum cost.
   b Copy the diagram onto a piece of paper and fill in the circles. Use A to indicate the use of angle, and FS for flat strip. Explain your choice of member in each case.

Questions

8 Many large modern buildings are constructed 'around' a framework of **concrete** beams. Concrete is good in compression, but poor in tension. A 'pure' concrete beam therefore has a certain weakness.

A hospital building under construction

a With your understanding of a beam under load, explain what this weakness is.

b Explain how the steel-reinforced concrete beam shown reduces this problem.

Reinforced concrete beam

9 If wire were used to make this structure rigid, a single member would not do the job.

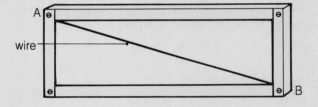

a Explain why, and show where a second member would have to be fitted.

10 If member **AB** in the above structure was an **I** girder or angle girder for example, a second member would **not** be needed to make the structure rigid.

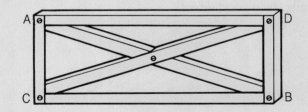

CD in the structure shown can therefore be removed without affecting its rigidity. Any member which can be removed from a frame structure without affecting its rigidity is called a **redundant member**.

Identify redundant members in the structures shown. (All members are good in compression.)

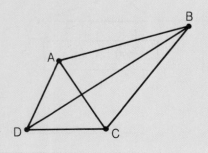

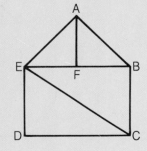

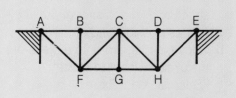

Moments

Have you ever been to a circus and watched a 'high-wire act'? The artist is able to perform balancing tricks, by using the **principle of moments**.

Moments is the strange name given to a simple idea. We can begin to explain moments by thinking about children on a see-saw.

Derrico-Alazanas high-wire act

The see-saw

It's not much fun playing on a see-saw when your big brother or sister does this.

To use the see-saw properly, the heavier person must sit closest to the pivot. You can work out exactly where each child should sit using the principle of moments.

Moments explained

The 'turning effect' produced by each child on the see-saw is called a moment, and it is dependent upon two factors:

1 The **force** produced as a result of the child's weight, and
2 the 'leverage' gained by the **length** of the beam (the **distance** from pivot to child).

The **force** multiplied by the **distance** is called the **moment** of the force.

moment = force × distance

In the see-saw shown, the 600 N force is trying to turn the beam clockwise. Its moment about the pivot is

$600 \times 1 = 600$ Nm (clockwise moments).

The 300 N force however, is trying to turn the beam anticlockwise. Its moment about the pivot is

$300 \times 2 = 600$ Nm (anti-clockwise moments).

Only when the 'clockwise moments' equal the 'anti-clockwise moments' (as in this example) will the beam balance.

Since the unit of force is the newton, and the unit of distance is the metre, you will notice that the unit of moment is the newton metre, Nm.

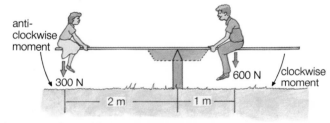

A see-saw in equilibrium

Questions

11 To test your understanding of moments, answer the questions below. (Assume, in each case, that the beam has no weight.)

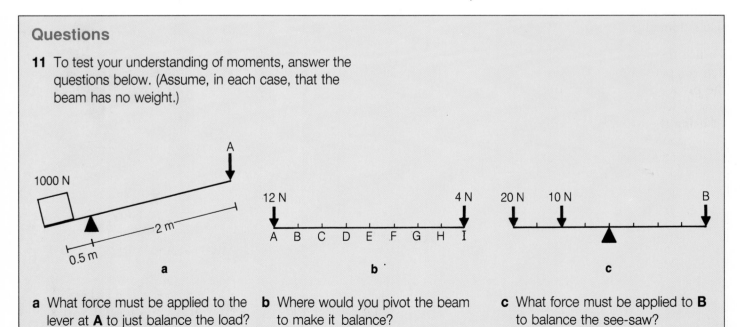

a What force must be applied to the lever at **A** to just balance the load?

b Where would you pivot the beam to make it balance?

c What force must be applied to **B** to balance the see-saw?

Design problem

Using the idea of moments, Andrew and Carmel set about solving the design problem which their teacher had written on the blackboard.

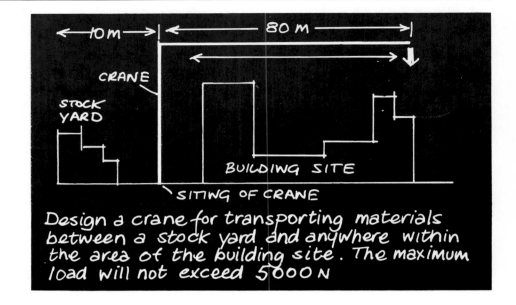

Design a crane for transporting materials between a stock yard and anywhere within the area of the building site. The maximum load will not exceed 5000 N

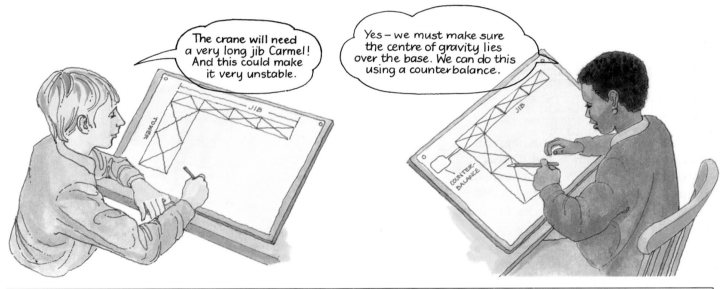

The crane will need a very long jib Carmel! And this could make it very unstable.

Yes – we must make sure the centre of gravity lies over the base. We can do this using a counterbalance.

Questions

12 The diagram shows the final solution chosen to satisfy the brief.

a If the crane was used to lift the maximum load (as shown), what must be the weight of the counterbalance for maximum stability?

b If the position of the load was moved along the jib, the crane would become unstable and could topple over. Explain this, and show how this could be prevented.

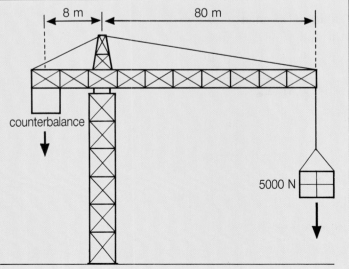

The cantilever

A beam which is supported at one end only is called a **cantilever**. Some examples of cantilever structures are shown.

When a cantilever is required to carry a large load, **bending moments** must be taken into account.

Some bridges are constructed as shown here, with a central section inserted between double cantilevers. Notice that the cantilever beams are thicker at their centres. This is necessary because of bending moments.

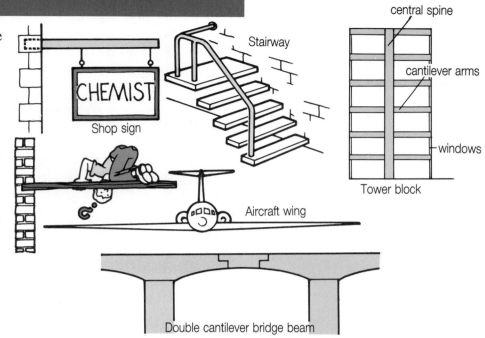

Shop sign · Stairway · central spine · cantilever arms · windows · Tower block · Aircraft wing · Double cantilever bridge beam

CHEMIST

Bending moments explained

When a force is applied to a beam, as shown here, the beam experiences 'stress' to some degree at all points between **A** and **B**. It is at **A**, however, where most stress occurs, and where the beam is most likely to break. (You can prove this by experimenting with a thin piece of wood bent over the edge of a table.) We say that the greatest **bending moment** is at **A**.

Bending moment is the product of the **force** and the **distance** between the force and the point of bending.

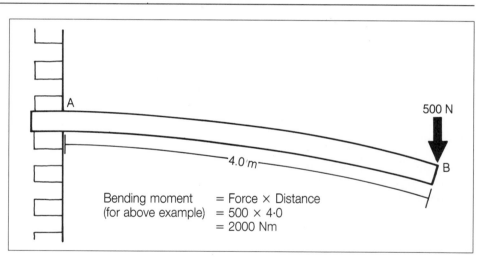

A

500 N

4.0 m

B

Bending moment = Force × Distance
(for above example) = 500 × 4·0
= 2000 Nm

Questions

13 a What is the bending moment at **A** and **B** for the cantilever shown opposite?

b Explain why the beams in the cantilever bridge above are made 'thicker' at their centres.

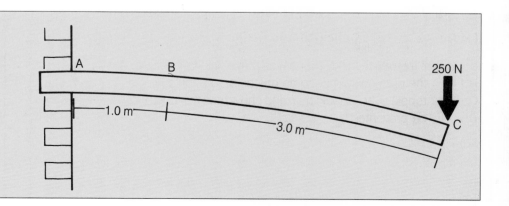

A

B

250 N

1.0 m

3.0 m

C

Structures mini-project – Bridge

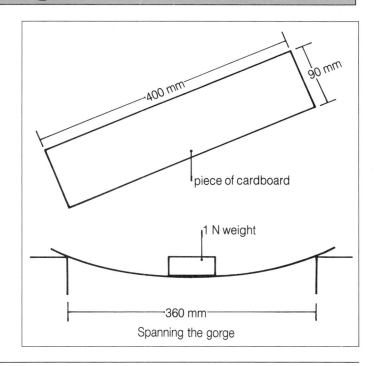

What to do first

1 Find a piece of cardboard and cut a strip 400 mm long by 90 mm wide. This will be used for the 'roadway' of your bridge.

2 Using two tables, or two blocks of wood, create a 'gorge' 360 mm wide.

3 Span the gorge with the cardboard, and load it with a 1 N weight. The card should sag 'badly'. If it doesn't, add more weight until it does. **Remember this weight**.

piece of cardboard

1 N weight

360 mm

Spanning the gorge

Brief

Using the card as the 'roadway', and Artstraws for the remaining structure, **design** (on paper) a bridge. The bridge must carry up to twenty times the original load on the card. No straws must be be positioned below the 'roadway'.

Useful information

Before you begin designing, examine the straws from which your bridge will be constructed.

Try stretching one of the straws – in other words, put it in **tension**.

Then put a straw under **compression**. You will discover that straws are much stronger in tension than under compression.

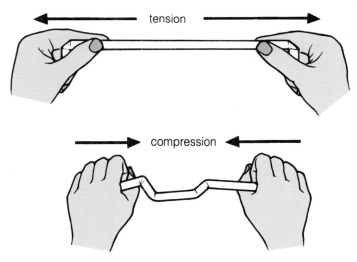

tension

compression

Use this knowledge to help you to design a successful bridge.

Analyse the designs for tension and compression and see if each straw member is 'up to' the job you are giving it. If not, modify the design.

Note When you have considered several designs, **choose** the one which you think will best satisfy the brief. You will then be ready to begin construction work.

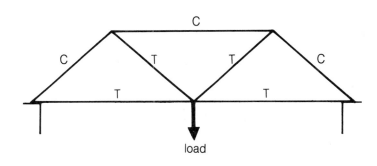

load

Construction work

For this project you will need:
  1 piece of thin card –
    400 mm × 90 mm
  15–20 Artstraws
    (420 mm length)
  1 glue gun and glue stick
  20–30 1 N (100 g) slotted
    weights
  Paper, pen, pencil and ruler.

Learning from the project

Test your bridge at several stages as the work progresses.

Gently load it as shown, and notice **how** and **where** it begins to fail – but don't allow members to become damaged.

Final test

When the bridge is complete, load it until it eventually fails. Take careful note of how and where it fails.

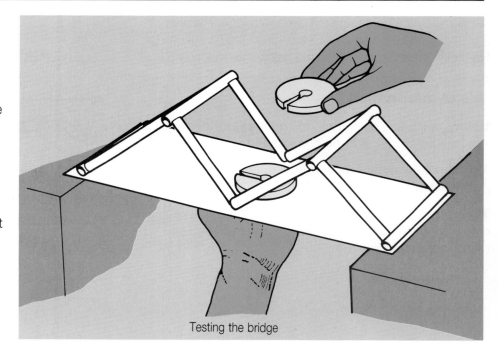

Testing the bridge

The report

You should now write a report containing the following:

1 The project brief.
2 Any information on frame structures which you made use of.
3 Sketches showing several possible designs which you considered.
4 Notes explaining your choice of design.
5 Any important information concerning the construction work.
6 Notes concerning the tests you made, and any modifications made as a result of these tests.
7 Notes concerning the final test – describe how the various parts of the structure failed, and under what kind of loading.
8 An evaluation of the project – identifying successful and unsuccessful features in the design.

Structures mini-project — Cantilever

Brief

Using an empty kitchen roll tube as the tower, and Artstraws for the remaining structure, design and construct a 'double' cantilever.

The right-hand beam must carry twice the load of the left-hand beam. (6 N and 3 N minimum.) The structure must be free-standing (not attached to the base), and it must be stable.

Before construction, analyse your designs (as for the bridge project).

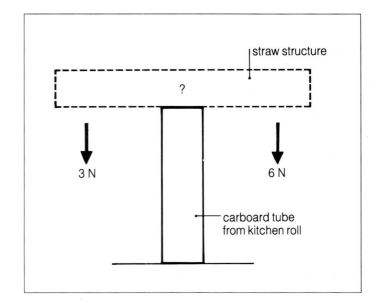

Construction work

For this project you will need:
    1 empty kitchen roll tube
    10 Artstraws (420 mm long)
    1 glue gun and glue stick
    2 slotted weight hangers
    18 1 N (100 g) slotted weights
    Paper, pen, pencil and ruler.

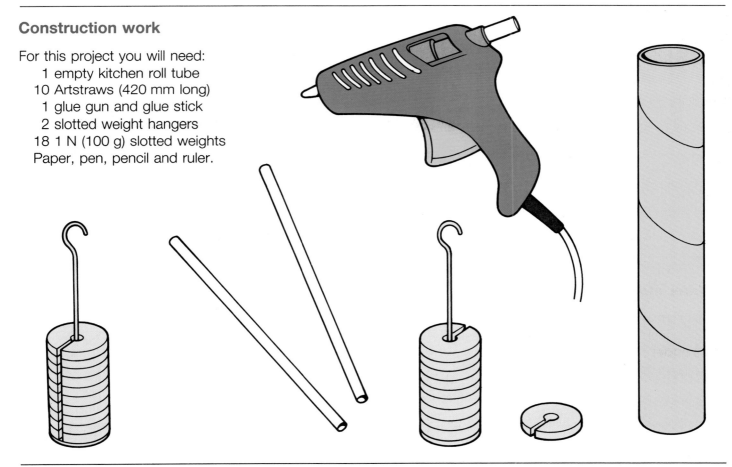

Report

Write a report as for the bridge project (page 64).

Project briefs

A number of project briefs are given below. Follow the design process (outlined in Chapter 1) as you try to satisfy the briefs. Any suitable materials can be used to realize the projects including wood strips, Artstraws and cardboard.

1 Playframe – activity centre

A local authority has provided a safe 'woodchip' play area in a city centre park.

Design and build a scale model of a playframe–activity centre to be positioned on the site. The structure should provide for a range of play activities and can include moving structures (swings etc.) providing that they do not endanger other users.

woodchip play area

2 Pop group's mobile stage

A local pop group requires a stage and canopy for use on a summer tour of open air concerts.

Design and construct a scale model of a suitable design. The design should be made from lightweight sections which can be erected, dismantled, stored and transported easily.

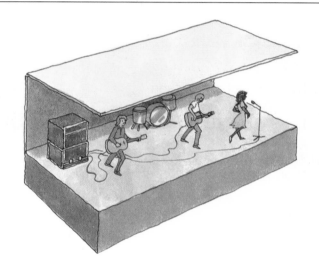

3 Water storage tank

A water storage tank is required for an industrial plant. The tank will contain 10 000 gallons of water (mass approximately 50 000 kg) and be positioned 8 metres above the ground.

Design and construct a model of the tower using Artstraws. The model should be 25 cm high, and support a mass of 1.5 kg.

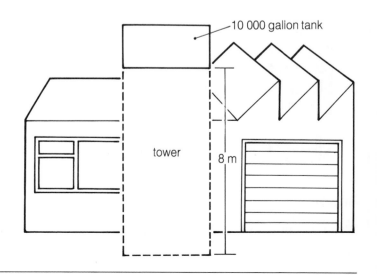

10 000 gallon tank

tower

8 m

4 Footbridge

An additional car park is to be provided for a 'superstore' to cater for peak hour shopping periods. The car park will be situated across a busy road from the store and will therefore require an access bridge. The store is situated on raised ground 4 metres above the car park level.

Design and build a scale model of a footbridge suitable for pedestrians, pushchairs, wheelchairs and shopping trolleys.

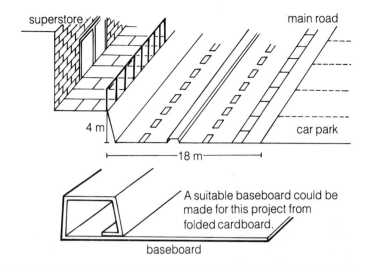

A suitable baseboard could be made for this project from folded cardboard.

baseboard

5 Rapid assembly shelter

Famine and disaster relief agencies are often required to provide emergency shelter for homeless families.

Design and construct a 1/10 scale model of a quick-assembly shelter from suitable materials. The shelter should enable four adults to stand comfortably and sleep a family of six. It must be constructed from sections which can be fitted together easily, **or** be in the form of a 'fold-down' assembly. The shelter must protect the occupants from wind, rain, and sub-zero temperatures.

Shelters in use: Leninakan after the earthquake, 1988

6 Cantilever grandstand

A cantilever type grandstand canopy is required for a football stadium.

Design a 1/100 scale model of the canopy which will provide adequate protection from the weather, and construct a 1/4 length section of the model.

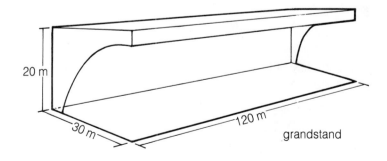

grandstand

Further ideas for projects

- Baby's play pen
- Model kit car chassis and body shell
- Suspension bridge

- Collapsible child's play house
- Novel style greenhouse
- Dry ski slope.

Examples of school technology projects

Lightweight pushchair
(Caroline Cunningham – 4th year)

Brief   I enjoy working with children in the school creche. My idea is to design and make a light pushchair which can be folded easily.

Solution

Cantilever (Teacher's brief)

Brief   Design and construct a cantilever using Artstraws. It must be capable of supporting a mass of 2 kg (20 N), at a distance of 35 cm from the bench.

One pupil's solution

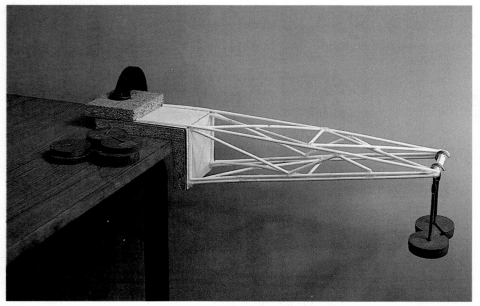

Road-bridge (Teacher's brief)

Design and construct a road bridge to cross a (model) gorge 80 cm wide. The structure should be made from 6 mm square wooden strips, hardboard, and glue. The island in the river at the bottom of the gorge can be used to support the structure if required. The maximum length of any one member must not exceed 45 cm. The bridge must not be attached to the gorge.

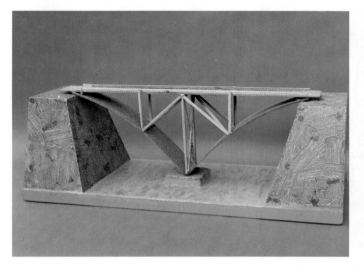 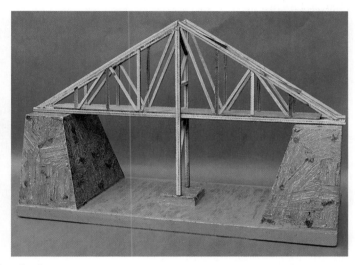

Two pupils' solutions

Fairground ride (Teacher's brief)

Brief Design and construct a 'fairground ride' toy using any suitable materials. The toy can have moving parts, but must be safe for young children to use.

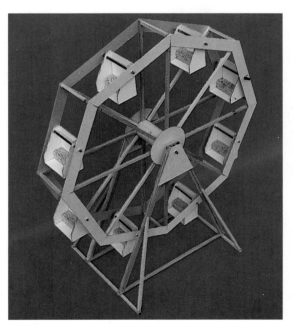 

Two pupils' solutions

CHAPTER FIVE

Mechanisms

Logging machinery

Wind generator

Water wheel

Tractor and plough

Food mixer

Oil derrick

Scissor jack

Forklift truck

The technological advances made by people through the ages have been closely linked with their ability to harness energy. The beauty of energy is that it can be transferred from one form into another. For example, the kinetic energy (or motion energy) of rushing water can be transferred, by a water wheel, into rotary kinetic energy. Similarly, a modern aerogenerator transfers the kinetic energy of the wind into electrical energy in the wires of the generator. These, and all the other 'energy converters' shown on this page are of course examples of **machines**.

Mechanisms

All machines, however basic or complex, are made up of simple **mechanisms**. A mechanism is a device which changes an input motion and force, into a desired output motion and force.

The car jack shown uses a **screw** and **nut mechanism**. This changes the 'round and round' motion (or **rotary motion**) at the screw into a straight line motion (or **linear motion**) at the nut, and changes a **small force** at the screw into a **large force** at the nut. In this way, only a small effort is required by the motorist, to raise the heavy load through the action of the scissor mechanism.

Unlike the scissor jack, most machines today have their mechanisms hidden from view within the body of the machine or behind panels. For aesthetic, ergonomic and safety reasons therefore, we rarely see them. You can be sure however, that wherever **movement** takes place, whether in a simple device like a door handle or a complex technological system, mechanisms will be found.

This chapter is all about different mechanisms, how they work, and how they can be used.

Pulley systems

Rotary motion is the most common type of motion to be found in machines.

In many machines, rotary motion must be **transmitted** from one shaft to another. On the pillar drill shown, for example, rotary motion is transmitted from the motor shaft to the output shaft or spindle. A pulley system is one kind of mechanism which can do this. In the illustration Jill is examining the drill's pulley system with her teacher.

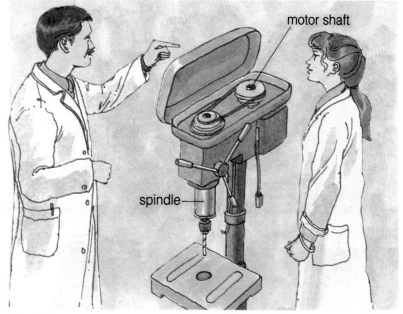

Pillar drill

Pulleys explained

A **pulley** is simply a wheel with a groove in its rim.

Using two pulleys and a flexible drive belt (to link the pulleys together), rotary motion and **torque** can be transmitted from one shaft to another. Torque, which can be described as the **turning force**, is explained fully on pages 100 and 101.

Features of belt and pulley transmission systems

The main advantages of belt and pulley transmission systems are that they are: **quiet** in operation, require **no lubrication**, and are **relatively cheap** to produce. They are used in domestic appliances for these reasons.

The main disadvantage is that slip can occur. They should only be used therefore where slip will not affect the operation of the machine.

In certain circumstances, slip can actually be useful. For example, if a machine like a pillar drill jams, the drive belt can slip. This could protect the user from injury, and protect the drive motor from damage.

Some examples of the use of belt and pulley transmission systems are shown.

Appliances using pulley systems

Washing machine – rear panel removed

Lawnmower

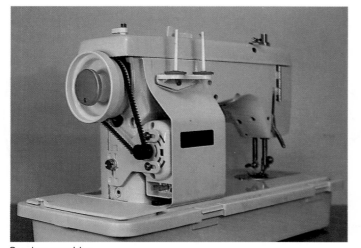

Sewing machine

Motor car engine

Shop window display project

The photograph shows one pupil's solution to the following **brief**:

Design a kinetic shop window display to attract the attention of the public and advertise a product.

The display is belt and pulley driven and uses a crank and slider mechanism to operate the saw. The crank and slider is described on page 90.

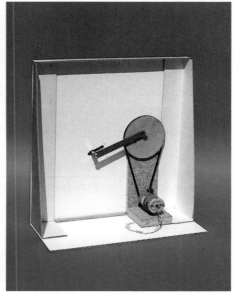

Speed ratio

The speed at which a machine's output shaft rotates, will depend upon the function of that machine. In the case of a record player for example, the output shaft must rotate at 45 rpm (45 revolutions per minute) and 33 rpm.

The rotary speed of the output shaft depends upon the **speed ratio** of the pulley system, and the speed at which the motor shaft rotates.

Record deck

Speed ratio explained

When a small pulley is used to drive a large pulley, the large pulley rotates **more slowly** than the small pulley. This can be explained by looking at the diagram of the transmission of motion by a pulley system.

If the 'driver' pulley has a circumference of say 8 cm, and the driven pulley a circumference of 24 cm, then for **one complete turn** of the driver pulley, 8 cm of drive belt is 'moved along'. The driven pulley therefore will only rotate through **one third of a turn**, as 8 cm of drive belt moves along.

Now, since the driven pulley only rotates through one third of a turn for each complete turn of the driver pulley, the driven pulley will only rotate at one third of the speed of the driver pulley.

The **ratio** between the rotary speed of the **driver** pulley and the **driven** pulley is known as the **speed ratio**. In the example above, the speed ratio is 3 : 1.

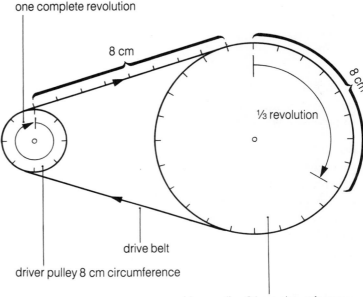

one complete revolution

8 cm

8 cm

⅓ revolution

drive belt

driver pulley 8 cm circumference

driven pulley 24 cm circumference

The transmission of motion by a pulley system

Calculating speed ratio – pulley system

A quick way of working out the speed ratio of a pulley system is to use this equation.

$$\text{speed ratio} = \frac{\text{circumference of driven pulley}}{\text{circumference of driver pulley}}$$

In above example,

$$\text{speed ratio} = \frac{24}{8} = \frac{3}{1} \text{ or } 3 : 1$$

- -

A more convenient way of working out speed ratio (or **velocity ratio** as it is usually called), is to use the equation shown here. The answer will be the same.

$$\textbf{Velocity ratio} = \frac{\textbf{diameter of driven pulley}}{\textbf{diameter of driver pulley}}$$

Rotary shaft speeds

Once the velocity ratio of a system is known, the rotary speed (or **rotary velocity**) of a given shaft can be calculated.

The pulley system shown has a velocity ratio of 2 : 1. If you could rotate the input shaft at exactly 60 rpm, the output shaft would rotate at half this speed, i.e. 30 rpm.

The equation for calculating the rpm of the driven shaft is given below.

$$\text{RPM (of driven shaft)} = \frac{\text{RPM of driver shaft} \times \text{diameter of driver pulley}}{\text{diameter of driven pulley}}$$

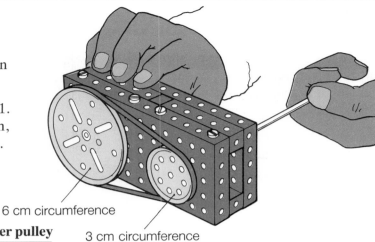

6 cm circumference

3 cm circumference

Pulley system made from Meccano

No-slip belt and pulley system

Where a quiet, no-slip drive is required, a special toothed belt and pulleys can be used.

Some motor car engine timing mechanisms use this system. In a car engine it is essential that the crankshaft and camshaft rotate 'in step' with one another. Any slip would cause serious damage to the engine.

Motor car engine timing mechanism

Questions

1 The air compressor below is driven via a pulley system from a motor running at 300 rpm as shown.
   a What is the velocity ratio of the pulley system?
   b At what speed does the compressor shaft rotate?

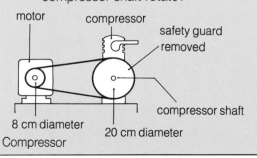

motor   compressor

safety guard removed

compressor shaft

8 cm diameter
Compressor

20 cm diameter

2 The diagram shows a stepped cone pulley system as used on some pillar drills. By changing the position of the V belt, three different shaft speeds can be obtained.
   a In which position must the belt be engaged to provide the highest drill speed?
   b If the drive motor runs at 1400 rpm, what is the highest drill speed?
   c What is the slowest speed at which the drill will run?

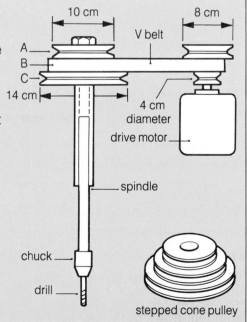

10 cm   8 cm

V belt

A
B
C

14 cm

4 cm diameter
drive motor

spindle

chuck

drill

stepped cone pulley

Chain and sprocket systems

Where it is essential to have no slip, but also a very **strong** drive linkage, a **chain and sprocket** system can be used.

Probably the most familiar use for this system is on the bicycle.

Milk race cyclists

Chain and sprocket explained

A **sprocket** is a toothed wheel, and a **chain** is a length of loosely jointed links.

Rotary motion and torque is transmitted between shafts by the traction between the chain and sprockets.

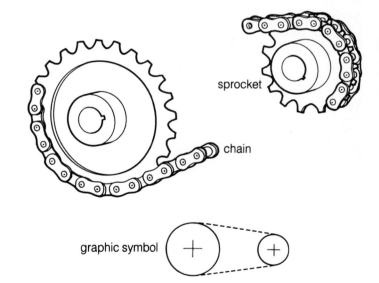

sprocket

chain

graphic symbol

Features of chain and sprocket transmission systems

The main advantage of a chain and sprocket transmission system is the positive, **no-slip drive**. This is essential in machinery where the relative position of the moving parts must not change.

The disadvantages include: the relatively high **cost**, the need for **lubrication** to reduce wear, 'backlash' between chain and sprockets, and **noisy** operation.

Some applications of the chain and sprocket transmission are shown.

Appliances using chain and sprocket systems

Motorcycle

Motor mower

Small printing machine

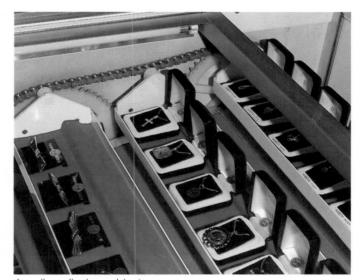

Jewellery display cabinet

Conveyor belt project

The photograph shows a pupil's idea for a sand quarry conveyor system. Sprockets and chain are used to link the conveyors providing a positive drive. This system also allows the position and angle of the belts to be changed to suit most conditions.

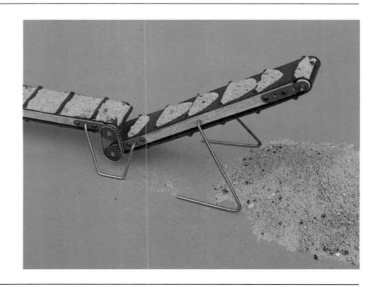

Velocity ratio

The velocity ratio of a chain and sprocket transmission system depends upon the **number of teeth** on the driven and the driver sprockets.

When a small sprocket is used to drive a large sprocket, the large sprocket rotates more slowly than the small sprocket. This can be explained by looking at the diagram of transmission of motion by the chain and sprocket.

If the driver sprocket has say 12 teeth, and the driven sprocket has 24 teeth, then for one **complete turn** of the driver sprocket, 12 links of chain are moved along. The driven sprocket therefore, will only rotate through **half a turn** as 12 links move along.

Now, since the driven sprocket only rotates through **half** a turn for each complete turn of the driver sprocket, the driven sprocket will only rotate at **half the speed** (or velocity) of the driver sprocket.

The **velocity ratio** of the above system therefore is 2 : 1.

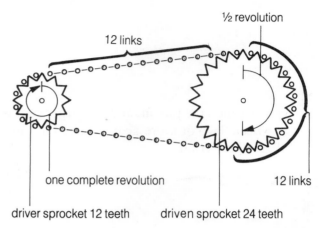

The transmission of motion by the chain and sprocket

Calculating velocity ratio – chain and sprocket

A quick way of working out the **velocity ratio** of a chain and sprocket transmission system is to use this equation,

$$\text{velocity ratio} = \frac{\textbf{number of teeth on the driven sprocket}}{\textbf{number of teeth on the driver sprocket}}$$

In above example,

$$\text{velocity ratio} = \frac{24}{12} = \frac{2}{1} \text{ or } 2 : 1$$

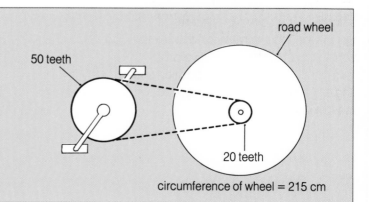

Gear systems

The **gear train** is another mechanism for transmitting rotary motion and torque. Unlike a belt and pulley, or chain and sprocket, no **linking device** (**belt** or **chain**) is required. Gears have **teeth** which interlock (or **mesh**) directly with one another.

Neena has used gears in this simple winch model.

These are called **spur gears**. The name probably originates from their resemblance to spurs worn by horse riders in olden days.

When spur gears of different sizes are meshed, the smaller gear is called the **pinion**, and the larger gear is called the **wheel**. Two or more gears meshed in this way is called a **gear train**.

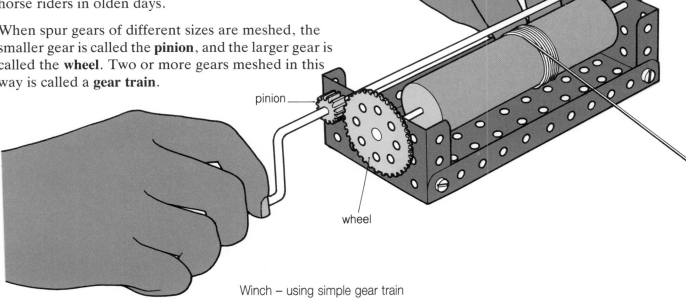

Winch – using simple gear train

Spur gears explained

The diagram shows a simple gear train where **A** is the driver gear, and **B** is the driven gear.

When A makes one complete turn, its 15 teeth move past point **X** on the diagram. Since the gears are meshed (and cannot slip), 15 teeth on the driven gear also pass point **X**. For **each complete turn** of the driver gear therefore, the driven gear only rotates through a **quarter of a turn**.

Now, since the driven gear only rotates through a quarter of a turn for each complete turn of the driver gear, the driven gear will only rotate at a quarter of the speed (or velocity) of the driver gear.

The velocity ratio of the above system therefore (and **gear ratio**) is 4 : 1.

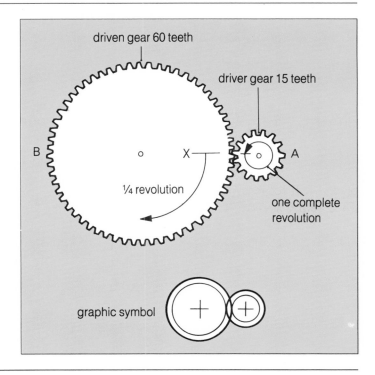

Calculating gear ratio – simple gear train

To calculate the gear ratio of a simple gear train, use the equation shown here.

$$\text{Gear ratio} = \frac{\textbf{number of teeth on driven gear}}{\textbf{number of teeth on driver gear}}$$

For previous example,

$$\text{Gear ratio} = \frac{60}{15}$$

$$= \frac{4}{1} \text{ or } 4 : 1$$

Compound gear train

Sometimes a simple gear train cannot provide a big enough gear ratio.

In the picture, Julie is testing one of her designs for a cot mobile. It was important to make the mobile's arms rotate slowly to relax and calm the baby. On this prototype she experimented with a compound gear train.

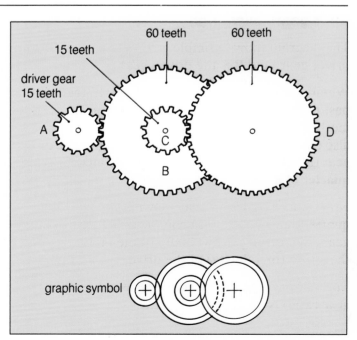

The compound gear train explained

The diagram shows the compound gear train used for the cot mobile. Notice that four gears are used and that gears **B** and **C** are **fixed together** on the same shaft.

When the driver gear **A** makes one complete turn, gear **B** will rotate through a quarter of a turn. Now, since gear **C** is fixed to the same shaft as gear **B**, it too makes a quarter of a turn. Gear **D** therefore will only rotate through a $\frac{1}{4}$ of a $\frac{1}{4}$ of a turn, i.e. $\frac{1}{16}$ of a turn. The gear ratio of this compound gear train therefore, is 16 : 1.

driver gear
15 teeth

15 teeth

60 teeth

60 teeth

A

C

B

D

graphic symbol

Calculating gear ratio – compound gear train

To calculate the gear ratio of a compound gear train, use the equation shown here.

$$\textbf{Gear ratio} = \frac{\textbf{no. of teeth on B}}{\textbf{no. of teeth on A}} \times \frac{\textbf{no. of teeth on D}}{\textbf{no. of teeth on C}}$$

In previous example,

$$\begin{aligned}
\text{gear ratio} &= \frac{60}{15} \times \frac{60}{15} \\[2mm]
&= \frac{4}{1} \times \frac{4}{1} \\[2mm]
&= \frac{16}{1} \text{ or } 16 : 1
\end{aligned}$$

Idler gear

When two spur gears are meshed in the normal way, the driver gear and the driven gear **rotate in opposite directions** to one another.

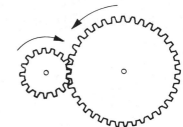

Direction of rotation of gears

However, by making use of an extra gear, called an **idler**, the driver and the driven gears can be made to rotate in the **same direction**.

Note   It is important to understand that an idler gear does **not** alter the gear ratio of a system, neither does it change the velocity ratio.

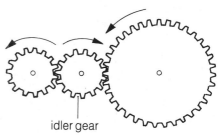

idler gear

Simple gear train with idler gear

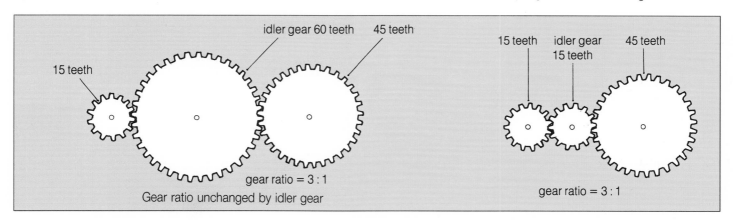

idler gear 60 teeth   45 teeth

15 teeth

gear ratio = 3 : 1

Gear ratio unchanged by idler gear

15 teeth   idler gear 15 teeth   45 teeth

gear ratio = 3 : 1

Features of spur gear transmission systems

The main advantage of a spur gear transmission system is its **compactness**. Another important feature is the **minimal backlash** between gears.

The main disadvantage (of machined metal gears) is **high cost**. Inefficiency due to friction is another problem – this can be reduced by lubrication.

Some examples of the applications of spur gear transmission systems are shown.

Appliances using gear systems

Lathe gearbox

Gearbox from washing machine programme timer

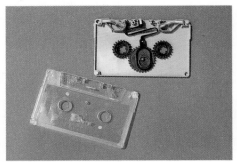

Cassette tape head cleaner

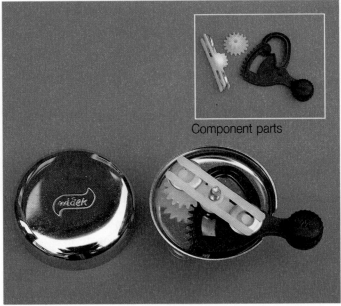

Component parts

Cycle bell

Semi-automatic record deck

Printing machine project

The photograph shows a pupil's hand-operated fabric printing machine. The print roller is driven through spur gears, and the pressure roller and ink roller are driven by friction.

The print design is cut into a piece of cycle inner tube which slides onto the print roller.

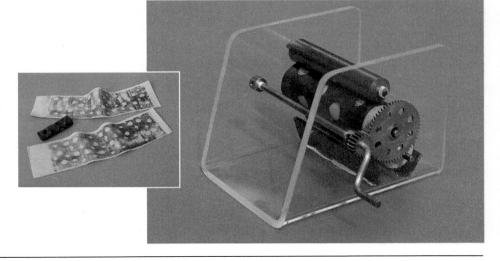

Questions

5 A simple gear train is shown. Driver gear **A** has 20 teeth. When shaft **A** is rotated 10 times, shaft **B** rotates 5 times.
   a How many teeth has gear **B**?
   b What is the gear ratio of the system?
   c If shaft **A** rotates at 60 rpm, at what speed does shaft **B** rotate?
   d If shaft A rotates anti-clockwise, in which direction does shaft **B** rotate?

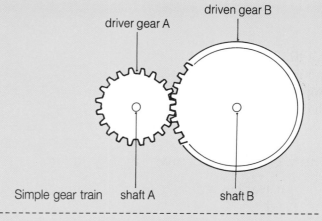

driver gear A
driven gear B
Simple gear train   shaft A   shaft B

---

6 a What is the name of the transmission system shown?
   b What is the gear ratio of the system?
   c If shaft **C** rotates at 36 rpm, at what speed will shaft **D** rotate?

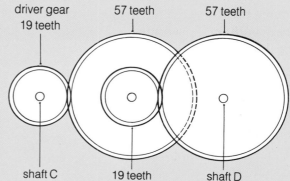

driver gear 19 teeth   57 teeth   57 teeth
shaft C   19 teeth   shaft D

---

7 a What is the gear ratio of the transmission system shown?
   b If gear **E** rotates clockwise, in which direction will gear **F** rotate?

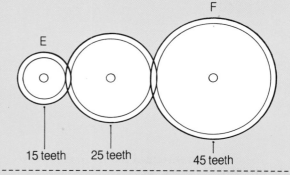

E   F
15 teeth   25 teeth   45 teeth

---

8 The black box shown contains a simple gear train. When shaft **G** is rotated 10 times, shaft **H** rotates 8 times.
   a Using two gears chosen from those listed below, sketch the transmission system which the box contains.

   Gears – 35 teeth, 30 teeth, 25 teeth, 20 teeth.

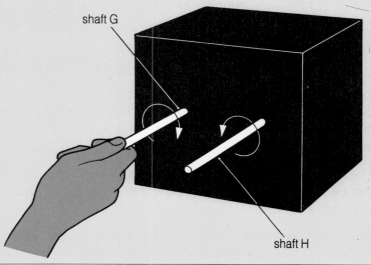

shaft G
shaft H

Worm and wormwheel

All the rotary mechanisms described so far transmit motion between **parallel** shafts. The **worm** and **wormwheel** however, transmit motion between shafts which are at **right angles**.

The worm and wormwheel explained

A worm gear has just **one tooth** in the form of a screw thread, or spiral.

Each time the worm makes one complete revolution, just one tooth on the wormwheel moves past point **X** on the diagram.

To make the wormwheel make one complete revolution therefore, the worm must rotate 60 times (in the example shown).

Now, since the worm must rotate 60 times for each complete revolution of the wormwheel, the worm must rotate 60 times faster than the wormwheel. The velocity ratio (and gear ratio) of the above system therefore is 60 : 1.

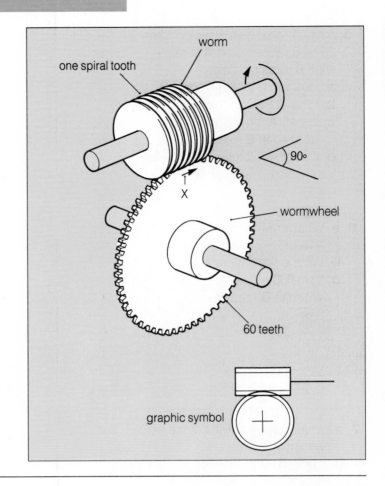

Calculating gear ratio – wormwheel

To calculate the gear ratio of a worm and wormwheel, use the equation shown here.

$$\text{Gear ratio} = \frac{\textbf{number of teeth on wormwheel}}{\textbf{number of teeth on worm}}$$

In previous example,

$$\text{Gear ratio} = \frac{60}{1} \text{ or } 60 : 1$$

Features of the worm and wormwheel transmission system

Probably the most important characteristic of a worm and wormwheel is the very **high gear ratios** which are possible. The ability to transmit motion through right angles, and the very quiet operation of the gears, is also important.

The main disadvantage (of metal gears) is their high cost. Plastic gears however can be produced more cheaply, especially if injection moulded in large quantities.

Some applications of the worm and wormwheel are shown.

Appliances using the worm and wormwheel

Guitar machine heads

Cassette recorder

Motor car windscreen wiper mechanism

Model railway engine

Industrial motor unit

Model railway engine

Dockside crane project

The photograph shows a pupil's dockside crane model. It was made using a variety of constructional materials and components.

A worm and wormwheel has been used to advantage in this model. A very useful feature of a worm and wormwheel is that the gears can only be driven by turning the worm shaft. If you try to turn the wormwheel shaft, the system 'locks up'. This makes the crane safe to use because when the drive motor is switched off, the load will not come crashing down.

Dockside crane project

The conversion of rotary motion into linear motion

Many technological problems involve movement in a straight line (or **linear motion**). Linear motion can be produced by the **conversion** of rotary motion using a **rack** and **pinion**.

The rack and pinion explained

A **rack** is a '**flat**' **gear** whose teeth mesh with the teeth of a pinion.

If the pinion is rotated about a fixed centre, the rack will move 'sideways' in a straight line.

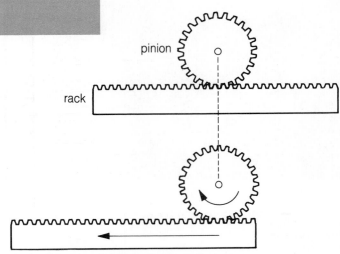

Rack and pinion (rotary to linear motion)

Linear to rotary motion

A rack and pinion can also be used to convert linear motion into rotary motion.

If the pinion is free to rotate – but cannot move sideways – linear motion of the rack will produce rotary motion in the pinion.

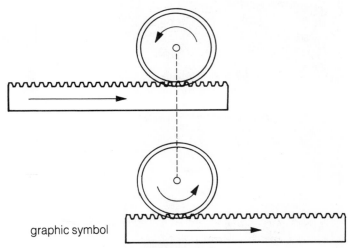

Rack and pinion (linear to rotary motion)

Velocity ratio (Rotary to linear motion).
The ratio between the pinion speed and the linear rack speed for a rack and pinion depends upon three factors.

1 The rotary speed of the pinion,
2 the number of teeth on the pinion,
3 the number of teeth per centimetre on the rack. This can be explained by looking at the diagram shown.

If the pinion has say 20 teeth, then for each complete revolution it makes, 20 pinion teeth will move past point **X** on the diagram. Now since the rack and pinion are meshed, 20 rack teeth must also move past point **X**. If the rack has 5 teeth per centimetre, then for each rotation of the pinion, $20 \div 5 = 4.0$ cm of rack will move past point **X**.

If the pinion rotates at say 10 rpm therefore, the rack will move at a linear speed of 40 cm per minute.

Some applications of the rack and pinion are shown.

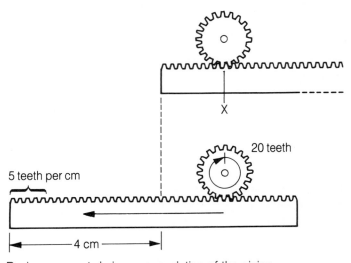

Rack movement during one revolution of the pinion

Appliances using rack and pinion systems

Sluice gate at lock

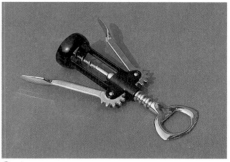

Corkscrew

Pillar drill

Microscope

Camera tripod

Sliding door project

The photograph shows a pupil's sliding door model. The door is driven by a rack and pinion. You can read about the electrical circuit used to control the door in Chapter 6.

Question

9 If the pinion has 20 teeth and the rack has 5 teeth per centimetre, how long would it take for the door to open (or close) if the pinion shaft rotates at 24 revolutions per minute? The door must move 8 cm to fully open (or close).

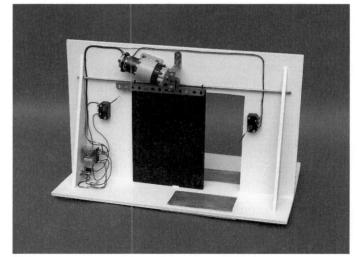

Sliding door project (Fraser Campbell – 5th year)

Screw mechanisms

The **screw mechanism** is another device which converts rotary motion into linear motion.

The screw mechanism explained

A screw is simply a spiral groove cut into the surface of a round bar.

When threaded into a tapped hole, or nut, the screw's rotary motion produces linear motion as one thread 'climbs' into the other.

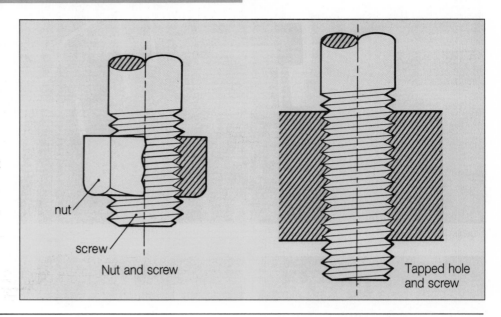

Nut and screw

Tapped hole and screw

Rotary to linear motion

The linear movement produced by the rotation of the screw is determined by the **pitch** of the thread. For each complete rotation of the thread, a nut (for example) will move a distance equal to the pitch of the thread.

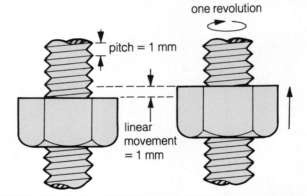

one revolution

pitch = 1 mm

linear movement = 1 mm

Types of thread

Two basic thread types are produced, the **'V' thread** and the **square thread**.

'V' threads are most commonly used for nuts and bolts, set screws and other fastening devices. The large amount of friction between the threads is used to advantage to prevent the devices from coming unscrewed.

Much less friction occurs with the square thread. These are used to advantage therefore for the moving parts of machines and tools.

Some applications of the screw mechanism are shown. Notice that in each case, a rotary motion input produces a linear motion output.

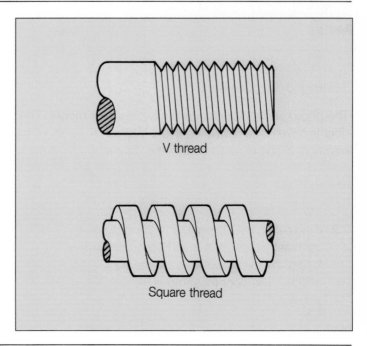

V thread

Square thread

Appliances using screw mechanisms

Playdough extruder

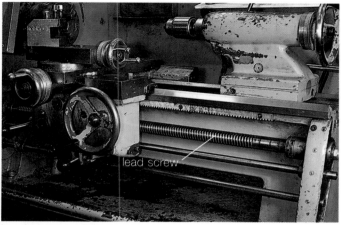

Lead screw on lathe

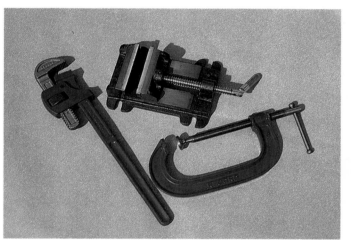

G cramp, machine vice and Stillson mole wrench

Corkscrew

Horse jump project

Claire has a pony and enjoys amateur show jumping. When practising alone however, she finds it a nuisance having to keep dismounting to raise (or lower) the rail. She decided therefore, to try to solve the problem. This is the solution she developed.

The horse jump model was designed to allow the rail to be raised or lowered by turning a crank handle. The handle is set at the correct height to be operated from horseback. The system uses two screw mechanisms, and other mechanisms described earlier.

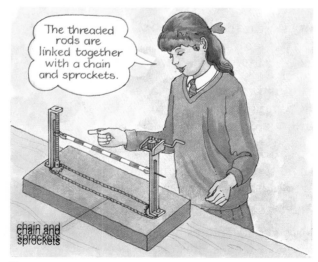

Horse jump project

The crank mechanism

A crank is a device through which **rotary motion** and **torque** can be applied to a shaft. The simplest device is a **crank handle**.

When a number of cranks are incorporated into a shaft, it is called a **crankshaft**.

The most common application of the crankshaft is in the motor car engine.

A *crankshaft*, *connecting rod* and *piston*, is one example of a **crank and slider** mechanism (described below).

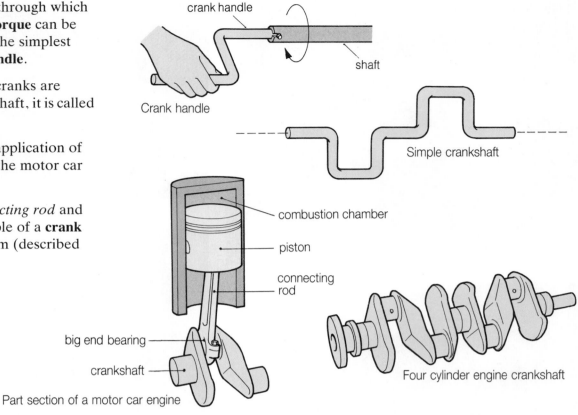

Crank handle

Simple crankshaft

Part section of a motor car engine

Four cylinder engine crankshaft

Crank and slider mechanism

The **crank and slider** is another mechanism which can convert rotary motion into linear motion.

By rotating the crank, the slider is forced to move backwards and forwards as shown. This backwards and forwards motion is called **reciprocating motion**.

Alternatively, if the slider produces the input motion (as in the case of a piston in a motor car engine) the crank is forced to rotate.

The **distance moved** by the slider, is dependent upon the **length of the crank**.

As the crank rotates through 180°, the slider moves a distance equal to **twice** the length of the crank.

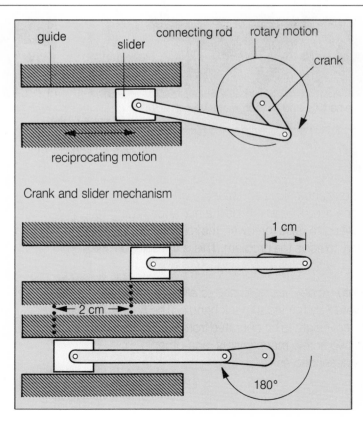

Crank and slider mechanism

Questions

10 The photograph shows a power hacksaw as used in some school workshops. The sketch outlines the crank and slider mechanisms which it uses.

If the **stroke** of the hacksaw blade is 12 cm, what is the length of the crank?

Power hacksaw

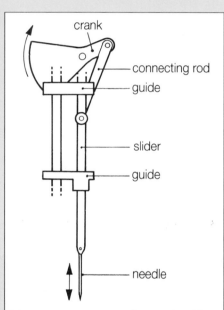

11 The photograph shows a domestic sewing machine. The sketch outlines the crank and slider mechanism which it uses to produce reciprocating motion at the needle.

At its slowest operating speed, the needle moves down 120 times per minute. At what speed does the crank rotate?

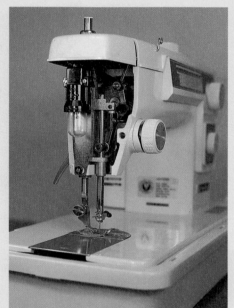

Sewing machine

12 Design a mechanism for a simple **machine press**. The mechanism must be driven from an electric motor whose output shaft rotates at 120 rpm.

The press head must move up and down continuously and make two 'down strokes' per minute. The head must rise and fall a distance of 3 cm.

The block diagram should help you to solve this problem.

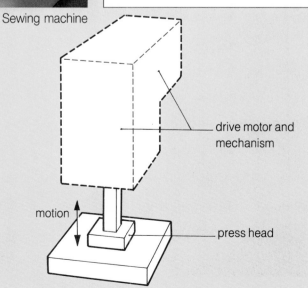

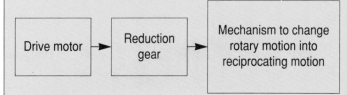

Drive motor → Reduction gear → Mechanism to change rotary motion into reciprocating motion

Cams

Yet another mechanism which can convert rotary motion into linear motion (and reciprocating motion) is the **cam** and **follower**.

Cam and follower explained

A **cam** is a specially shaped piece of metal (or other suitable material) which is fixed to an axle or shaft.

A **follower** is a device designed to move up and down as it follows the shape, or **profile** of the rotating cam. The follower may be held firmly against the cam profile by gravity, or more often by the action of a spring.

The **profile** of a cam determines the distance travelled by its follower. For the **pear-shaped** cam shown, the distance moved by the follower is equal to d_2 minus d_1 ($d_2 - d_1$).

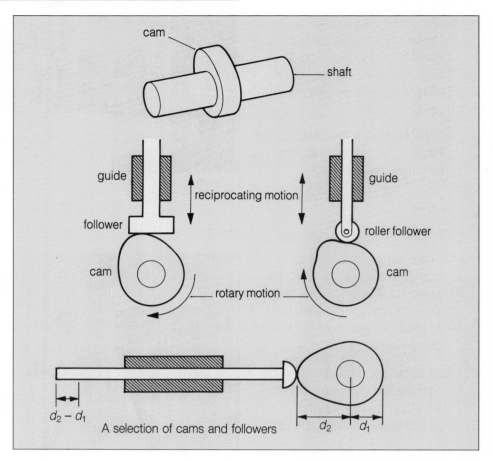

A selection of cams and followers

Appliances using cam and follower systems

Motor car engine

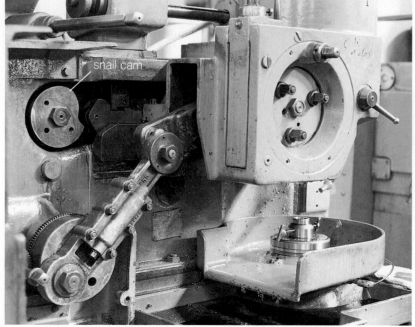

Gear cutting machine (shaper)

Appliances using cam and follower systems

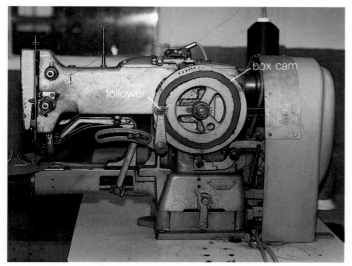

Staying machine (used in shoe making)

Washing machine program timer

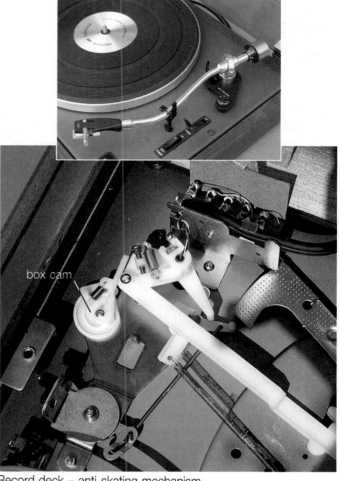

Record deck – anti-skating mechanism

Ram mechanism

Cams are used to **operate microswitches** in many different kinds of machines. The photograph shows a teacher's demonstration 'ram mechanism'. This is controlled by microswitches and a cam. You can read about the application of a ram mechanism, and how it is controlled, on page 162.

Levers and linkages

Levers

A simple **lever** is a rigid bar which pivots at a point called the **fulcrum**. A lever changes an input motion and force into a desired output motion and force.

A screwdriver, for example, acts as a lever when used to open a tin of paint. The input force is called the **effort**, and the output force is called the **load**.

Many kinds of tools contain lever systems, but sometimes they are disguised. See if you can identify the **fulcrum**, **effort** and **load** in the tools shown.

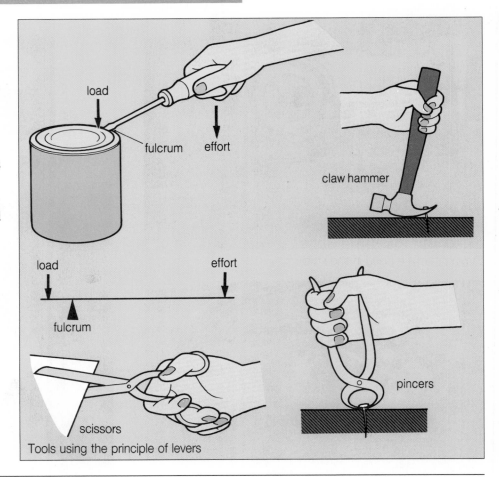

Tools using the principle of levers

Velocity ratio – levers

Velocity ratio can be explained by examining a lever in use.

Using this lever, Jack can move a load over a distance of 20 cm by exerting an effort over a distance of 80 cm.

The ratio of the distance moved by the effort to the distance moved by the load is called the velocity ratio.

To calculate velocity ratio, use this equation.

$$\textbf{Velocity ratio} = \frac{\textbf{distance moved by effort}}{\textbf{distance moved by load}}$$

In this example,

$$\text{Velocity ratio} = \frac{80}{20} = \frac{4}{1} \text{ or } 4 : 1$$

The larger the velocity ratio of a lever, the larger the load which can be moved for a given effort. This is explained below.

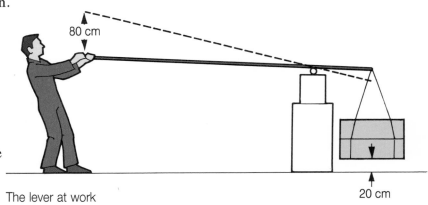

The lever at work

Mechanical advantage

Using this lever, Jack can raise a load of 1200 newtons using an effort of just 300 newtons.

If he wasn't using the lever, four times this effort would be required. We say therefore, that the lever has a **mechanical advantage** of 4.

To calculate mechanical advantage, use the equation shown here.

Mechanical advantage $= \dfrac{\textbf{load}}{\textbf{effort}}$

In this example,

Mechanical advantage $= \dfrac{1200}{300}$

$= 4$

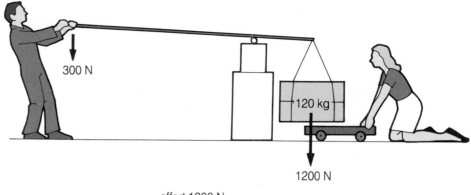

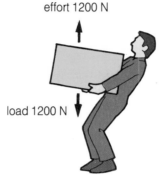

Moments

The mechanical advantage gained by a lever can be explained by the principle of **moments**.

When the effort force is applied to a lever, the lever rotates about the fulcrum. The 'turning effect' produced is called a **moment**. The moment depends upon the **force**, and the **distance** at which the force acts from the fulcrum.

$$\textbf{moment} = \textbf{force} \times \textbf{distance}$$

When a lever is in **equilibrium** – that is, when the effort force just 'balances' the load force – the moments to the right and the left of the fulcrum are equal. (See diagram.)

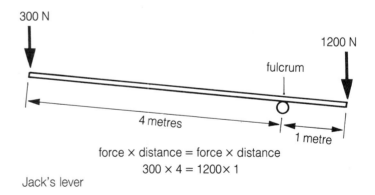

force × distance = force × distance

$300 \times 4 = 1200 \times 1$

Jack's lever

Question

13 What effort would be required to raise the load in the previous example if the long arm of the lever was 6 metres long?

Types of lever

There are three different types, or **classes** of lever – each with the effort, load and fulcrum arranged in different ways.

A crowbar is one example of a **class 1 lever**. To increase the mechanical advantage of a class 1 lever the fulcrum must be moved closer to the load. However, we 'pay' for this increased mechanical advantage by having to move the effort over a greater distance.

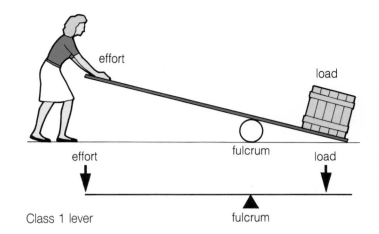

Class 1 lever

The bottle opener is an example of a **class 2 lever**.

The mechanical advantage of a class 2 lever is increased by moving the load nearer to the fulcrum. However, the 'cost' is the same as described for the class 1 lever.

To calculate the turning forces at the effort and load, the principle of moments is applied as shown in the diagram.

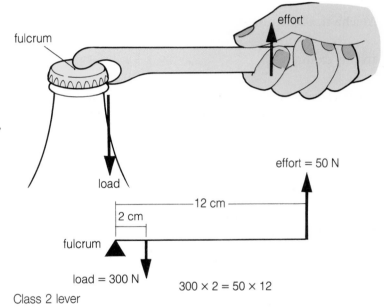

$300 \times 2 = 50 \times 12$

Class 2 lever

The arm provides a good example of a **class 3 lever**.

Unlike the class 1 and 2 levers, a class 3 lever has a **mechanical disadvantage**. The input force (the effort) is greater than the force produced at the load. However, the distance moved by the load is greater than the distance moved by the effort.

When a mechanical system requires a large output movement for a small input movement, we have to 'pay' by providing a large effort.

To calculate the turning forces at the effort and load, the principle of moments is applied as shown in the diagram.

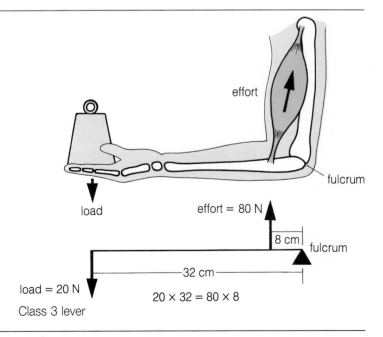

$20 \times 32 = 80 \times 8$

Class 3 lever

Linkages

Many machines and other devices use link mechanisms to make them operate. Sonal has used a fairly complex link mechanism in her 'crazy snake' project.

Crazy snake project

Linkages explained

A linkage is simply an assembly of levers designed to transmit motion and force.

By carefully designing the linkage, a given input motion and force can be transferred into the required output motion and force. Some examples are shown here.

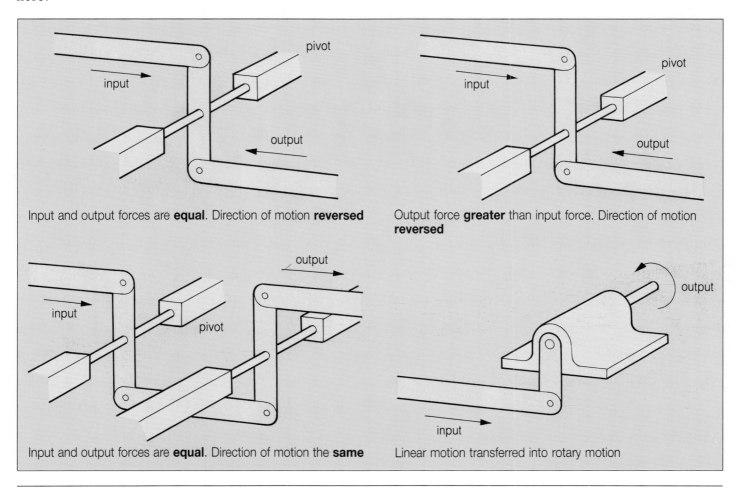

Input and output forces are **equal**. Direction of motion **reversed**

Output force **greater** than input force. Direction of motion **reversed**

Input and output forces are **equal**. Direction of motion the **same**

Linear motion transferred into rotary motion

Appliances using link mechanisms

Motor car windscreen wiper mechanism

Small printing machine

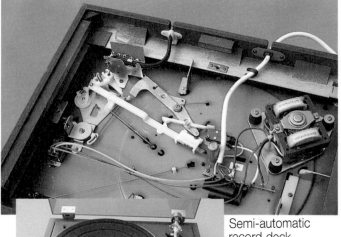

Semi-automatic record deck

Motor car steering linkage

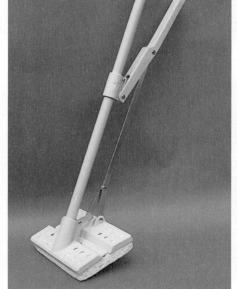

Refuse lorry — lifting and crushing mechanism

Squeeze mop

Buggy brake mechanism

Questions

14 a What force is required at **E** to just balance the crowbar?

b If the 'long arm' of the crowbar was 0.5 metres longer, what force would be required at **E**?

15 a What class of lever is this wheelbarrow?

b What is the effort force required to support the barrow as shown?

16 Make a list of the devices shown here and label them class 1, class 2 and class 3 levers.

17 The black boxes contain different link mechanisms. Sketch the linkages which you think they contain.

18 Sketch the link mechanism which you think is contained in the black box, giving suitable measurements to provide the output force obtained from the given input.

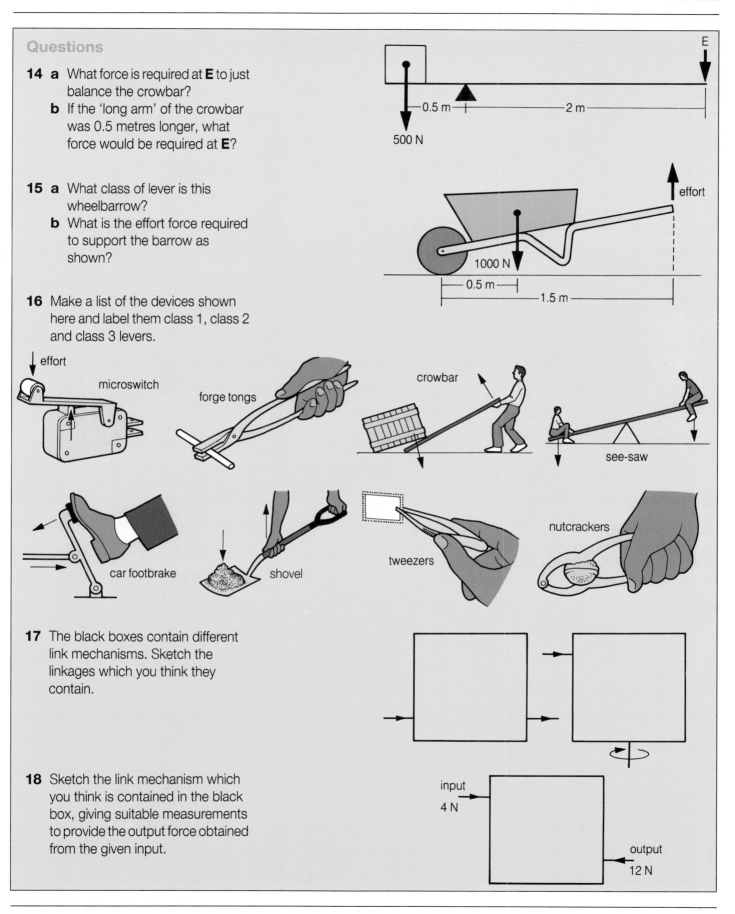

The transmission of force

Many examples of the transmission of movement (or **motion**) have been given in this chapter. However, machines do **work**, and therefore mechanisms must transmit **force** as well as motion. (Work = force × distance moved – see Chapter 9.)

John's teacher has set up a simple experiment to demonstrate the transmission of force. A heavy load is attached to a piece of string, which is wrapped around an axle, and John has to try to 'wind it up'.

John finds it difficult because such a large **turning force** is required.

By using a second axle and a transmission system however (a gear train in this example), a much smaller turning force is required. John can now raise the load very easily.

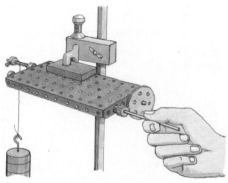

The explanation

Imagine how easy it would be to turn the axle in the first experiment if there was an 'arm' attached to it as shown in the diagram. The action is rather like a lever. In fact, just like a lever, the longer the arm, the easier it would be to produce a turning motion. The 'arm' in fact multiplies the turning force applied to the axle. We call the turning moment (or force F × distance r) a **torque**.

Now, when two gears are meshed, as shown, they act rather like levers. Each gear tooth can be regarded as the end of a lever. When shaft **A** is turned, 'lever **A**' applies a force to the end of 'lever **B**'. The **longer** lever '**B**' is made therefore, the greater the **torque** which is applied to the shaft **B**.

We can make 'lever **B**' longer of course, by using a gear with a greater number of teeth. Further, the smaller we make gear **A**, the greater the force which appears at the end of 'lever **A**'. A gear system therefore, not only transmits motion, but also transmits and converts torque.

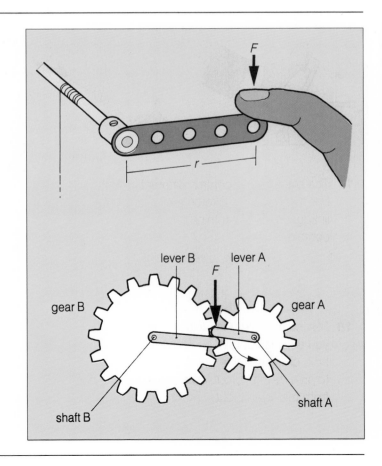

The importance of torque conversion

Motors used in school technology projects tend to be small, low-powered types. The shaft usually turns fairly quickly, and with very little torque.

If you tried to use such a motor to drive directly to the wheel of a small vehicle, for example, the motor just wouldn't cope, and would possibly 'burn out'.

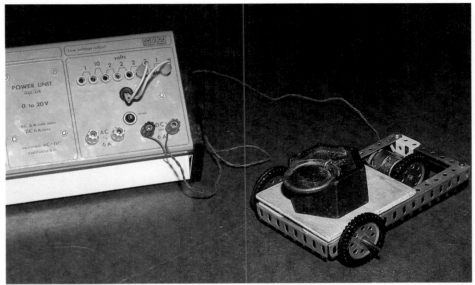

Motor provides insufficient torque to drive the loaded vehicle

You can feel just how much torque is required to drive a small vehicle, by turning the axle with your fingers.

To successfully drive this vehicle from its motor, the high-speed low-torque output must be converted into a **low-speed**, **high-torque** output. To do this, a transmission system will be needed.

By using a suitable transmission system, both models and full-size machines can be made to operate at the correct speed and with enough torque to do the job.

By turning the axle by hand, you can feel just how much torque is required

Questions

19 The black box shown contains a transmission system. Two pupils use the box in a 'test of strength' by applying turning forces as shown. Pupil A finds it very easy to beat pupil B.

   a Sketch two different transmission systems which would give pupil A the best possible chance of winning.

   b Explain why pupil A can win so easily using your chosen systems.

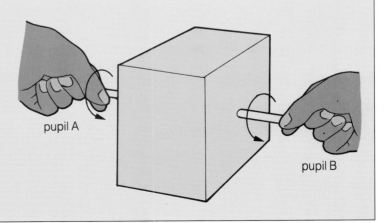

pupil A

pupil B

Project briefs

A number of project briefs are given below. Follow the design process (outlined in Chapter 1) as you try to satisfy the briefs. Any suitable materials and construction kits – Lego, meccano, etc. – can be used to realize the projects.

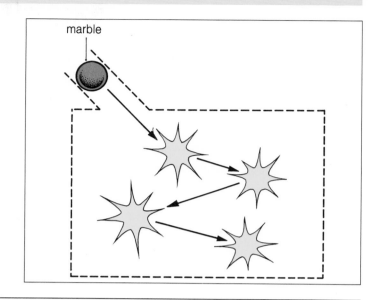

1 Mechanical toy

Design and construct a mechanical toy which is 'driven' by the energy of a moving marble. As the marble moves, it should trigger all sorts of interesting visual and sound effects.

2 Alternative energy vehicle

Energy can be stored in a stretched spring or elastic band. This is sometimes called strain energy.

Design and construct a small vehicle which is driven by strain energy. Test the completed vehicle for maximum speed, hill climbing ability, and maximum distance travelled.

$$\text{speed} = \frac{\text{distance covered (m)}}{\text{time taken (s)}}$$

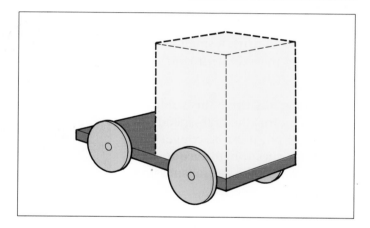

3 Builder's lift

A small building firm requires a lift to carry bricks, mortar and other building materials up the scaffolding.

Design and build a model of a suitable lift. The lift must be simple in operation and easy to install. It can be either hand-operated, or driven by an electric motor. The lift must be completely safe in its operation – for example, if the driving force is removed the lift must not be able to 'crash' to the ground.

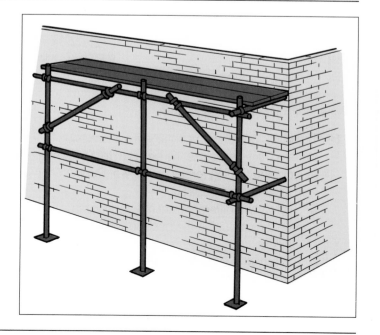

4 Shop window display

A shopkeeper requires a window display unit for a jeweller's shop. The purpose of the unit is to display watches in a novel way to attract the attention of passers by.

Design and construct a display unit which makes use of movement to attract attention. The unit can display either a number of watches, or a single watch.

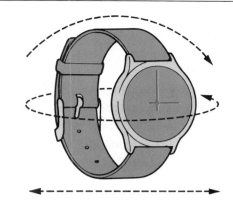

5 Coin sorter

'Mixed up' 1p and 2p coins require sorting into separate containers.

Design and construct a device which will accept the mixed up coins, separate them and store them separately.

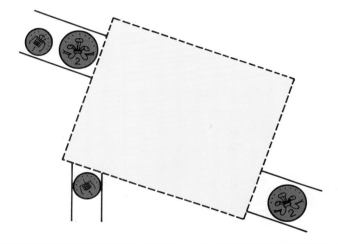

6 Fun park cable car

With the hope of attracting more visitors, a local 'fun park' wishes to install a cable car ride.

Design and construct a scale model of one section of the ride. This should include towers, winding gear and cars. For the purpose of the model, the winding gear can be driven using a crank handle. The system must be designed for maximum safety and the cars must provide protection against the wind, rain and snow.

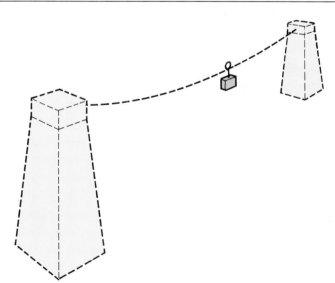

Further ideas for projects

- Swing bridge
- Fairground ride
- Slow-moving rough terrain vehicle

- Pull-along toy
- Walking robot
- Gardening aid for the elderly

- Mechanical game
- Child's pedal toy
- Automatic aluminium/steel drinks can sorter

Examples of school technology projects

Energy converters (Teacher's brief – 4th years)

Brief – Unlike the fossil fuels which will eventually run out, some energy sources can be used over and over again. These are called **renewable** energy sources and include the wind, waves, tide and solar energy (energy from the sun). Design and construct a machine which can harness one of these energy sources to do useful work.

Some solutions

Water turbine which can raise a load.
Nikki Berridge 4th year.

Wind turbine which can both raise and lower a load. Adrian Horsburgh and Michael Freeman 4th years.

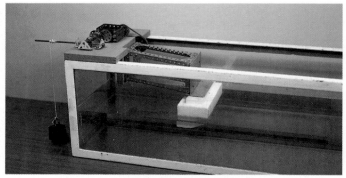

A wave energy machine which can raise a load. (Teacher's demonstration model).

A water turbine which can generate electricity. Samantha Veitch – 4th year

Log sorting machine (Philip Beasley – 5th

Brief – When I was on holiday in Canada I went to a Timber Mill where I got the idea for my project. I want to design and make a machine which will separate long logs from short logs and scraps.

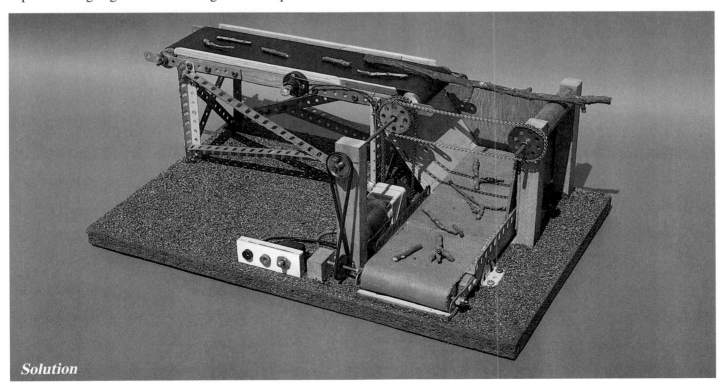

Solution

Sorting device (Susan Riley – 4th year)

Whilst visiting a local industrial complex, I became fascinated with the machine used for sorting and packaging.

Brief – I would like to test my ingenuity by designing a device for sorting out discs or ball bearings of different diameters, or cotton reels of different colour.

Solution – Ball bearing sorter

Robot arm (David Cox – 4th year)

After watching the TV reports of the Chernobyl nuclear accident I began to understand some of the dangers of nuclear energy, particularly for those who had to work on the site of the power station.

Brief – To design and construct a remote-controlled robot arm for use in a dangerous environment.

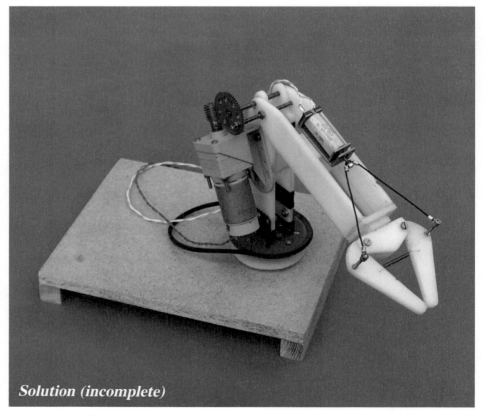

Solution (incomplete)

Railway level-crossing barrier (Leslie Hind – 5th year)

My hobby is model railways.
I have an O gauge layout which I am gradually adding to, but the accessories are very expensive.
I would like to buy a level crossing but I cannot afford one.

Brief – To design and make a suitable level crossing using cheap materials and components, and to produce a set of plans for its construction which I could sell to other enthusiasts.

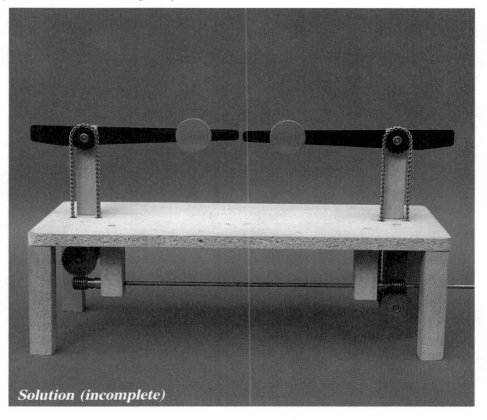

Solution (incomplete)

Car park barrier (Matthew Lock – 4th year)

My neighbour works as a gateman at a small inner city company. His job is to operate a car park barrier by hand when employees' cars arrive and leave. This can be a very miserable job, especially when it is cold and wet.

Brief – Design a semi-automatic car park barrier which can be controlled from inside the gateman's hut.

Solution

CHAPTER SIX

Control electrics and electronics

Automatic sliding door

Payphone in use

Aircraft
autopilot

Vending machine exterior

Drinks

Vending machine interior

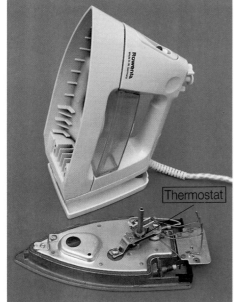

Steam iron

Thermostat

Automatic washing machine

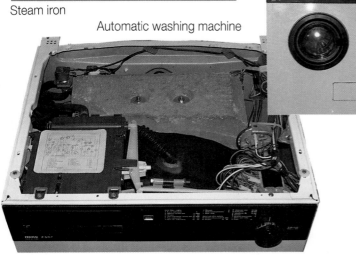

Factory robots

There is hardly any area of present day human activity that does not depend in some way on **electrical** or **electronic devices**.

Most of the devices in these pictures will be very familiar to you. Without these, and numerous other electrical 'servants', our lives would be very different.

All the devices shown here contain electrical or electronic **control systems** – that is, circuits which control the way the device operates.

A steam iron for example, uses electricity to heat an element which applies heat to the clothes. The temperature of that element however, must be controlled. The circuit which does this contains a special component called a thermostat. This is an example of a very simple control system.

An automatic washing machine is much more complex. It controls the flow of water into and out of itself, the temperature of the water, the speed of rotation of the drum, and so on – in other words, the complete 'wash cycle'.

Some of the most sophisticated control systems however, belong to the 'robots'. One example of a robotic device is the robot arm. These are increasingly taking over production processes in factories. Robots can work much faster than a human operator, performing a wide variety of tasks. They can work in dangerous environments, rarely make mistakes, and never get bored.

A true robot has an 'electronic brain'. This is used to store and process the information which controls the actions of the robot. If the robot is required to do a new job, it can have its 'memory' rubbed clean and a new set of instructions given – this is called programming.

Many interesting control projects can be built at school. Before learning about control circuitry however, it will be useful to revise some basic electrical theory.

Basic electrics – revision

Voltage and current

A battery is a source of electrical energy – it provides the 'pressure' which causes electricity to flow. We measure this electrical pressure in **volts**, **V**. The higher the **voltage**, the greater the pressure.

The flow of electricity is called **current** and is measured in **amps**, **A**

If a single battery makes a bulb glow dimly, two batteries connected in **series** as in circuit 2 will make it glow brighter. This happens because when batteries are connected in **series** their voltages 'add up'. Two similar batteries connected in series produce twice the electrical pressure. The greater the electrical pressure (in a given circuit) the higher the current.

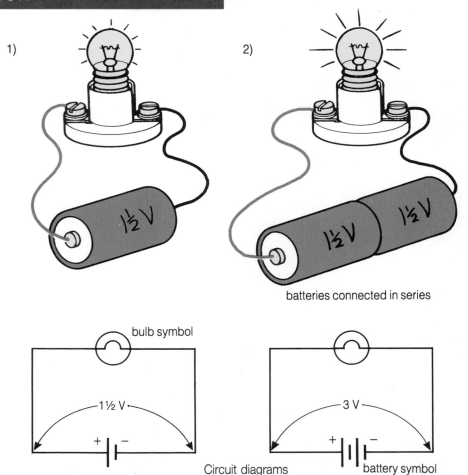

batteries connected in series

Circuit diagrams

When batteries are connected in **parallel** however, their voltages do **not** 'add up'. The voltage provided by the two batteries in circuit 3 is the same as by the single battery in circuit 1.

Even so, there are reasons for connecting batteries in parallel: two batteries last longer than one, and can supply a higher current, should it be required.

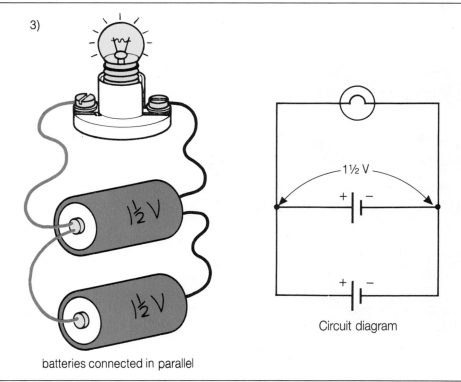

batteries connected in parallel

Circuit diagram

Resistance

Anything which opposes the flow of current in a circuit is said to offer **resistance**. We measure resistance in **ohms** Ω.

Resistance wire, and components called **resistors** are specially made to resist the flow of electricity. Connecting wire however, has a very, very low resistance – it allows electricity to flow freely.

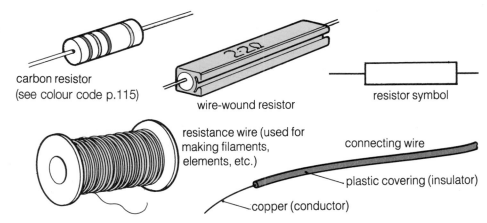

carbon resistor (see colour code p.115)

wire-wound resistor

resistor symbol

resistance wire (used for making filaments, elements, etc.)

connecting wire

plastic covering (insulator)

copper (conductor)

All electrical components offer some resistance to the flow of electricity. The filament in a bulb is a resistor which glows and gives off light.

The brightness of a bulb gives an indication of how much current is flowing in a circuit. Use this knowledge to decide which of the circuits shown offers least resistance and which offers the most.

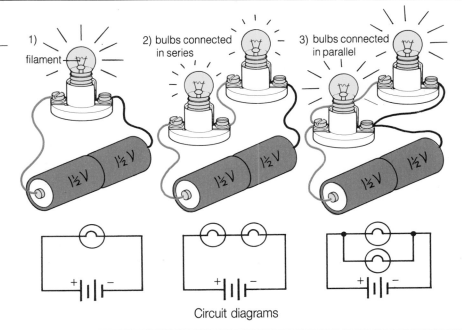

1) filament

2) bulbs connected in series

3) bulbs connected in parallel

Circuit diagrams

When resistors or resistive components are connected in **series**, the effect is to add more resistance to the circuit. The total resistance can be found by simply adding up all the resistance values.

To calculate the value of resistors in series, we use the equation:

$$R_T = R_1 + R_2 + R_3 \text{ etc}$$
(total)   (resistor values)

What is the effective resistance of R_1 and R_2 connected like this?

100 Ω R_1 100 Ω R_2

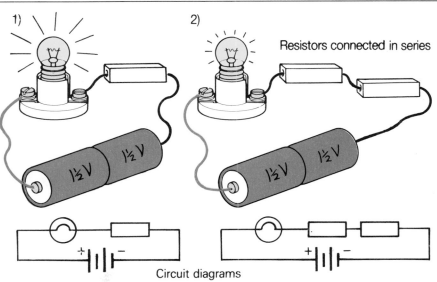

1)

2) Resistors connected in series

Circuit diagrams

When resistors, or resistive components, are connected in **parallel**, the effect is to **reduce** the resistance in the circuit. That is why the bulb in circuit 5 is brighter than the bulb in circuit 4.

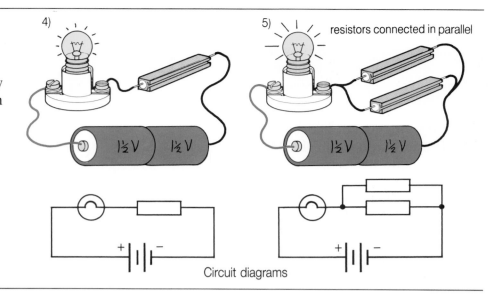

Circuit diagrams

To calculate the value of resistors in parallel, we use the equation:

$$\frac{1}{R_T} = \frac{1}{R_1} + \frac{1}{R_2} + \frac{1}{R_3}$$

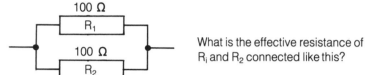

What is the effective resistance of R_i and R_2 connected like this?

Variable resistor (potentiometer)

A variable resistor can be used to adjust the flow of current in a circuit.

When the resistor's spindle is rotated, a sliding contact puts more or less resistance material in series with the circuit.

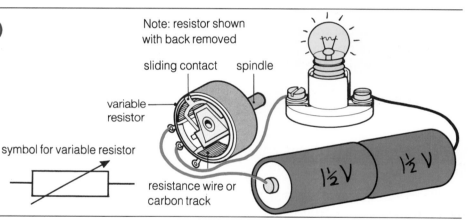

Note: resistor shown with back removed

Other resistive components

Light dependent resistor (or LDR)

An LDR is a component whose resistance depends upon the amount of **light** falling on it.

When the LDR in this circuit is slowly covered up, the bulb gets dimmer and finally goes out. What does this tell you about how the resistance of an LDR varies? Try to complete this sentence:

As the light falling on an LDR decreases, the resistance of the LDR ....

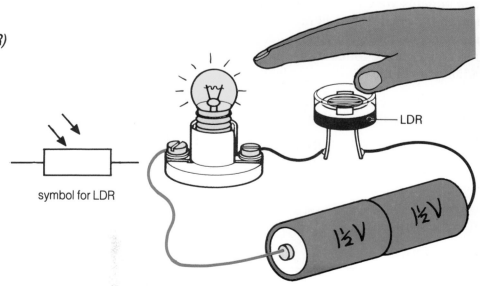

Thermistors

A thermistor is a component whose resistance varies with **temperature**.

Two types of thermistor are made: those whose resistance increases with increasing temperature (these are said to have a positive temperature coefficient $+t$), and those whose resistance decreases with increasing temperature (these are said to have a negative temperature coefficient $-t$).

Which type of thermistor is being used in the experiment illustrated?

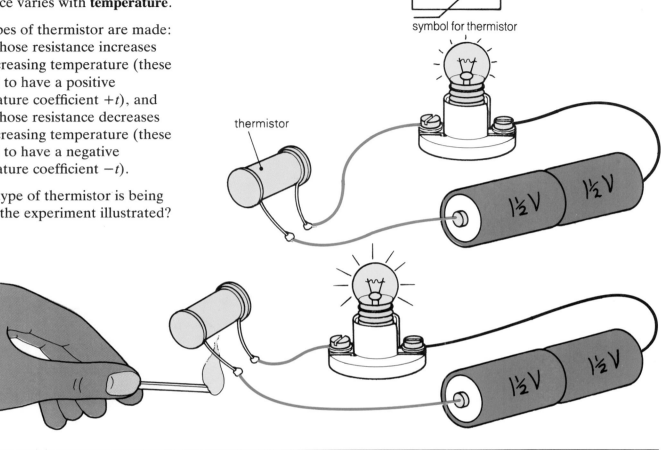

symbol for thermistor

thermistor

Ohm's law

Earlier in this chapter we saw that we could increase the current flowing in a circuit by increasing the electrical pressure (or voltage). We also saw that by **increasing** the resistance in a circuit we could **reduce** the flow of current.

In 1826 George Ohm understood this, and went on to discover a special relationship between **voltage, current** and **resistance**. He discovered that the current passing through a resistor was proportional to the voltage across it. In other words, if the voltage across a resistor was doubled, the current flowing through that resistor would double, and if the voltage was trebled, the current would treble, and so on. This became known as Ohm's Law.

From the above knowledge, Ohm derived this equation:

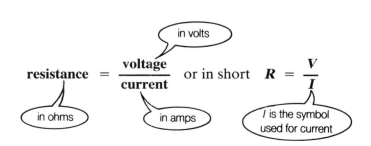

$$\textbf{resistance} = \frac{\textbf{voltage}}{\textbf{current}} \quad \text{or in short} \quad R = \frac{V}{I}$$

in volts

in ohms

in amps

I is the symbol used for current

Measuring current, voltage and resistance

Ammeters are used to measure the flow of **current** in a circuit. They must be connected in **series** with the circuit components. In this way, the current flowing in the circuit also flows through the ammeter and therefore can be measured.

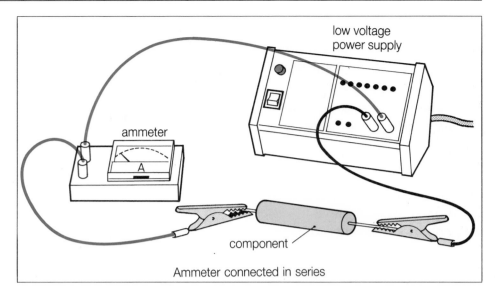

Ammeter connected in series

Voltmeters however, must be connected across (or in **parallel** with) circuit components. They are connected in this way because their job is to measure the electrical pressure (or voltage) across a component.

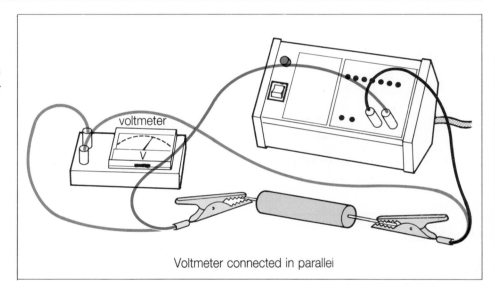

Voltmeter connected in parallel

The resistance of a component can be found using the Ohm's Law equation. First we must measure the current passing through the component, and the voltage across it.

For the carbon resistor in the diagram:

$$R = \frac{V}{I}$$

$$= \frac{10}{0.1}$$

$$= 100\,\Omega$$

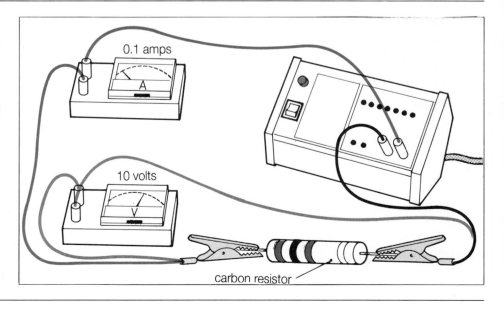

carbon resistor

Simple Ohm's Law calculations

The teacher is explaining that $R = \dfrac{V}{I}$ can be used not only for calculating resistance, but **voltage** and **current** too. She has shown that the equation can be rearranged for this purpose, and also how to use it in calculations.

If you have difficulty with rearranging the equation, ask your teacher for help.

Resistor colour codes

Some resistors have their resistance value shown using numbers. These tend to be the lower value types.

Most resistors are coded using coloured bands. The first three bands (closest together) give the value of the resistor in ohms Ω.

The fourth band indicates how accurate the given value is. The most expensive resistors carry a red 4th band. A red fourth band means that the resistor's value will be within 2% of the stated value, gold 5%, and silver 10%.

Example

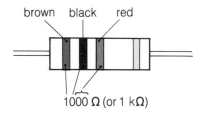

brown   black   red

1000 Ω (or 1 kΩ)

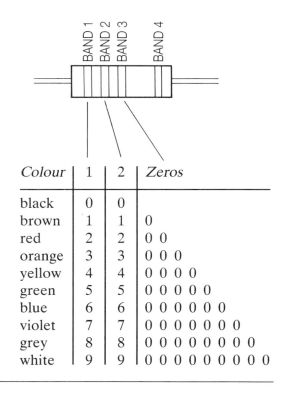

Colour	1	2	Zeros
black	0	0	
brown	1	1	0
red	2	2	0 0
orange	3	3	0 0 0
yellow	4	4	0 0 0 0
green	5	5	0 0 0 0 0
blue	6	6	0 0 0 0 0 0
violet	7	7	0 0 0 0 0 0 0
grey	8	8	0 0 0 0 0 0 0 0
white	9	9	0 0 0 0 0 0 0 0 0

Questions

1 a Calculate the value of resistor R in this circuit.
  b How much current would flow if the value of R was doubled?

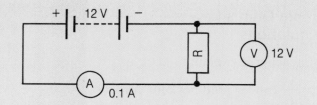

2 a Calculate the current flowing in this circuit.
  b What would be the ammeter reading if the resistor's value was halved?

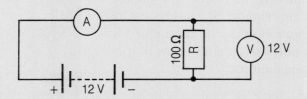

3 a Calculate the voltage across R in this circuit.
  b How much current would flow if the voltage across R was doubled?

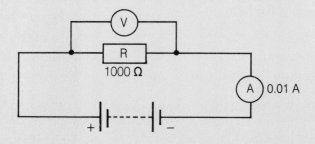

4 a Calculate the current flowing through R_1.
  b Calculate the current flowing through R_2.
  c What will be the reading on the ammeter?
  d What is the **total** resistance in this circuit?
    (Note – an ideal ammeter has no resistance.)
    Use the equation $R_T = R_1 + R_2$

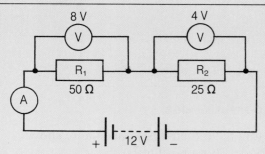

5 When 12 V is applied across a 10 Ω resistor, a current of 1.2 A flows.

When two 10 Ω resistors are connected in **parallel**, twice as much current flows (2.4 A). The total effective resistance of R_1 and R_2 in parallel therefore must be less than 10 Ω.

What will this value be? You can check your answer by using the equation:

$$\frac{1}{R_T} = \frac{1}{R_1} + \frac{1}{R_2} \cdots \cdots$$

You may need your teacher's help with this calculation.

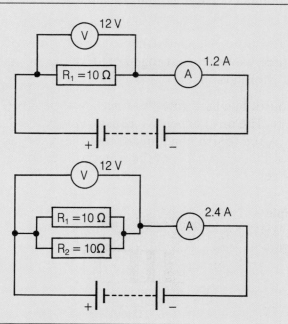

Control electrics

The switch

We all make use of switches every day. We use them to turn on lights, radios, hairdriers and numerous other devices. A switch is used for making and breaking an electrical circuit. Only when the circuit is 'made', by switching on, will current flow.

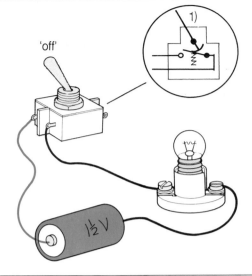
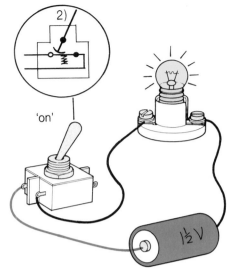

Switch names and symbols

The simplest type of switch is represented by the symbol shown here. Notice that it has two parts, a **pole** and a **contact**. It is called a **single pole single throw** switch (SPST).

It is given this name because its single pole can be 'thrown into contact' in one position only.

Three more switch symbols are shown here. Can you work out how they got their names?

All sorts of switches are available. Some of the more common types are shown below.

pole   contact

Symbol for single pole single throw (SPST) switch

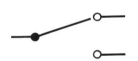

Symbol for single pole double throw (SPDT) switch

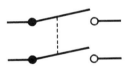

Symbol for double pole single throw (DPST) switch

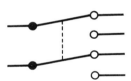

Symbol for double pole double throw (DPDT) switch

Toggle switch

Microswitch

Slide switch

Push button switch

Reed switch

Rotary switch

Note   Some switches return to their 'unswitched', state after the operating force has been removed. Microswitches, reed switches and some press switches do this.

The contacts on these switches are often labelled **N/C** or **N/O**. **N/C** stands for 'normally closed'. This is the contact which is connected to the pole when the switch is not activated. The **N/O**, or 'normally open' contact, connects to the pole when the switch is activated.

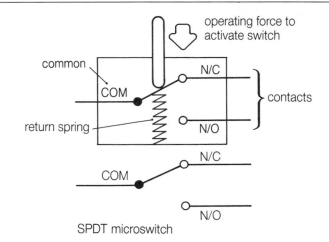

SPDT microswitch

Questions

6 The control of electric motors is common in technology. Sometimes this simply involves turning them on and off. The circuit shown here is designed to operate in this way.

Using the circuit symbols given, draw the circuit diagram for this control circuit.

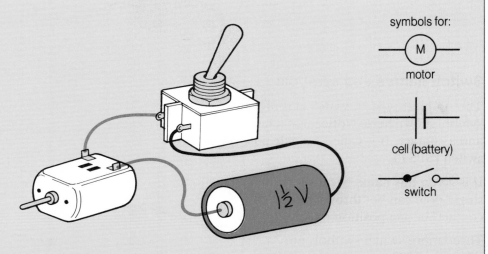

symbols for:

motor

cell (battery)

switch

7 a What type of switches are S_1 and S_2?
   b Which switch or switches must be operated to light bulb B_2?
   c When both bulbs are on, will they be at full or half brightness?

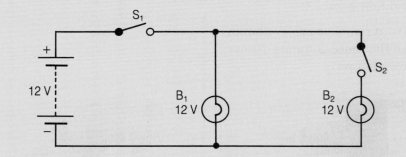

8 a What type of switch is S_1?
   b Which bulb or bulbs are 'on' when S_1 is in the 'up' position? Will the bulb or bulbs be at full or half brightness?
   c Which bulb or bulbs are off when S_1 is in the 'down' position?

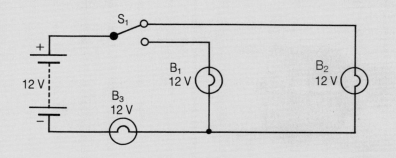

9 The landing light in most houses is controlled by a circuit similar to that shown. When S_1 and S_2 are in the 'up' position, the light is on.

a What other switch positions will turn the light on?

b What positions will turn the light off?

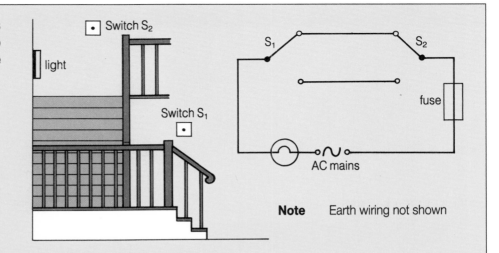

Note   Earth wiring not shown

10 The control circuit for a stamping machine is shown. For reasons of safety, the machine must not be operated without a safety guard in position.

a Explain how the circuit prevents this from happening.

b Are PS_1 and MS_1 connected in series or parallel?

Note   Earth wiring not shown

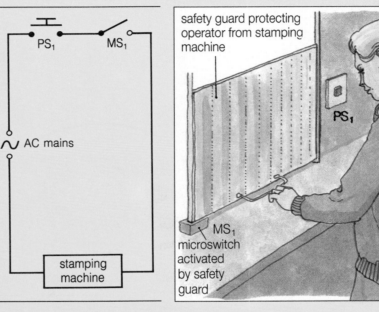

11 This wood-turning lathe has two doors which allow access to the belt and pulley 'gearbox'. For reasons of safety, the lathe will not start unless **both** doors are closed.

Complete the circuit diagram which will allow the safe operation of this machine. Use the symbol shown for the microswitches.

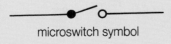

microswitch symbol

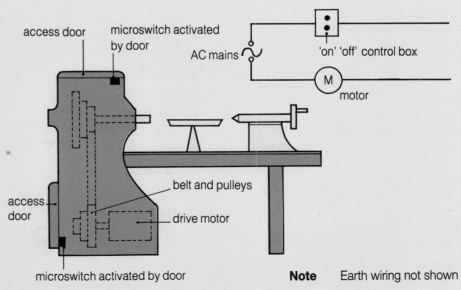

Note   Earth wiring not shown

More advanced switching circuits

It is often necessary to change the direction of rotation of a motor shaft. This is so in the case of lifts and automatic sliding doors for example.

Joanne is working on a vehicle project which requires its motor to be reversible. Her teacher explains that a **DC motor** can be reversed by changing the direction in which the current flows through the motor. This can be done by reversing the wires to the battery. (See circuit diagrams.) A more convenient way however, is to use a switch.

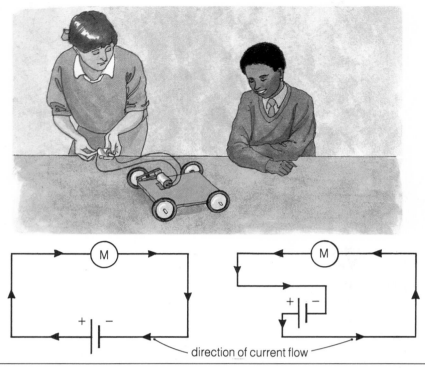

direction of current flow

Switched reversing circuit

If a double pole double throw (DPDT) switch is connected to a motor as shown here, you can **change the direction** of current flow through a motor at the 'flick of the switch'.

Circuit explained

With the switch in the 'up' position, current flows through the motor from right to left as shown. Let us assume that this causes the motor to run clockwise.

When the switch is flicked to the 'down' position, the current flows through the motor from left to right, causing the motor to run anti-clockwise.

Joanne used the above circuit to control her vehicle, but also added two microswitches as shown. She added these to make the vehicle stop if it bumped into a wall or other object. Switches which operate in this way are called **limit switches**.

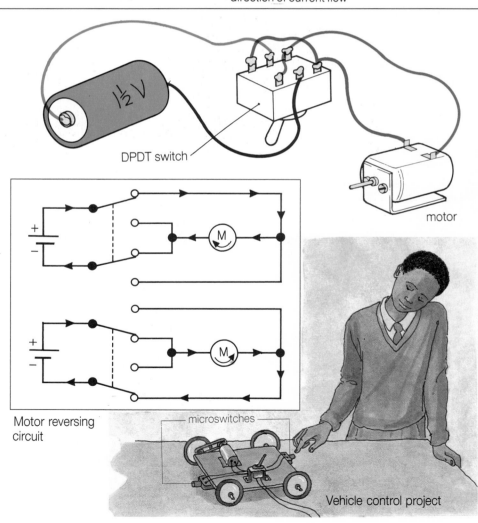

DPDT switch

motor

Motor reversing circuit

microswitches

Vehicle control project

Question

12 Joanne's vehicle moves backwards when the switch is in the down position. Which microswitch would stop the vehicle if it bumped into something when travelling forwards?

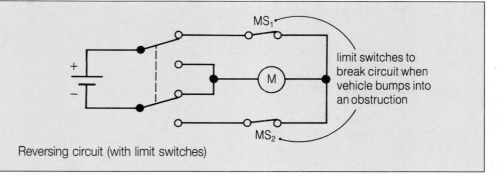

limit switches to break circuit when vehicle bumps into an obstruction

Reversing circuit (with limit switches)

Control using relays

Fraser has built a model sliding door, and has learnt to control it using a reversing circuit and limit switches. The limit switches stop the motor when the door is in the open and closed positions.

However, he really wanted the movement of the door to be fully automatic. His teacher explained that he could do this if he learnt about relays.

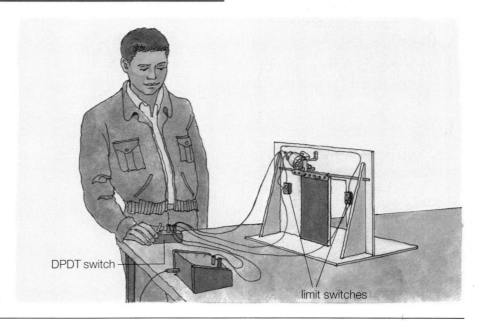

Sliding door project

DPDT switch

limit switches

The relay

A relay is a switch which is turned on and off by an electromagnet.

Look at the diagram of the construction of a relay. When a small current flows through the coil it produces a magnetic field which magnetizes an iron core. This attracts the armature which forces the switch contacts to touch. When the current is turned off, the switch contacts open again.

A relay is a very useful type of switch because it can be turned on and off in all sorts of different ways. This is illustrated in the following questions.

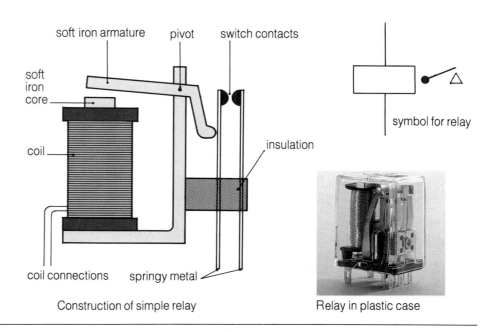

Construction of simple relay

symbol for relay

Relay in plastic case

Questions

13 The relay in this circuit can be turned on and off by light using an LDR. (See LDRs page 112.)

If light is shone onto the LDR, does the motor turn on or off?

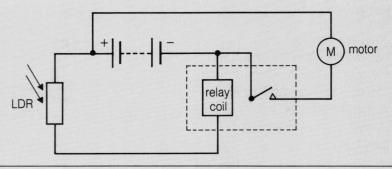

14 The relay in this circuit can be turned on and off by heat using a thermistor. (See thermistors page 113.)

Will a rise or fall in temperature cause bulb B1 to turn on?

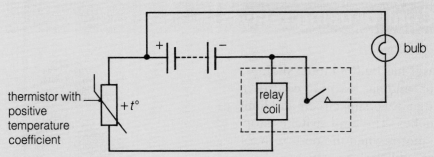

15 The relay in this circuit can be turned on and off by magnetism using a reed switch. (See reed switches page 118.)

a Will the alarm be on or off when the magnet is moved away from the reed switch?

b Can you suggest a use for this circuit?

Note This circuit shows an important property of a relay. It enables a safe low voltage circuit to operate a high voltage or high current circuit – the two circuits are completely separate.

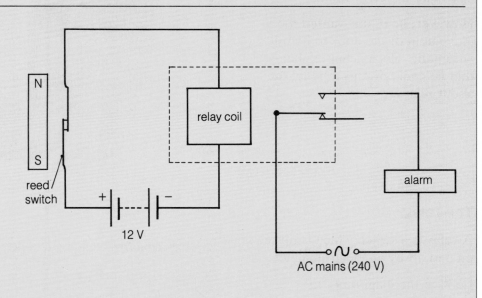

Relay buzzer

The relay coil in this circuit has been connected in series with its own switch. When operating, the relay switches on and off very rapidly, producing a buzzing sound. A relay can therefore be used to make a crude buzzer.

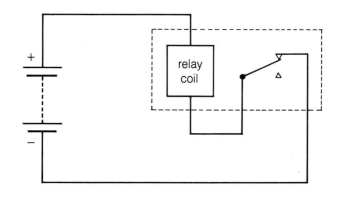

Question

16 Why does the relay in this circuit switch on and off continuously?

A project – using relays

The 'fast reaction' game

Using the circuit shown, design and make a 'fast reaction' game.

The game

Three people are involved in the game – two players and an operator. The operator (whose hand must be hidden from view) presses switch S_1 to light bulb L_1. The players (with their fingers poised 2 cm above their press switches) watch and wait for the light to come on. On seeing the light, they press their own switch as quickly as possible. The person whose reaction is faster wins because their light and relay switch on. At the same time, their relay disconnects the opponent's circuit.

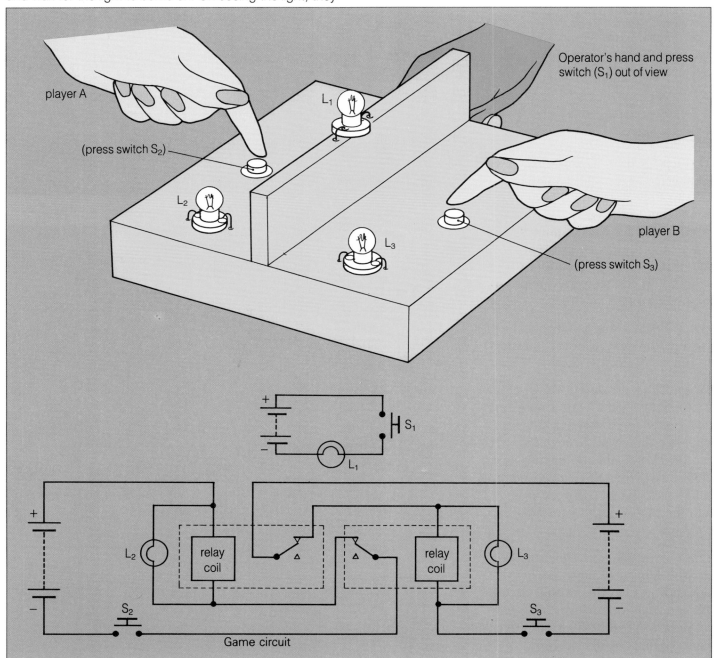

More complex relay circuits

The relay reversing circuit

The standard switch-operated motor reversing circuit is shown on page 120. This of course is a manually operated circuit (operated by the finger). When semi-automatic, or automatic control is required, the **relay** reversing circuit can be used.

The diagrams show two useful relays for school technology projects.

Two-pole changeover relay

Four-pole changeover relay

base numbers

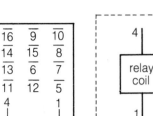

base numbers

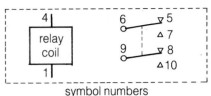

symbol numbers

symbol numbers

RS Components 'Continental' series (185 Ω) relays

The circuit

The relay reversing circuit is very similar to the switch reversing circuit. The motor must be connected to the relay's switch contacts, and the poles must be connected to the power supply, in the normal way. In addition, the relay coil is connected to the power supply via a switch, PS_1.

When PS_1 is **not** pressed (Fig. 1), current flows to the motor causing it to run – say clockwise.

When PS_1 is pressed however (Fig. 2), the relay 'flicks over' (energizes) and current is directed in the opposite direction through the motor. Hence, the motor runs anti-clockwise. When PS_1 is released the relay 'flicks back' (de-energizes) and the motor once again runs clockwise.

On its own, the above circuit doesn't appear to have any advantages over the normal circuit. As you read on however, you will learn how it can be built up into a very useful control circuit.

Fig 1

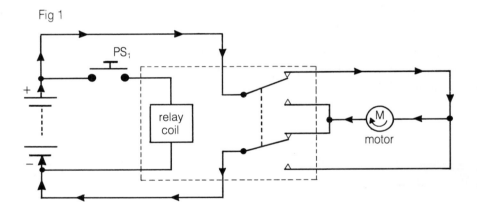

Fig 2

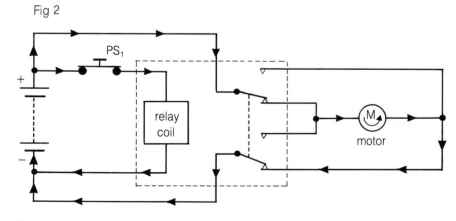

Relay reversing circuit

The relay latch

When a relay is operated via a press switch, the relay will only remain energized whilst your finger is on the button. In some control circuits however, it is necessary for the relay to remain energized after the button is released. This can be achieved using the relay **latch** circuit described below.

Relay latch explained

In the relay latch circuit, two extra wires are connected in a special way. We will call these wires XX. (See diagram.)

When PS_1 is pressed, current flows to the relay coil in the normal way via PS_1. However, current also flows via wires XX, and through part of the relay's own switch.

When PS_1 is released therefore, although current can no longer flow to the relay coil via PS_1, it continues to get there via wires XX. The relay therefore cannot switch off. It is said to be 'latched'.

Below, you can see how Fraser used the relay reversing circuit **and** the relay latch to control his automatic sliding door.

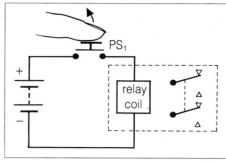

Relay de-energizes when PS_1 is released

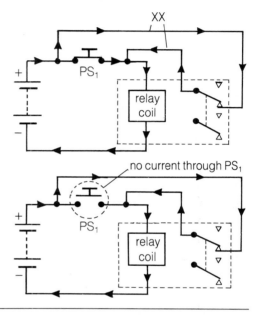

no current through PS_1

Relay latch circuit

Fraser's sliding door project – continued from page 121

The control circuit explained

Note   The relay used in this circuit is a 4 pole changeover type.

Microswitch MS_1 is a limit switch which stops the motor when the door is in the closed position. When either pressure pad PP_1 or PP_2 is pressed, the relay energizes and latches. The motor now drives the door open until it hits a second limit switch – microswitch MS_2 – which forms part of the latch circuit. When MS_2 opens, the latch is 'broken' and the relay de-energizes. The motor therefore runs in the reverse direction, closing the door. When the door is fully closed, MS_1 is 'opened' and the motor stops again.

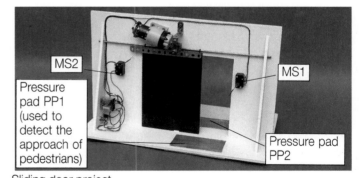

Sliding door project

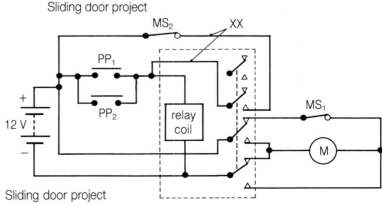

Sliding door project

Projects using the relay latch

'Steady hand' game

The diagram here shows the traditional 'steady hand' game.

Re-design the circuit to include a latch. This will ensure that the buzzer remains on after the first contact is made.

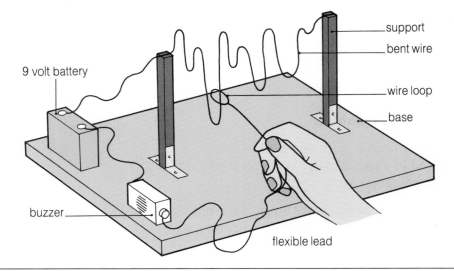

Simon's money box project

Simon challenged Fraser to steal his special money box. However, the project had a design fault.

Using Fraser's suggestion, re-design the circuit so that the alarm remains on even if the thief does press the switch.

A commercial relay latch circuit

Workshop power supplies

Factory and school workshops must be fitted with emergency stop buttons by law. The circuit shown here illustrates how this can be done using a relay latch circuit.

To switch on the power, a key switch is turned on momentarily, and then turned off – this causes the relay to latch. 'Stop' buttons are connected in series in the latch 'wires'.

If either stop button is pressed, the latch is broken and the relay de-energizes – cutting the power to the machinery.

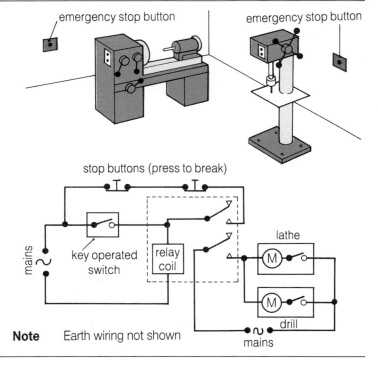

Note   Earth wiring not shown

Control electronics

The diode

A diode is a component which allows current to flow in **one direction only**. It creates a kind of 'one way street' in an electrical circuit.

The most common diodes consist of a junction of 'p-type' and 'n-type' silicon **semiconductor** materials.

The diagrams here show the 'one way street' effect of a diode.

A diode has two leads known as the 'anode' and 'cathode'. Only when the anode is connected to the positive side of a power supply, and the cathode to the negative side of the power supply, will current flow. When connected in this way a diode is said to be **forward biased**.

Some common silicon diodes

symbol for diode

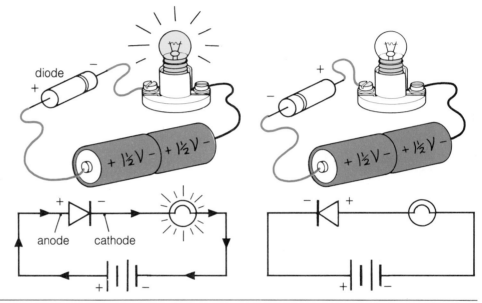

Light emitting diodes

Special diodes are made which emit light. These are called light emitting diodes (or LEDs).

LEDs are used mainly as visual indicators that a circuit is working or an appliance is 'on'. Like ordinary diodes, LEDs allow current to flow in one direction only.

LEDs normally work at around 2 volts. In order to obtain the correct working voltage for the LED in a circuit, a resistor is normally placed in series with the LED. Ohm's Law can be used to calculate the value of this resistor.

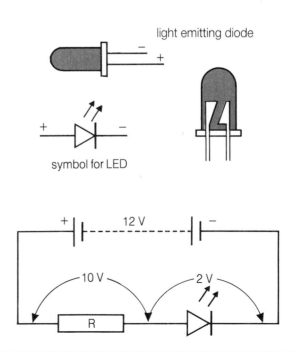
light emitting diode

symbol for LED

Calculating resistance value

When two or more components are connected across a power supply in this way, they are said to form a **potential divider**. The components divide the power supply voltage between them. If the LED requires 2 V across it, 10 V must be 'dropped' across the resistor.

If the LED requires say 10 mA (1000 mA = 1 A) to operate it, the value of R can be calculated as shown here:

$$R = \frac{V}{I}$$
$$= \frac{10}{0.01}$$
$$= 1000\ \Omega.$$

'Game of chance' project – using diodes

Susan and Steven have designed and made a 'game of chance' which uses diodes.

Both players gamble by pressing either button A or B. The player whose turn it is spins the disc. The player whose light remains on after the disc has stopped is the winner.

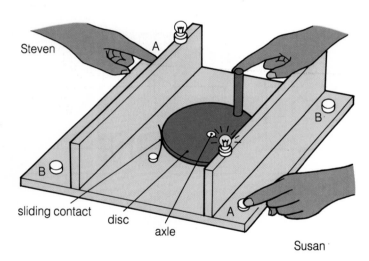

Steven

sliding contact · disc · axle

Susan

Game of chance explained

Look closely at the game circuit. Steven has gambled with button A. Susan has gambled with button A and has spun the disc. The disc has stopped as shown. Susan's light is on – she wins 2 points.

Trace the circuits to see why Susan's light is on whilst Steven's is off. Remember, a diode only allows current to flow in one direction.

There are three other possible results for this gamble: Susan could win 1 point, if both her and Steven's lights stayed on, OR Steven could win 1 point if his light stayed on but Susan's went off, OR neither player would gain a point if both lights went off.

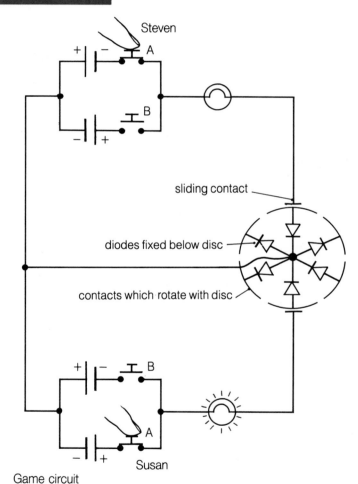

Steven

sliding contact

diodes fixed below disc

contacts which rotate with disc

Susan

Game circuit

Questions

17 a Which position must the diodes be in to give Susan a 1 point win for this gamble?
  b Which position must they be in to give Steven a 1 point win?

Transistors

Tom's dilemma

Tom asked his teacher for some help with a design problem. He was working on an aid for the disabled – a bathwater level alarm for the blind.

The purpose of the alarm was to allow a blind person to leave a 'running bath' unattended until the alarm signalled that the bath was ready.

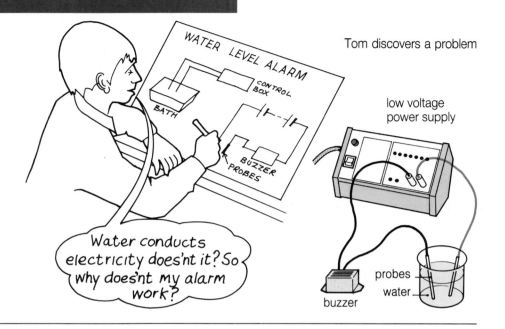

Tom discovers a problem

low voltage power supply

probes
water
buzzer

Tom's problem explained

Although Tom was correct – water does conduct electricity – the **resistance** of water is very high. The current flowing in Tom's circuit was too small to operate the buzzer.

Tom measured the current – it was only 0.001 A (1 mA).

When he measured the current needed to operate the buzzer, he discovered that 0.025 A (25 mA) was required.

His teacher explained that a **transistor** could solve his problem.

ammeter
0.001 A

buzzer
water
(high resistance)

Measuring the circuit current

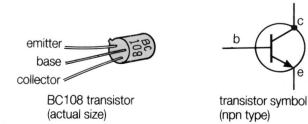

0.025 A

buzzer

Measuring the buzzer current

Transistors explained

A transistor is another **semiconductor** device. It is made of three layers of n- and p-type semiconductor material.

The three layers are called the **emitter, base** and **collector**.

Transistors are available in a wide variety of shapes and sizes, but there are only two basic types. (Only npn-types will be used in this book.)

emitter
base
collector

BC108 transistor
(actual size)

c
b
e

transistor symbol
(npn type)

What do transistors do?

We can begin to answer this question by looking at a simple transistor circuit.

In diagram 1, switch S1 is open and in this condition current will **not** flow in any part of the circuit.

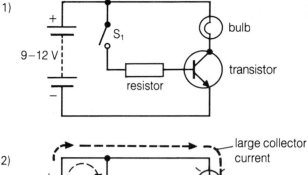

When S1 is closed however, a **very small** current flows through the base of the transistor via resistor R. When this happens the transistor 'turns on' allowing a **larger** current to flow through its collector, via the bulb. (See diagram 2.)

Can you see that the transistor has used a small current to turn on a large current?

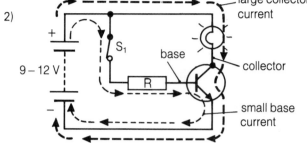

Tom's problem solved

Using the above knowledge, Tom designed and built this experimental bathwater level alarm circuit.

He connected the probes in the transistor's base circuit, and the buzzer in the transistor's collector circuit.

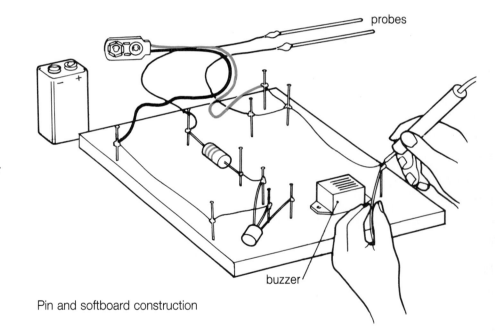

Pin and softboard construction

How the circuit operates

The tiny current passing through the water (between the probes) provides the base current to turn the transistor 'on'. The buzzer is then driven by the transistor's larger collector current.

Note   Resistor R is included in this circuit to protect the transistor. If the base current became too large, the transistor would be damaged.

Project note   Caution – transistors will be damaged if they, or the power supply, are connected the wrong way round.

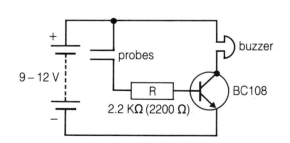

Electronic systems

At this point it will be useful to look at an important problem-solving approach to electronics which concentrates on the '**building blocks**' of electronic devices – this is called **the systems approach**.

The solution to all electronic problems can be represented by a **block diagram**. The most basic systems will contain just two building blocks – an **input device** and an **output device**. An example is shown here.

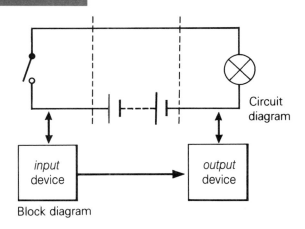

Circuit diagram

Block diagram

Even the most complex electronic systems will only contain two further types of building blocks: **control devices** and **interface devices**, although in any one system there can be a great many individual blocks.

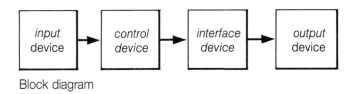

Block diagram

Input, control and output explained

Tom's bathwater level alarm (page 130) contains *three* of the basic building blocks.

His input device is a **moisture probe**. An input device is a sensing device which reacts to changes in the environment (in this case to the presence of moisture in the bath).

The control device is a **transistor** (and protective resistor). A control device is something which responds to changes at the input, and reacts by controlling the output (in this case by turning on a buzzer).

The output device is a buzzer. An output device is something which gives out information or performs a physical function (in this case it provides an audible warning).

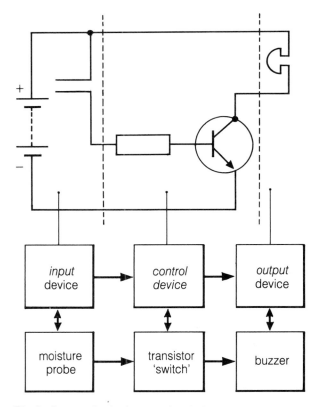

Block diagram for bath water level alarm

Input, control and output components

Electronic components make up the building blocks in electronic systems. Some were identified in Tom's circuit – some others are listed below.

input	control	output
variable resistor (see page 112) symbol	transistor (see page 129) symbol (npn transistor)	bulb symbol
light-dependant resistor (see page 112) LDR symbol	op-amp (see page 140) symbol	light-emitting diode (see page 127) LED symbol
thermistor (see page 113) symbol	555 timer (see page 149)	solenoid
touch sensor symbol	logic gates (see page 152) symbols	motor

Control systems

There are two basic types of control system – **open loop** and **closed loop** systems.

Open loop describes a system in which the building blocks simply connect together in a linear way, and where a particular input produces a particular output.

Tom's water level alarm is an example of an open loop system. Another example is shown here.

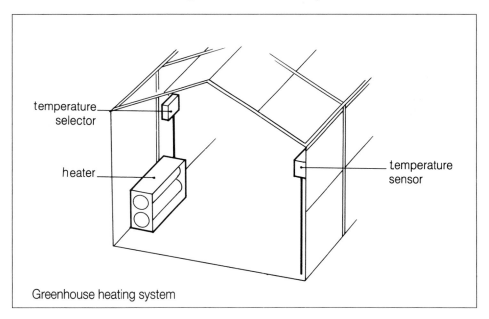

Block diagram for automatic sliding door

Closed loop describes a system which has **feedback**. Feedback involves the use of a sensor to detect changes at the output and to feed information back to the control device, which may then modify the output.

The greenhouse heating system, shown here, is an example of a closed loop system. It comprises: an electric heater, a temperature selector unit and a temperature sensor. Look carefully at the block diagram for this system.

Greenhouse heating system

The sensor constantly monitors the greenhouse temperature and feeds information (in the form of an electrical signal) back to the control device (in the heater). The control device compares this signal with the signal from the selector unit. When these two signals are the same, the control device 'knows' that the required temperature has been reached and it turns off the heater.

In conclusion, a closed loop system has a means of checking what is happening at the output, and if necessary, changing what is happening. However, an open loop system cannot do this.

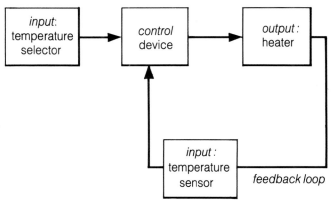

Block diagram with feedback

Transistor circuits – continued

By making a number of simple changes to Tom's circuit shown on page 130, a wide range of control problems can be solved.

Lorna has designed a **water pollution indicator** for use in rivers and canals. In her circuit, the input device is an LDR and the output device is a bulb.

Water pollution indicator

How the indicator works

Polluted water often contains suspended particles, which affect the passage of light. When light is shone through the water towards the LDR therefore, the amount of light reaching the LDR will depend upon the level of pollution. (See diagrams.)

The resistance of an LDR depends upon the amount of light falling on it. (See page 112.) As the light level increases, so the resistance decreases. The ORP12 LDR has a resistance of 10 million ohms (10 MΩ) in the dark, and as little as 130 Ω in bright light.

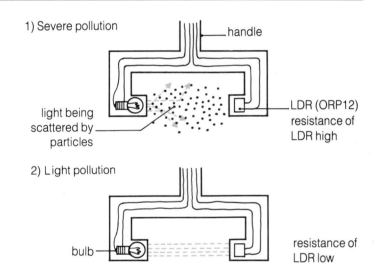

1) Severe pollution — handle

light being scattered by particles

LDR (ORP12) resistance of LDR high

2) Light pollution

bulb

resistance of LDR low

How the circuit works

If you ignore the variable resistor (VR) for a moment, the operation of the circuit can be explained as follows.

When the LDR is in darkness (in polluted water) its resistance is high. Insufficient base current flows to turn on the transistor, and the indicator bulb is off.

In less polluted water however, the resistance of the LDR falls. This allows sufficient base current to flow to turn the transistor on. The transistor's collector current passes through the indicator bulb, making it glow.

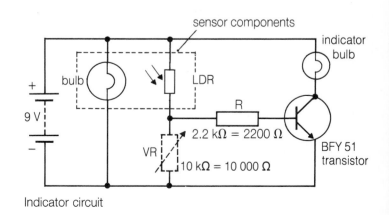

Indicator circuit

What does the variable resistor do?

In the actual circuit, current flowing through the LDR 'splits' taking the two routes shown.

Now, the current flowing in the base circuit depends upon the voltage across VR, which in turn depends upon the resistance of VR and of the LDR. By adjusting the variable resistor therefore, we can set the circuit to operate at a particular light level (and therefore at a particular level of pollution).

Project note   See page 137.

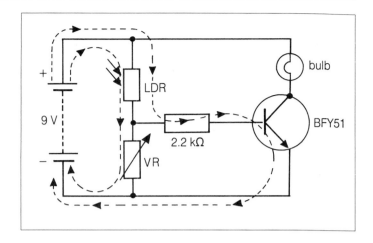

Circuit design information

Collector current

For each kind of transistor, there is a maximum collector current which must not be exceeded. A BC108 transistor, for example, has a maximum collector current (or I_c) of 100 mA.

If the device to be 'turned on' requires more current than the transistor can provide, a **relay** can be utilised.

The circuit shown here, for example, enables a fan motor (which draws 2 A) to be switched on when a preset temperature is reached.

Note   When a relay de-energizes it releases a surge of electrical energy which could destroy a transistor. By connecting a diode across the transistor (as shown in the diagram), the energy is diverted away from the transistor which is thus protected from damage.

A relay is an example of an interface device. An interface provides a control link between two circuit functions, but keeps the circuitry separate.

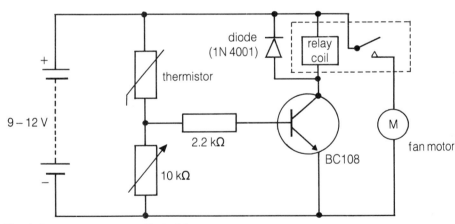

Circuit for a temperature activated fan

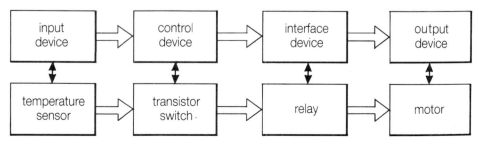

Block diagram for a temperature activated fan

Transistor gain

We have seen that a small current flowing in the base of a transistor will 'turn on' a larger collector current. This is known as current amplification.

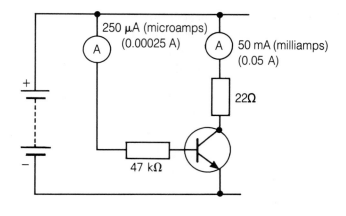

The ratio 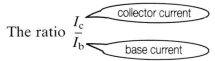 $\dfrac{I_c}{I_b}$

is a measure of this amplification which we call the transistor's current **gain**. The symbol for transistor current gain is h_{fe}.

$$h_{fe} = \frac{I_c}{I_b}$$

$$= \frac{0.05}{0.00025}$$

$$= 200$$

for the transistor in the circuit shown.

The Darlington Pair amplifier

The amplification of a single transistor is often not sufficient in a circuit. If the amplified current of one transistor is fed into the base of a second transistor however, the amplification can be increased many times.

If the gain of each transistor shown here is 100, for example, then the combined gain of the two transistors is in excess of 10 000. Can you see why?

This method of connecting transistors is known as a Darlington Pair.

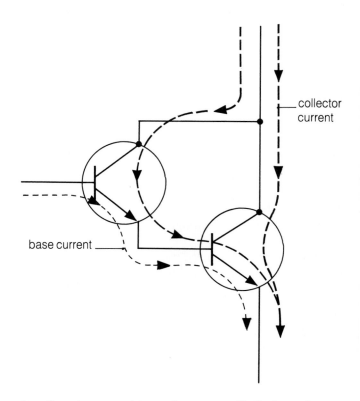

Coupling of two transistors – known as a Darlington pair

Project notes

Lorna's Water Pollution Indicator, shown on page 134, did work using a single transistor. However, the circuit was far more **sensitive** (could detect smaller changes of light intensity) using the Darlington Pair circuit shown here.

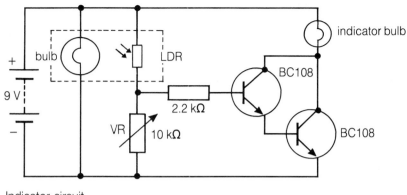

Indicator circuit

A printed circuit board construction was used for this project.

A note for teachers – printed circuit board, etch resist pens, chemicals, trays etc, can be obtained from component suppliers.

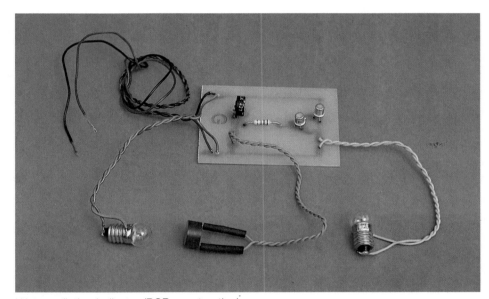

Water pollution indicator (PCB construction)

Light activated switch

The circuit shown here is a modification of the Water Pollution Indicator circuit.

By replacing the indicator bulb with a relay (and protective diode) the circuit may be used to control other devices in response to changing light levels. Further modifications include the replacement of the LDR with a thermistor – to produce a temperature activated switch; or metal probes or plates – to produce a moisture activated switch.

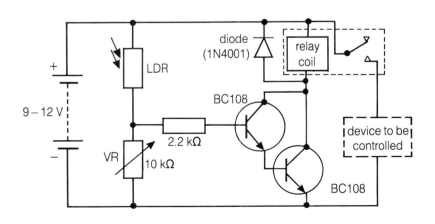

Projects

Touch sensitive switch

The circuit shown can be used in any project which requires something to be switched on by the touch of a finger. The circuit can be used to turn on a lamp or buzzer for example, or control an electric motor.

How the circuit works

The finger is used to 'connect' the touch plates. The tiny current which flows through the finger-tip becomes the base current which turns the transistor on. The transistor's collector current is used to energize a relay, which in turn can be used to switch on other devices.

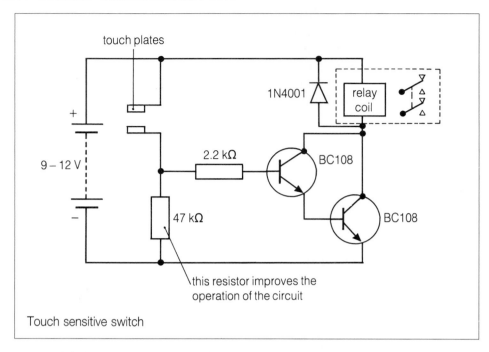

Touch sensitive switch

Circuit modification

In the above circuit, the relay will de-energize the moment the finger is removed from the touch plates. If you require the relay to remain on however, the modification shown here can be used.

This is another example of a **latching circuit**. Can you see why the relay remains on?

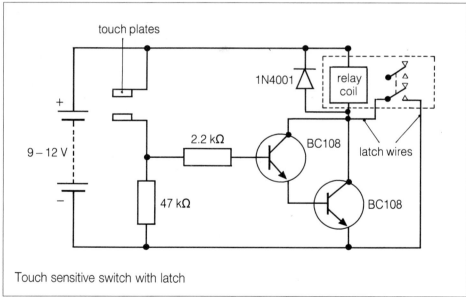

Touch sensitive switch with latch

Note   You can use a second touch-sensitive switch as an 'off' switch to work in conjunction with the above circuit. To do this, wire the second relay's contacts **in series** with the first relay's 'latch wires'. When the second circuit is activated therefore, the latch in the first circuit will be broken.

'Fast reaction' game (alternative circuit)

The diagram shows an alternative circuit for the 'fast reaction' game described on page 123.

How the circuit works

If PS_2 is pressed **first** (by player A), TR_2 turns on – due to the connection of its base circuit, and L_2 lights. Now, when TR_2 switches on, the voltage at its collector falls to zero (you can check this using a voltmeter). If PS_1 is pressed a fraction of a second later therefore, TR_1 will **not** turn on, since there is no voltage available to produce a base current. The reverse applies of course, if PS_1 is pressed first.

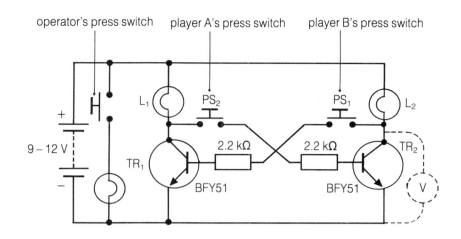

Reaction trainer

Think of a situation in which a person's 'fast reaction' is important. This could be whilst driving a car or taking part in a sport, for example.

Briefs

Either
1 Design and construct a simulator which could be used to **compare** the reactions of two people in your chosen situation.

Or
2 Design and construct a simulator which could be used to **improve** the reaction of an individual in your chosen situation.

Note

For brief number 2, you might find it useful to refer to the section on timing circuits in this chapter (pages 145–150).

Integrated circuits

The circuits discussed so far have been made up from **discrete** (or separate) components such as resistors, transistors etc. Integrated circuits (or ICs) however, are complete circuits in themselves. ICs contain very small 'chips' of silicon, into which numerous components have been formed. Each silicon chip is mounted in a plastic case and is connected to pins set in the side of the case.

The 741 operational amplifier, or **op amp**, is a particularly useful IC for school technology projects. Its basic operation is described below.

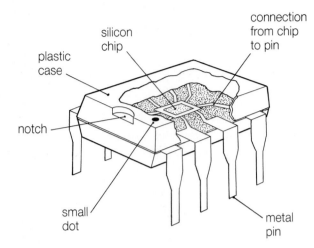

741 operational amplifier IC

The 741 operational amplifier

The op amp chip contains a complex circuit. We can neither see it, nor could we repair it if it went wrong. It is only necessary therefore to understand what it can do, not how it does it.

On page 130, we mentioned the amplification of a transistor and learnt about **current gain**. In the case of the op amp however, it is more appropriate to consider **voltage gain**.

The standard symbol for an amplifier is a triangle. It has an input (into which the 'signal' is sent) and an output (from which the amplified signal is obtained).

If the amplifier had a gain of say 10, and the voltage at the input was +0.5 volts, we would expect the output to be +5 volts (0.5 × 10 = 5).

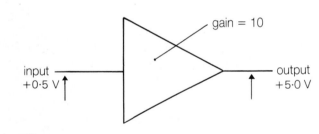

Amplifier

Unlike the amplifier described above, an op amp has **two** inputs. These are called the **inverting**, and **non-inverting** inputs. The amplifier uses these inputs in a special way. It amplifies **the difference** between the two input voltages.

For example, if +0.5 volts was applied to the non-inverting input, and +0.1 volts was applied to the inverting input, the op amp would amplify 0.4 volts (the difference) to give an output of +4 volts.

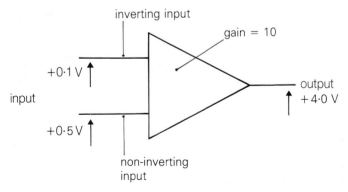

Operational amplifier

If the input voltages were reversed however, i.e. +0.1 volts on the non-inverting input and +0.5 volts on the inverting input, the op amp would still amplify the difference between the two input voltages, but the output would be −4 volts (**minus** 4 volts).

The effect of applying the larger voltage to the **inverting** input therefore, is to **invert** the output (make it go negative).

Note For the purpose of the explanation, the op amp described above was said to have a gain of 10. In reality however, an op amp's gain can be in excess of 100 000.

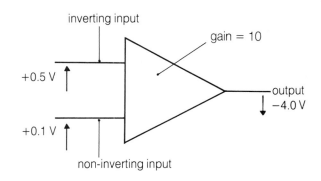

Experimental op amp circuit

The circuit described below can be used to investigate and experiment with the 741 op amp. For ease of understanding, the circuit has been explained in several stages.

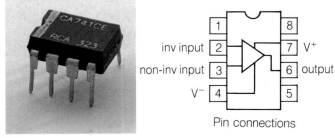

741 op amp

The power supply

The diagram shows an op amp connected to its power supply. Notice that two batteries have been connected in a special way. Three terminals are provided: a common (0 volts), a positive supply (+9 volts) and a negative supply (−9 volts). This is called a **dual rail power supply**.

Notice that the inputs have been labelled '+' and '−'. This has nothing to do with the power supply. '+' is the symbol used to indicate the non-inverting input, and '−' indicates the inverting input.

Inputs and outputs

In the diagram, three resistors have been added to form a potential divider – 'dividing up' the +9 V supply as shown. These will be used to provide the inputs.

Two LEDs have been connected across the output (in series with a resistor). These will be used to indicate the 'state' of the output.

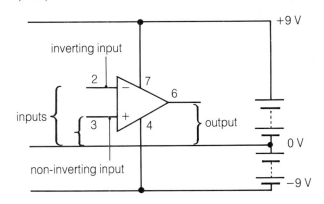

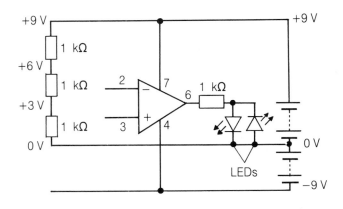

The experiment

'Flyleads' can be used to connect the non-inverting input to +6 volts, and the inverting input to +3 volts, as shown.

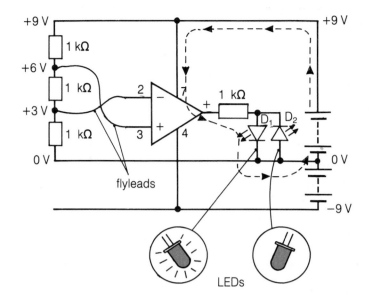

With this arrangement, the difference between the two voltages will be amplified, and the output will go **positive**. Current will therefore flow in the output as shown, and D_1 will pass current and 'glow'. D_2 however, will **not** pass current, because its anode is not connected to the positive supply. (See diodes page 127.)

Note   As we have stated, the gain of an op amp is typically 100 000. However, the 3.0 volts difference between the two inputs can only be amplified up to the maximum supply voltage (9 volts in this case) and not 300 000 volts, as you might expect.

If the flyleads are reversed as shown (connecting the non-inverting input to +3 volts and the inverting input to +6 volts), the output goes to −9 volts. Current will therefore flow in the output as shown, and D_2 will pass current and 'glow', but D_1 of course will not.

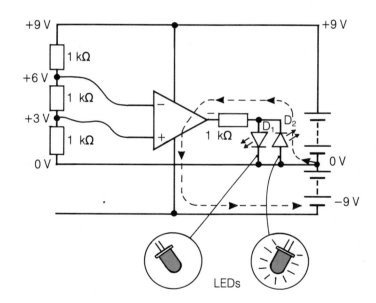

Conclusions

Because of the very large gain of an op amp we can assume that the output voltage will **either**,

1 be close to the positive supply voltage (when the non-inverting input is at a higher potential than the inverting input) **or**,
2 close to the negative supply voltage (if the inverting input is at a higher potential than the non-inverting input).

A useful op amp circuit

This circuit can be used as a very sensitive 'light activated switch'. It operates as follows:

When the LDR is illuminated its resistance is low and the voltage across it is low. When voltage V_1 is lower than V_2, the output of the op amp is negative. The transistor will therefore be off and the relay will not energize. When the LDR is in shadow however, its resistance rises and the voltage across it rises. If V_1 rises above V_2 the output of the op amp goes positive, the transistor turns on, and the relay energizes. The use of VR_1 enables the circuit to be adjusted to operate at a particular light level.

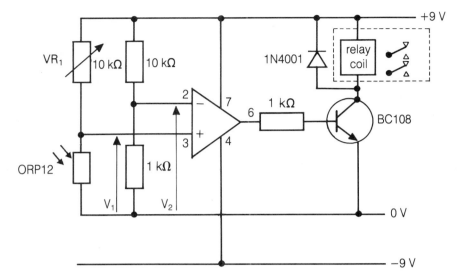

Light activated switch circuit

Projects

Car park exit barrier

Design an exit barrier system for a car park. The barrier must open when a vehicle breaks a light beam, and must remain open until the vehicle is clear of the barrier.

Note   If you use the op amp circuit for this project, the relay could be used to operate a motor reversing circuit to control the position of the barrier. (See page 124.)

Weighing machine

The photograph shows an experimental weighing machine which uses two 741 op amps.

The machine was designed to sense a 2 N weight, a 1 N weight and zero weight. Two LEDs light when 2 N are present, one LED lights when 1 N is present, and when the scale pan is empty, neither LED lights.

Notice that variable resistor VR_1 has a small pulley attached to its spindle, around which is wound the thread. When weights are placed on the scale pan, the spring extends and the spindle of VR_1 is rotated.

How the circuit works

R_3, R_4 and R_5 form a potential divider to which the inverting inputs of op amps 1 and 2 are connected. The voltages at these inputs are approximately 4.0 volts and 4.8 volts as shown. R_1, R_2 and VR_1 form a second potential divider to which the op amp's non-inverting inputs are connected.

When the scale pan is empty, VR_1 is at its lowest resistance value and the voltage across VR_1 and R_2 is less than 4 volts. Hence the outputs of both op amps are negative, and neither LED lights. When a 1 N weight is placed on the scale pan however, the spindle of VR_1 is made to rotate, and its resistance rises. This causes the voltage across VR_1 and R_2 to rise above 4.0 volts (but to less than 4.8 volts). The output of op amp 1 therefore goes positive and LED 1 lights. With two 1 N weights on the scale pan, the spindle of VR_1 is further rotated, again increasing its resistance. The voltage across VR_1 and R_2 now goes above 4.8 volts and the output of op amp 2 goes positive – hence LED 2 also lights.

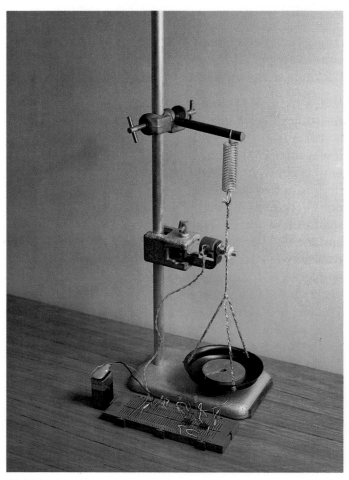

Weighing machine

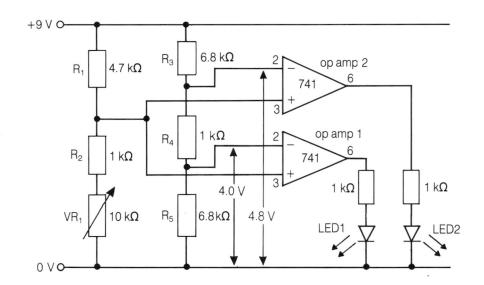

Note This circuit does **not** require a dual rail power supply. For each op amp, pin 7 is connected to +9 volts (in the normal way) and pin 4 connected to 0 volts. (These connections have not been shown on the circuit diagram.)

Timing circuits

In addition to simple 'timing' applications such as photographic timers, egg timers, cooker timers etc, **time delay** circuits are used to produce time delay sequences in control processes. The traffic lights at this Pelican crossing for example, operate using time delay circuits.

A number of useful timing circuits for school technology projects are described below. To understand how they work however, requires an understanding of **capacitors**.

Pelican crossing

Capacitors

A capacitor is a component which can store and release electrical energy. This can be demonstrated by doing the simple experiment described overleaf.

Capacitance is measured in farads, but the smaller values – microfarads (μF), nanofarads (nF) and picofarads (pF) are more convenient for our purposes.

There are two basic types of capacitor:

Polarized which tend to be the higher value types. These have a positive ($+$) and negative ($-$) lead which **must** be connected the correct way round in a circuit ($+$ to $+$ and $-$ to $-$).

Non-polarized which are low value types. These can be connected either way round in a circuit.

All capacitors have a maximum working voltage. This is shown using either numbers or a colour code.

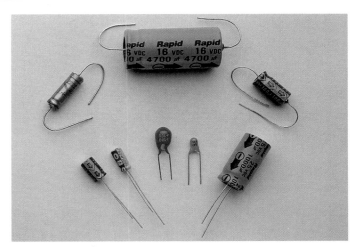

Polarized capacitors

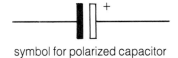

symbol for polarized capacitor

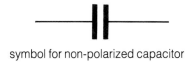

symbol for non-polarized capacitor

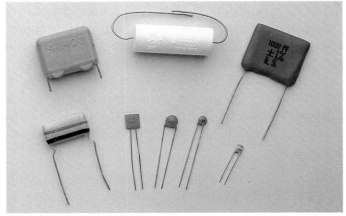

Non-polarized capacitors

The experiment

Connect a fairly large value capacitor across a 12 volt power supply as shown. This will cause the capacitor to 'charge up'. Remember to connect the positive side of the capacitor to the positive side of the power supply, and so on.

Then remove the charged capacitor and connect it across a 12 volt bulb. The stored energy will be released from the capacitor, causing the bulb to glow.

Within a few seconds, all the stored energy will be released and the bulb will go out.

Now repeat the experiment using **two** similar capacitors connected in **parallel**. What effect does this have? Discuss this with your teacher. Experiment with capacitors of other values too.

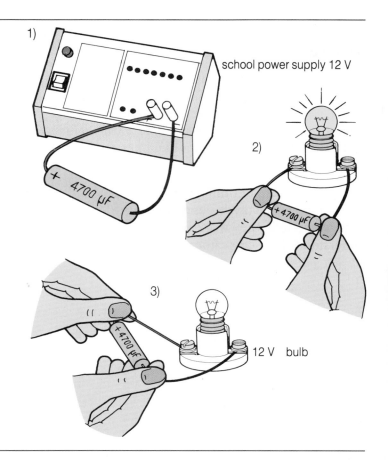

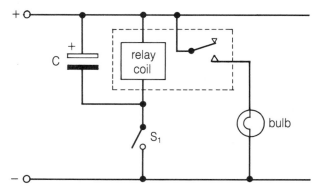

Time delay circuits

Circuit 1

This circuit is designed to keep a device turned on for a few seconds, after you have used the switch to turn it off.

The circuit explained

Notice that a capacitor has been connected in **parallel** with the relay coil in this circuit.

When S_1 is closed, the relay energizes and the bulb is switched on. At the same time the capacitor becomes charged. When S_1 is opened therefore, the relay does **not** turn off. It remains on for a few seconds as the capacitor discharges through the relay coil. The bulb therefore also remains on. As a capacitor discharges however, the current it delivers gets less and less until it is no longer sufficient to keep the relay energized. (See graph.)

Note   The bulb in this circuit can be replaced with any device which you wish to control.

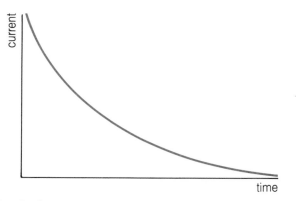

Graph of current against time for a discharging capacitor

Circuit 2

The operation of this timing circuit is quite different from Circuit 1. It can be used to turn a bulb on (or other device) for a short period of time, and then automatically turn it off. Notice that a capacitor has been connected in **series** with the relay coil in this circuit.

The circuit explained

When S_1 is closed, the capacitor charges via the relay coil. The charging current is high at first, but gradually decreases, until it is finally zero when the capacitor is fully charged. (See graph.)

When S_1 is first closed therefore, the relay energizes. It then remains energized until the capacitor's charging current falls below the minimum required to operate the relay. At this point the relay de-energizes. The larger the value of the capacitor, the longer the time delay.

Note To re-set the circuit, first open S_1, then press PS_1 (this will discharge the capacitor). When S_1 is closed again the circuit will operate as above.

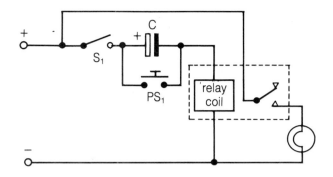

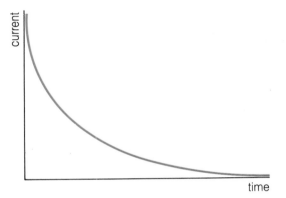

Graph of current against time for a charging capacitor

Circuit 3

This circuit produces yet another time delay sequence. When the circuit is activated, a delay occurs **before** the relay is energized and the bulb (or other device) is switched on.

The circuit explained

The operation of this circuit will be described in two stages.

1 When S_1 is closed, capacitor C charges via resistor R. As the capacitor charges up, the voltage across it rises (as shown by the graph). As the voltage across C rises however, the voltage across R falls. The total voltage across C and R will always equal the supply voltage.

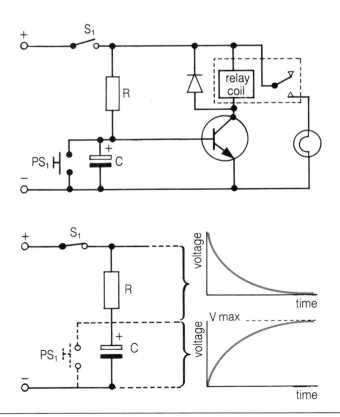

2 It has been shown that a small current flowing in the base of a transistor will turn the transistor on. However, a transistor will only begin to turn on when the voltage across its base emitter junction equals about 0.6 volts.

When S_1 is first closed therefore, the voltage across the capacitor (and therefore across the base emitter junction) is zero – the transistor will be 'off'. As the capacitor charges however, the voltage across it rises. When the voltage equals about 0.6 volts, the transistor will begin to turn on and at 0.7 volts will be fully on and the relay will have energized.

3 To re-set the circuit, first open S_1, then press PS_1 (this will discharge the capacitor). When S_1 is closed again, the circuit will operate as above.

Note   It is important to be aware that when a capacitor is charging (or discharging) **no current** flows between the capacitor's plates. Electricity is **stored** on the plates when the capacitor is charging, and is **released** on discharge. For a fuller explanation, you will need to read a more specialized electronics book.

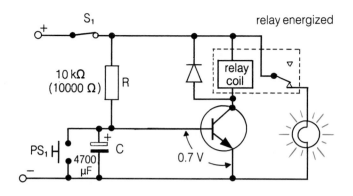

How quickly does a capacitor charge up?

R.C. time constants

When a capacitor charges via a resistor, the time it takes for the voltage across the capacitor to reach about $\frac{2}{3}$ of the supply voltage is known as the **time constant**.

To calculate the time constant for a given R.C. circuit, use the equation

$$t = C \times R$$

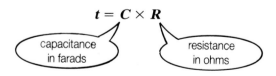

capacitance in farads   resistance in ohms

In the diagram,

$$t = 0.0047 \times 10\ 000$$

$$t = 47 \text{ seconds}$$

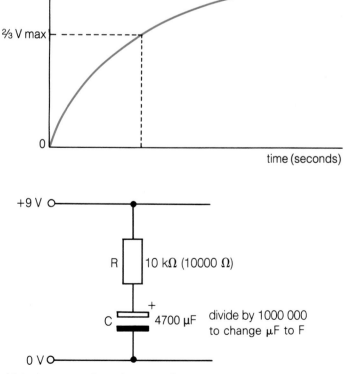

Voltage across C reaches 6 V ($\frac{2}{3}$ of 9 V) in about 47 seconds

Time constants and timing circuits

As we have said, in the timing circuit shown here, the transistor will begin to turn on when the base–emitter voltage equals about 0.6 V.

Now, since it takes $C \times R$ seconds (47 seconds) for the voltage across the capacitor to reach 6.0 V ($\frac{2}{3}$ of the supply voltage), it will take (approximately) $\frac{1}{10}$ of this time (4.7 seconds) to reach 0.6 V. The transistor therefore will begin to turn on after this time period.

Note To increase the time period, increase the value of C. If you increase the value of R very much, the circuit will fail to operate.

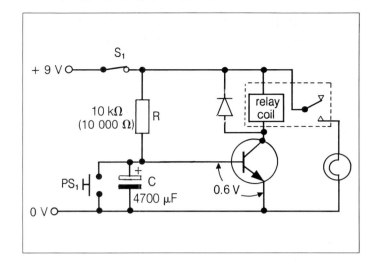

555 timer – integrated circuit

One of the disadvantages of circuits 2 and 3 described on the previous pages, is that they must be re-set manually (by pressing a switch) after each timing sequence. Further, only relatively short time delays can be produced by any of the circuits. These problems can be overcome by the use of the 555 timer IC.

As with the 741 op amp, we will only describe the operation of the IC, and not how its complex circuitry works.

555 timer IC

555 timing circuit explained (monostable operation)

The 555 timer circuit is designed to switch on a device for a pre-set period of time, and then switch it off (as in circuit 2).

To start the timing sequence, PS_1 is pressed momentarily.

Now, pin 3 (which is normally at 0 volts) immediately goes to +9 volts and the relay energizes. The relay then remains on for the period determined by the timing components R and C – it then turns off (as pin 3 goes back to 0 volts).

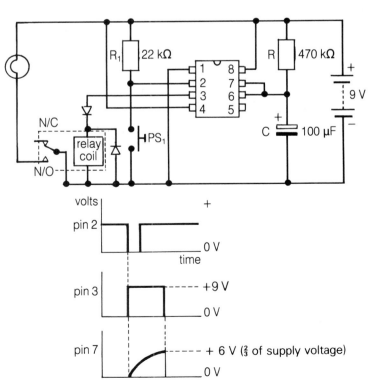

The graphs show the voltages on pins 2, 3 and 7 during the above sequence. At the same instant that the relay switches off, the capacitor is automatically discharged by the IC's internal circuitry. Hence the circuit is immediately made ready for the next timing sequence.

Note The device to be controlled (a bulb in this example) is turned on and off by the relay in the normal way.

Calculating delay time

For the 555 timer IC the delay time is given by the equation:

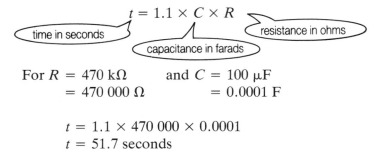

$$t = 1.1 \times C \times R$$

time in seconds | capacitance in farads | resistance in ohms

For $R = 470 \text{ k}\Omega$ and $C = 100 \text{ }\mu\text{F}$
      $= 470\ 000 \text{ }\Omega$ $= 0.0001 \text{ F}$

$$t = 1.1 \times 470\ 000 \times 0.0001$$
$$t = 51.7 \text{ seconds}$$

Project note R can be replaced by a 3 MΩ (3 000 000 Ω) variable resistor to give **variable** time delays of several minutes.

Project

Automatic porch light

Design an automatic porch light. The light must be activated by a **pressure pad**. After a short delay, the light must switch off.

This project could be made more sophisticated by adding a **light activated switch** circuit. This circuit would control the porch light – only allowing it to operate in the dark. Light activated switch circuits are shown on pages 122, 134 and 137.

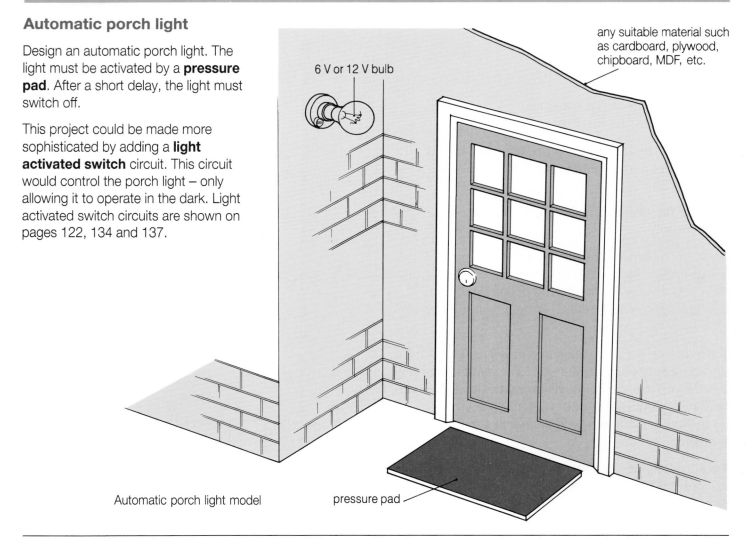

any suitable material such as cardboard, plywood, chipboard, MDF, etc.

6 V or 12 V bulb

Automatic porch light model

pressure pad

555 timer (astable operation)

The monostable operation of the 555 timer was described on page 149. **Monostable** means that the output of the IC (the voltage at pin 3) has *one* stable state (0 V). Although the output can be made to change to +9 V (for example), it always goes back to 0 V (its stable state) after a pre-determined period of time.

Astable refers to a system which has no stable state. The output of the 555 circuit shown here does not have a stable state – it changes between 0 V and +9 V continuously. The LED, therefore, flashes on and off continuously.

The **frequency** of an astable timer can be calculated as shown here.

Note 1 If you wish to adjust the frequency of the astable, replace R_2 with a variable resistor as shown 'dotted'.

Note 2 If you require *two* LEDs to flash on and off alternately, include a second LED (and resistor), where shown dotted.

Tone generator

By making a number of changes to the above circuit, a tone generator can be constructed. This has applications in alarms, musical instruments, Pelican crossing bleepers, and so on.

The note produced by the speaker can be changed by adjusting the 10 K variable resistor.

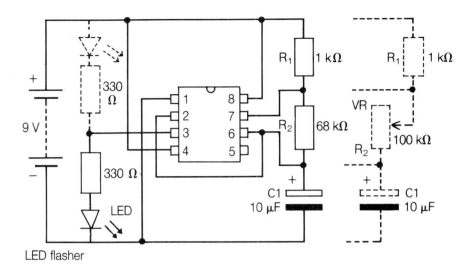

LED flasher

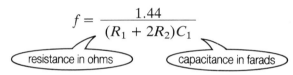

$$f = \frac{1.44}{(R_1 + 2R_2)C_1}$$

resistance in ohms   capacitance in farads

For above example:

$$f = \frac{1.44}{(1000 + 2 \times 68000) \times 0.00001}$$

$$f = \frac{1.44}{1.37}$$

$$f = 1.05 \text{ hz}$$
(Approximately one flash per second.)

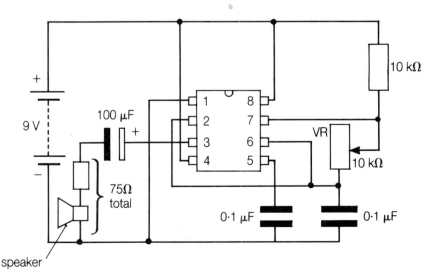

speaker

Tone generator

An introduction to control logic

The cartoon characters **Eyeball, Sensation** and **Muscles** will be used to explain **control logic**.

In these demonstrations, control logic will be used to help solve some design problems.

Eyeball

Sensation

Muscles

Brief   To design a system which will automatically take washing under cover when it rains **OR** when night falls.

Possible solution

(See diagram.) **Muscles** will be used to control the position of the washing and will be in charge of the crank handle. **Sensation** will be responsible for detecting rainfall, and **Eyeball** will keep a look out for nightfall.

Notice that Sensation and Eyeball each have a press switch. These are connected into a buzzer circuit which is used to tell Muscles when to wind in the washing. Muscles will hear the buzzer if either switch A **OR** B (or both) is pressed.

In logic, a circuit which behaves like these switches is called an **OR gate**. An OR gate gives an output when input A **OR** B (or both) is present – in this case, when switch A OR B is closed.

belt and pulley system

A
press switch

crank handle

B
press switch

buzzer

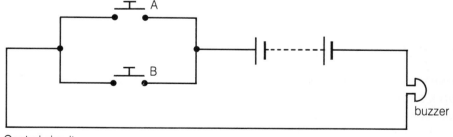

Control circuit

buzzer

Using this simple control circuit, the three characters are able to control the washing line to ensure that the washing is taken under cover at night, OR when it rains, or both.

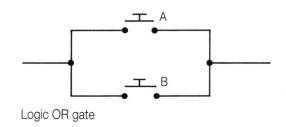

Logic OR gate

The language of logic

In the language of logic, when a switch is closed it is said to be at logic state **1**. In the circuit shown, switch A is at logic state **1**. An open switch is said to be at logic state **0**. Similarly, when a logic gate produces an output, the output is said to be at logic state **1**. No output, logic state **0**.

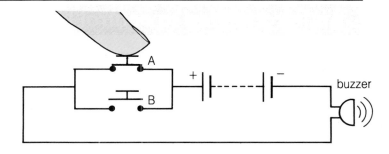

Most logic gates however, are electronic devices, not switches, and the inputs are in the form of **electrical pulses**. The inputs and output can only have two states (or voltage levels), 'high' or 'low'. 'High' (say +5 V) is referred to as logic **1**, 'low' (0 V) as logic **0**. The **OR** gate IC shown here operates in this way.

OR gate integrated circuit

Any OR gate can be represented with a block diagram. The block diagram for a two input OR gate is shown here.

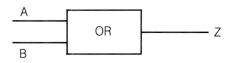

Truth table

We can represent the state of the inputs and output of a logic gate in a special table called a **truth table**.

The truth table for a (two input) OR gate is shown. Notice that the letter **Z** has been used to indicate the output. (Other letters are sometimes used.)

inputs		output
A	B	Z
0	0	0
0	1	1
1	0	1
1	1	1

Automating the washing line

Automation often involves replacing a human operator (or operators) with mechanical or electrical systems. In deciding what system to use therefore, it is useful to examine the operators' 'jobs'.

Sensation was responsible for detecting rainfall and therefore could be replaced by a **moisture sensing circuit**.

Eyeball detected changing light levels and therefore could be replaced by a **light activated switch**.

Finally, Muscles did the heavy work and could be replaced by a **motor reversing circuit** and a **transmission system**.

Demonstration 2

Brief   To design a system to automatically open a garage door when the car headlights are flashed. To add security to the system, the car must also be standing in a particular position when the lights are flashed.

Possible solution (See diagram.)   Muscles will be used to control the movement of the door and will be in charge of the winch. Sensation will be responsible for detecting the position of the car, and Eyeball will keep a look out for the car's headlights.

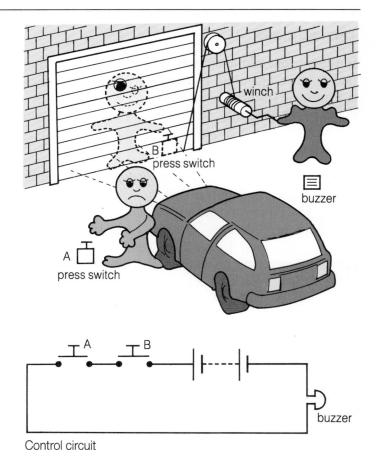

Again, both operators have press switches connected into a buzzer circuit. These are used to tell Muscles when to open the door. However, the buzzer will only sound when switches A **AND** B are pressed together.

In logic, a circuit which behaves like these switches is called an **AND gate**. An AND gate only gives an output when both inputs A **AND** B are present – in this case, when switches A AND B are closed.

Control circuit

Using this simple control circuit, the three characters are able to control the garage door and ensure that it will only open when the car headlights are flashed AND it is parked in the correct position.

Logic AND gate

Truth table

The truth table for a (two input) AND gate is shown here.

inputs		output
A	B	Z
0	0	0
0	1	0
1	0	0
1	1	1

Automating the garage door

Once again, Eyeball was responsible for detecting a change in light level, and therefore could be replaced by a light activated switch.

Sensation however, acted as a position sensor, and in this situation could be replaced by a **pressure pad**.

Finally, Muscles did the heavy work again and could be replaced by a motor reversing circuit and a transmission system.

The NOT gate

Now that you understand the principle of logic gates, and how they can be used in control circuits, the **NOT gate** can be explained in brief.

A **NOT gate** can be represented with the symbol shown. Notice that a NOT gate has a single input and a single output. The operation of a NOT gate is as follows:

When the input is at logic **1**, the output goes to logic **0**, and when the input is at logic **0**, the output goes to logic **1**.

The truth table for a NOT gate is shown here.

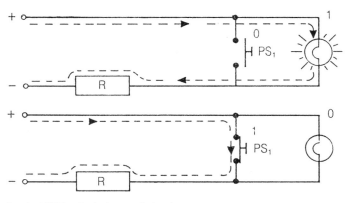

input	output
A	Z
0	1
1	0

The operation of a NOT gate can be illustrated using a simple switching circuit. When the input is at logic **0** (switch not pressed) the output goes to logic **1** (and the bulb is lit).

When the input is at logic **1** however, most of the current takes the path of least resistance (through the switch), the output goes to logic **0** (and the bulb goes out).

Logic NOT gate (using switches)

The NOT gate in a control circuit

A block diagram for an automatic watering system is shown. The design of the system ensures that the moisture content of the soil is constantly monitored.

However, because seedlings can be damaged if watered in bright (hot) sunlight, watering only takes place at night.

Trace the block diagram and see how the NOT gate prevents the AND gate from turning on the sprinkler during the daytime.

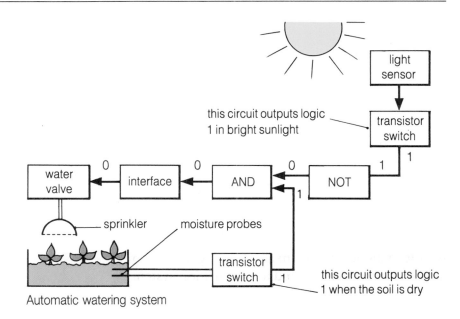

this circuit outputs logic 1 in bright sunlight

this circuit outputs logic 1 when the soil is dry

Automatic watering system

Circuit construction techniques

Tom's bathwater level alarm (shown on page 130 in this chapter) was built using a pin and board construction. This is one example of **modelling** – a method of construction which allows you to test and develop an idea quickly and easily.

More permanent, but still quite fast, methods of construction include the use of **matrix board** and **strip board**. With matrix board, small rigid pins are pressed into pre-drilled holes in the board and the components and connecting wires are soldered to these. Strip board looks similar to matrix board, but on one side it has strips of copper which join parallel lines of holes. The circuit is built up using these copper strips as connectors.

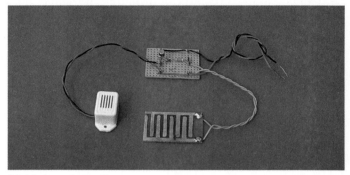

Matrix board circuit

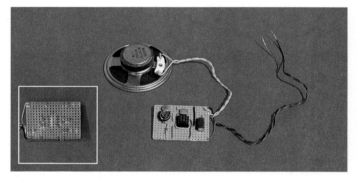

Strip board circuit

Printed circuit board (PCB)

Printed circuit board can be used to produce a permanent circuit when you are satisfied with a design after modelling.

PCB is clad with a thin coat of copper (sometimes on both sides) and does not contain any pre-drilled holes. One method of transforming this material into a **printed circuit**, ready for final assembly with circuit components is described below.

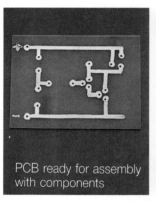

PCB ready for assembly with components

PCB

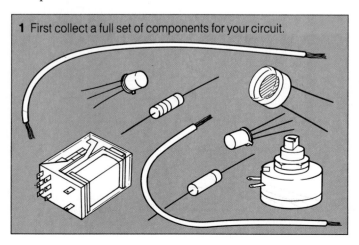

1 First collect a full set of components for your circuit.

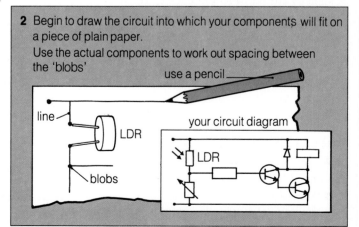

2 Begin to draw the circuit into which your components will fit on a piece of plain paper.
Use the actual components to work out spacing between the 'blobs'

use a pencil

line

LDR

your circuit diagram

LDR

blobs

3 After completing the circuit, attach it to a piece of PCB using Sellotape

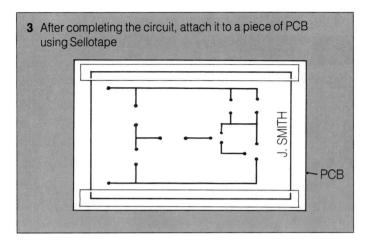

4 Now drill through each of the 'blobs' using a 1 mm drill whilst holding the work firmly over a piece of scrap wood.

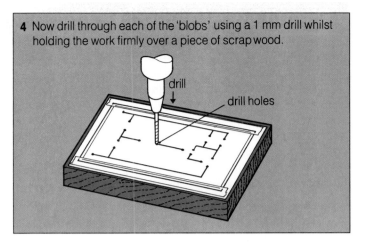

5 Remove the paper circuit from the PCB and clean the surface of the board using wire wool.
Now re-draw the circuit on the PCB using an **etch resist pen.**

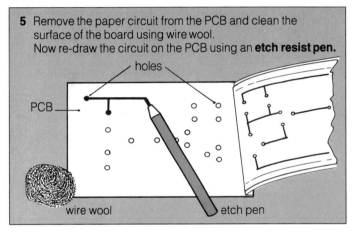

6 The circuit can now be etched in iron (III) chloride either in a tray, or preferably in a special etching bath.
Only do this with your teacher's supervision.

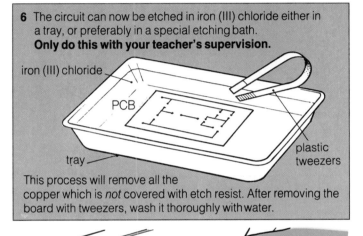

This process will remove all the copper which is *not* covered with etch resist. After removing the board with tweezers, wash it thoroughly with water.

Assembling the circuit

1 When you are ready to complete your circuit rub off the etch resist from the copper strips using wire wool.

2 Next insert the components in the correct position, from the underside of the board.

3 Using a soldering iron with a **clean** bit, heat up a joint, wait for a moment and then apply the solder to the joint. Remove the iron and solder and allow the joint to cool. Repeat for all the connections.

Note   Any movement of a joint before it sets will create a **dry joint** having a poor electrical connection.

4 When soldering transistors and diodes, or other components which can be damaged by heat, always use a **heatsink** – a pair of pointed pliers can be used for this purpose.

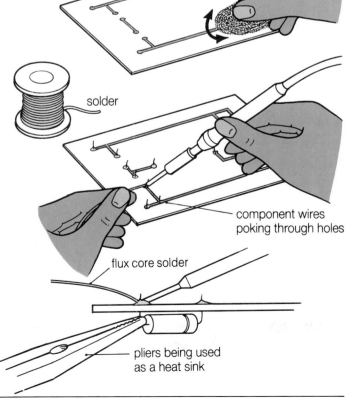

Questions

18 The block diagram of a fish tank environment alarm is shown here. The system is designed to monitor both water temperature and water level. If either are below a pre-set value, the system displays a visible warning.

Complete the block diagram by filling in the empty boxes.

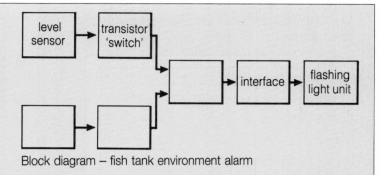

Block diagram – fish tank environment alarm

19 A stamping machine is loaded by hand with metal blanks. A light sensor detects the presence of the operator's arm. The machine 'stamps' when PS$_1$ is pressed, but only if the operator's arm has been withdrawn.

If the light sensor gives an output of **0** when the beam is interrupted, and the press switch gives an output of **1** when closed, what type of logic gate should be in the box X to allow the machine to operate safely?

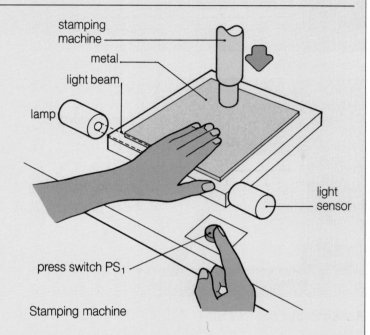

Stamping machine

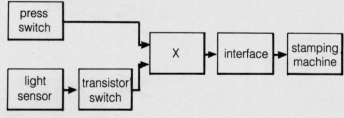

Block diagram – stamping machine

20 The block diagram of a control system is shown. If the input at A is logic **1** and at B is logic **0**, what are the values at C, D and E?

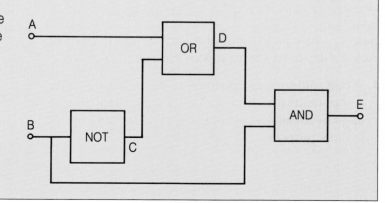

A	B	C	D	E
1	0			

Projects

A number of project briefs are given below. Follow the design process (outlined in Chapter 1) as you try to satisfy the briefs. A wide range of materials and components can be used in the realization of these projects, including construction kits.

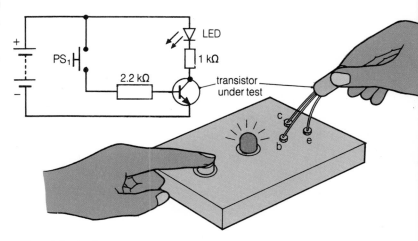

1 Transistor tester

A transistor tester is a very useful device to have available when building electronic circuits.

Design and construct a transistor tester using the circuit shown in the diagram.

If you have read Chapter 6 you should understand how the circuit works.

Transistor tester

2 Burglar alarm

Many people feel anxious about leaving their homes unattended at night and during holidays, because of the risk of being burgled.

Design and construct a burglar alarm system for a (model) room containing a window and a door. The alarm (a buzzer or bell) should be activated if either the window or door is opened. The alarm should continue to sound even if the window or door is closed again.

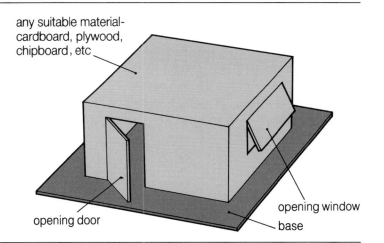

any suitable material-cardboard, plywood, chipboard, etc

opening window

opening door

base

3 Motor car courtesy light delay

A car's courtesy light is operated by microswitches activated by the car doors. The light automatically swiches on when a door is opened, and off when it is closed. It would be much more useful however, if the light remained on for a short time after the door was closed.

Design and construct a circuit to do this, and a model to demonstrate its operation.

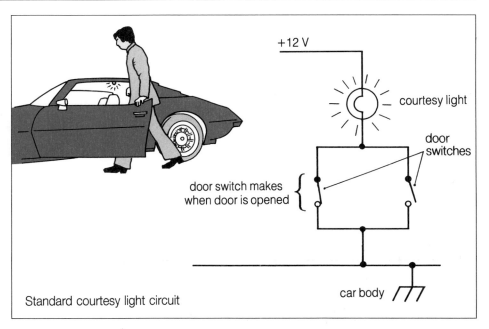

Standard courtesy light circuit

4 Goods transporter

Design and construct a scale model of a goods transporter vehicle for use in a warehouse. The flow chart below describes how the vehicle must operate.

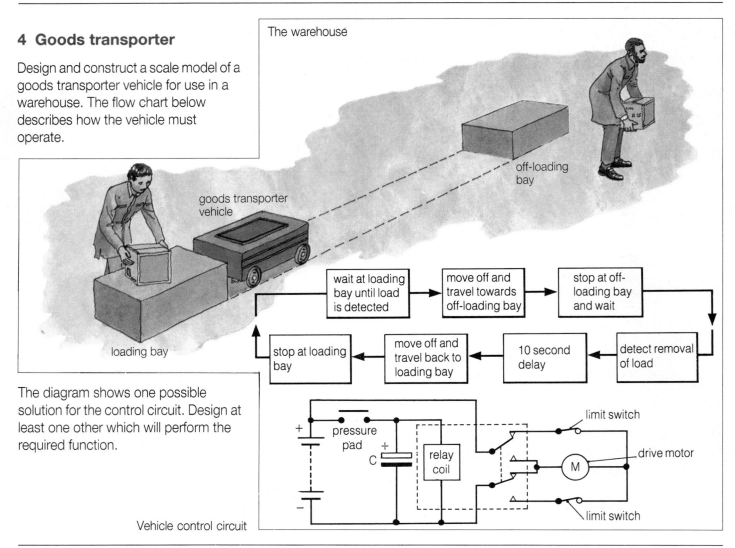

The diagram shows one possible solution for the control circuit. Design at least one other which will perform the required function.

Vehicle control circuit

5 Noughts and crosses

Design and construct an electronic noughts and crosses game.

One idea would be to use different coloured LEDs to represent the noughts and crosses. See if you can think of a more ingenious idea.

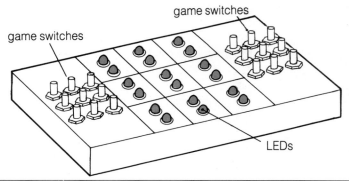

6 Self-balancing crane

Design and construct a model of a tower crane with a self-balancing jib.

The crane should be fitted with sensors which detect when the jib is out of balance, and a control system which automatically adjusts the position of the counterweight to re-balance the jib.

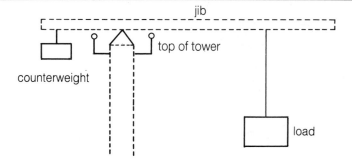

7 Damp detector

Young people buying their first houses often buy older properties. Damp can be a problem in some of these houses.

Design and construct a small, hand-held damp detector which could be marketed at around £10.

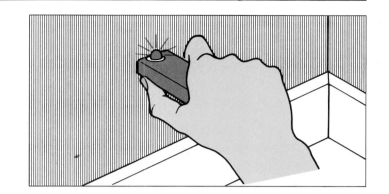

8 Personal safe

Design and construct a small safe with a combination lock, for keeping your private possessions secure.

One solution could include the use of rotary switches, connected in series, to form part of the control circuit, and a solenoid activated bolt.

To make the project more sophisticated, you could add a 'wrong combination' alarm, which once activated could not be switched off by the thief.

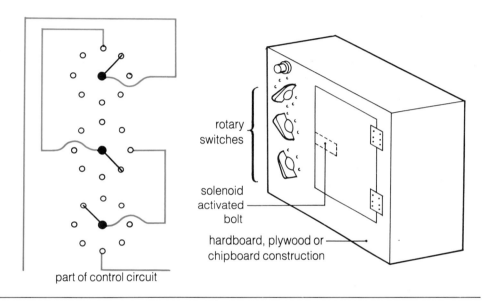

part of control circuit

rotary switches

solenoid activated bolt

hardboard, plywood or chipboard construction

9 Electronic ruler

Design and construct an electronic ruler which can be used to check the dimensions of small components.

The diagram should give you a clue to one possible solution. The control circuit can be similar to that used for the electronic weighing machine (page 144).

variable resistor

control circuit

rack

pinions

control knob

O	1.5
O	1.4
●	1.3
O	1.2
O	1.1
O	1.0

LED readout

component being checked

10 Automatic box-sorter

The diagram shows an idea for an automatic box-sorter. Tall boxes are detected by the light beam, but short boxes pass underneath undetected.

The circuit shown could be used to control the ram mechanism to push the tall boxes off the conveyor belt.

How the circuit works

When the light beam is broken, the relay contacts close, the motor runs, and the ram begins to move. When the drive shaft has rotated through a few degrees, the cam 'releases' MS_1, allowing its contacts to make. When the box is pushed out of the light beam therefore, and the relay de-energizes, the motor can continue to run until the cam once again opens MS_1.

The project

Using the above, or similar ideas, design and make an automatic box-sorter which will separate tall and short boxes and store them in two separate containers.

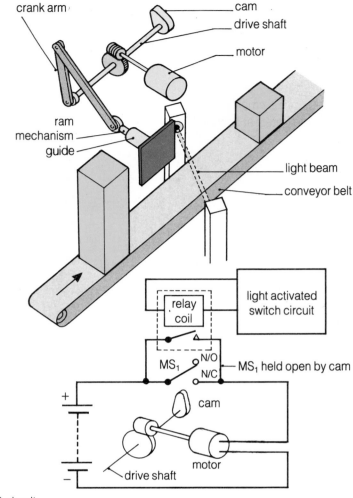

Ram control circuit

11 Personal alarm

Many people feel anxious about going out at night in some areas because of the fear of being attacked.

Design and construct a low cost personal alarm to help allay some of these fears. It must be easy to carry, and quick to activate in the case of an emergency.

Further ideas for projects

- Food or drink dispenser
- Cycle theft alarm
- Disco effects unit
- Automatic garage door
- Automatic watering system for a greenhouse
- Low-temperature alarm for the elderly
- Remote controlled robot arm
- Flashing shop sign

- Reaction timer
- Line following vehicle
- Electronic key
- Musical game
- Household aids for the handicapped
- Sports timer
- Baby alarm.

Examples of school technology projects

Some examples of 4th and 5th year technology projects are shown below. They may give you some ideas for your own projects. Try the **exercises** too – you will see just how easy it is to design quite complex circuits.

Stair-lift project

These photographs show the completed stair-lift project made by Pauline and Nick (as illustrated in Chapter 1).

See project brief and specification on pages 10 and 12.

Exercise Design a circuit suitable for controlling the stair-lift.

Plant care system (John Richardson – 5th year)

Brief Some greenhouse plants cannot tolerate very bright light. I wish to design a system which prevents light above a certain intensity reaching the plants.

Solution A light-activated switch circuit which controls a motor-driven gauze blind.

Exercise Complete the circuit diagram by including a light-activated switch circuit.

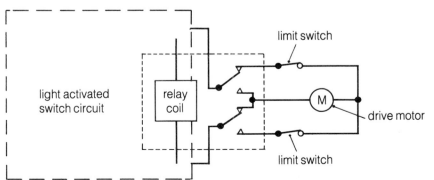

Fun robot (Jeremy Rooke – 5th year)

Brief   To design and construct a light-seeking robot toy. The robot should 'search' for a light beam (from a torch), lock on to it, and travel towards it. If the light beam is moved or interrupted, the robot must stop travelling forwards and begin to search for the light again.

Solution   A two wheel drive vehicle. The right wheel is driven continuously, but the left wheel is driven only when light from a torch falls on the LDR. See the circuit diagram shown.

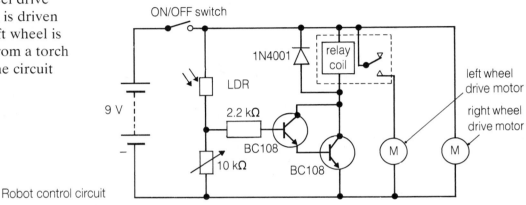

Robot control circuit

Factory lift (Andrew Timms – 5th year)

Brief   Design and make a passenger lift for use in a busy factory. The lift must work between two floors and does not need to have any doors. It must be possible to 'call' the lift from either floor.

Solution   See photograph and circuit diagram.

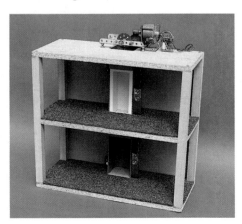

Exercise   Explain why the ground floor 'up' button and the first floor 'call' button are connected in parallel, whilst the first floor 'down' button and the ground floor 'call' button are connected in series.

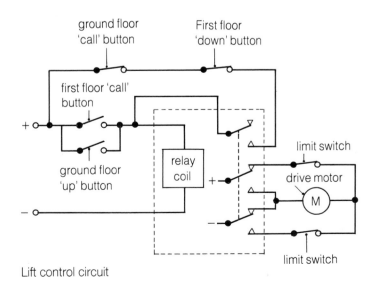

Lift control circuit

Fork lift truck (Robert Timson – 4th year)

Brief I want to design a remote-controlled fork lift truck. It will be used in a yard where dangerous chemicals are stored. The truck must be controlled by a hand-held control box.

Solution (See photograph and circuit diagram.)

Exercise The teacher suggested that limit switches could have been fitted to protect the fork lift motor from damage.

Explain this, and re-draw the circuit with the limit switches included.

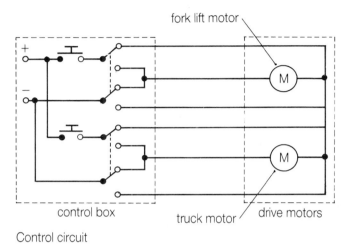

Control circuit

A warehouse lift (Neil Denny – 5th year)

Brief Goods which are delivered to the ground floor of a warehouse are off-loaded from lorries by hand. These must be transported to other floors in the warehouse to be stored.

Design and construct a convenient transport system to help with this work.

Solution A conveyor belt system which operates as outlined in the flow chart.

Exercise Design a circuit which could be used to operate the conveyor belt as outlined in the flowchart.

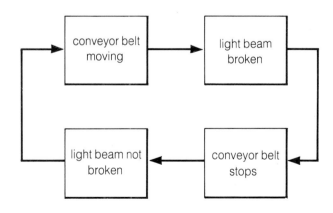

IN/OUT cat flap (Alex Burton – 4th year)

Brief I like to make sure that my cat is indoors at night. I want to make a cat flap which tells me when my cat is IN and when she is OUT.

Solution (See photograph and circuit diagram.)

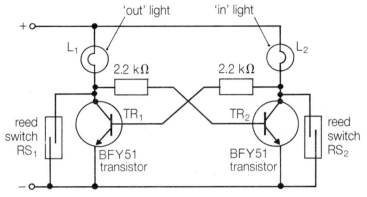

Information The control circuit used for this project is called a bistable multivibrator. (You may like to build a similar circuit and experiment with it.) When RS_1 is closed momentarily, TR_2 turns off. (Can you see why?) When TR_2 turns off, the voltage at its collector rises (you can check this with a voltmeter). A small current therefore flows in the base of TR_1 causing it (and L_1) to turn on. TR_1 remains on until RS_2 is closed momentarily. This causes the circuit to 'flip' turning L_2 on and L_1 off.

Tourist information map (Andrew Bruce – 5th year)

Brief I went on holiday to Majorca where I got lost several times. This gave me the idea for a useful project – to design and make an information map which helps you to locate places of interest.

Solution LEDs which flash at the required location for a pre-set period of time. The location is selected using a rotary switch. A press switch is used to activate the sequence.

Dispensing machine (Adrian Horsburgh – 5th year)

Brief To design a **gob-stopper dispenser** which uses a novelty theme and operates automatically when triggered by the customer.

Solution See photographs.

When a coin is inserted in the slot and the press button operated, the snooker player pots a gob-stopper into the collecting tray.

Notice the use of the large **cam** to operate the snooker player's arm.

Note The motor used to drive this cam is controlled by a circuit similar to that shown on page 162 (automatic box sorter project).

Burglar deterrent (Jonathan Munton – 5th year)

Brief To design a burglar deterrent for Mr Jones. He is a shift worker whose flat is unoccupied until he returns home each night at 10 o'clock. He lives in an area where burglaries are becoming fairly regular.

Solution A system which detects nightfall and responds by turning on the living room light and closing the curtains.

Exercise Design a circuit which could be used in this project.

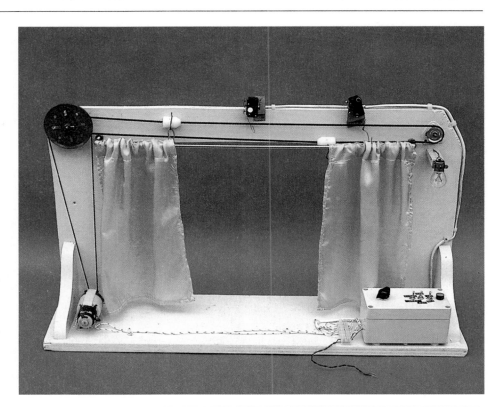

CHAPTER SEVEN

Pneumatics

Bus with pneumatically operated doors

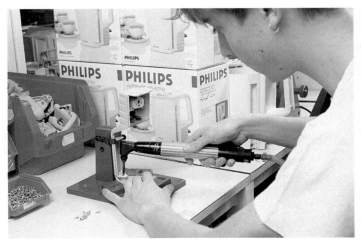

Pneumatic screwdriver

Machine used in shoe-making

Tyre bay equipment

Compressor and receiver

Pneumatic road drill

Air tanks on lorry

Example of pneumatically operated fairground ride

Pneumatics is all about using **compressed air** to 'make things happen'.

Compressed air is ordinary air which has been forced under pressure into a small space. Air under pressure possesses **energy** which can be released to do useful work.

For example, the doors on some buses and trains are operated using compressed air, and some lorries, buses and other large vehicles have air operated brakes. You can actually hear the air being used as these systems are operated.

Many different kinds of pneumatic tools are in use today, including the dentist's drill and the very familiar (and noisy) pneumatic road drill.

In industry, pneumatic systems have many applications. They are commonly used, for example, on automated production lines. This can involve, for example, moving materials, assembling products and packaging.

All the above systems rely for their operation on a constant supply of compressed air. This is usually provided by a **compressor**. A compressor is an 'air pump' driven by an electric motor or an internal combustion engine. The compressed air is usually stored in a strong metal tank called a **receiver**. The air is passed on to where it is needed along narrow plastic or metal pipes.

Understanding pneumatics is really very simple. All you have to do is to learn about the operation of a few basic components.

Understanding pneumatics

Jo has used two of the most basic pneumatic components, a **three port valve** and a **single acting cylinder**, in her stamping machine. The machine is designed to stamp dome shaped discs for use in the manufacture of medallions.

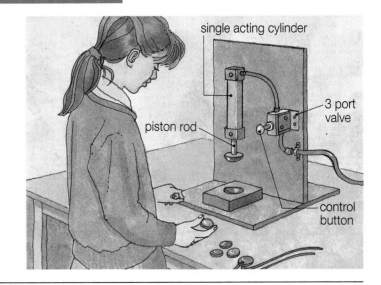

How the machine operates

A three port valve is a switch used to control the flow of air. The type shown here contains a component called a **spool** which moves inside the valve when the button is pressed or released. Its job is **to direct the flow of air** through the valve. Look at the picture of the valve and notice that when the button is pressed, compressed air from the supply is allowed to pass out of pipe 1 and into pipe 2 (which is connected to the cylinder).

Note The 'airways' into and out of the valve, which we have called pipes, are actually called **ports**. This is why the valve is called a three port valve.

A **single acting cylinder** uses compressed air to produce motion and **force**. It contains a piston which can slide 'up and down'. The piston is normally pushed 'up' into the cylinder by a spring. However, when the valve is operated as shown, compressed air enters the cylinder and forces the piston down. The air on the 'spring side' of the piston escapes through the vent hole.

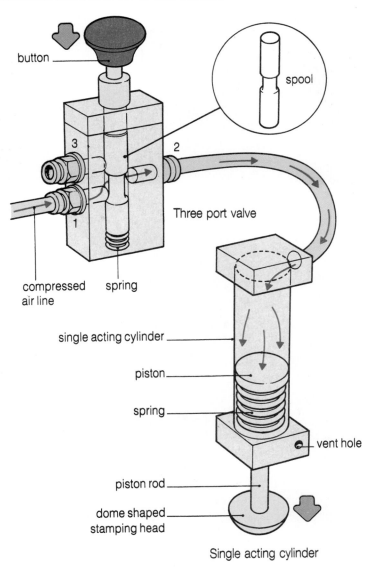

When the button is released, a small spring inside the valve pushes the spool back up. Notice that in this position, compressed air can no longer get from the supply to the cylinder. In fact the valve now allows the compressed air **in the cylinder** to escape down the pipe and out into the atmosphere through port 3. At the same time the spring in the cylinder pushes the piston back up. So by pressing and releasing the button, Jo is able to control her stamping machine.

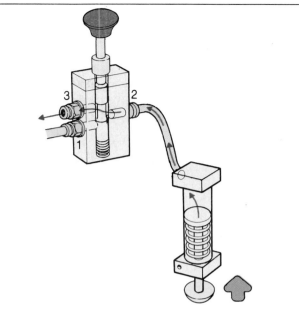

Component symbols

The above pictures make it very easy to understand how Jo's pneumatic circuit operates.

However, when drawing pneumatic circuits yourself it will be much easier to use **symbols** rather than pictures – although at first sight some pneumatic symbols look rather complicated. The symbol for the push button three port valve is shown here.

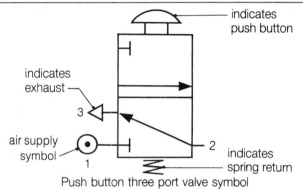

indicates push button

indicates exhaust

air supply symbol

indicates spring return

Push button three port valve symbol

The three port valve symbol explained

Just for a moment, look at the bottom half of the symbol, and ignore the top. Notice that the symbol shows port 1 'blocked off' (but ports 2 and 3 connected) just like in the real valve.

Now ignore the bottom half of the symbol and imagine that when the button is pressed the top part of the symbol slides over the bottom half as shown. This shows how the ports in the real valve are connected when the button is pressed.

So you can see that the bottom half of the symbol shows the connections inside the valve when the button is not pressed, and the top half shows the connections when the button is pressed.

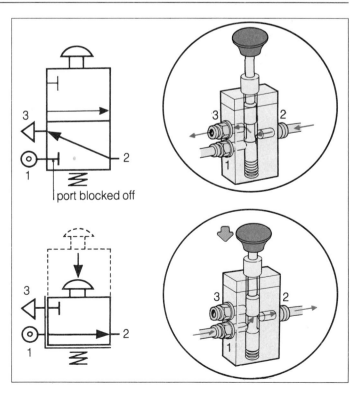

port blocked off

Single acting cylinder symbol

The symbol for a single acting cylinder really does not need any explanation. However, it is important to know that when the piston rod is 'out', the piston is said to be **positive**, and when it is 'in', it is said to be **negative**.

Note Single acting cylinders are used mainly where relatively small forces are required and where the linear motion is small. The piston's movement (or stroke) is actually restricted by the spring.

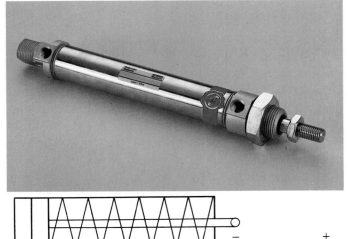

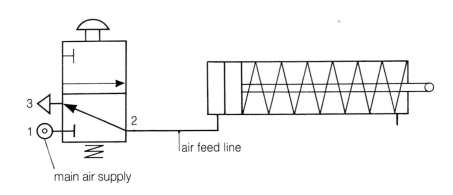

Symbol

Jo's pneumatic circuit

The diagram here shows the complete pneumatic circuit used in Jo's project drawn using circuit symbols.

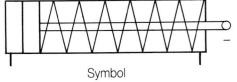

3

1

2

air feed line

main air supply

Question

1 Jo realised that operating her stamping machine **without a safety guard** was **dangerous**. She therefore redesigned the equipment to include a guard as shown here. By adding an additional valve she also made it impossible for the machine to be operated **unless the guard was in position**.

a Using the correct symbols, draw a circuit which would only allow the machine to be operated with the safety guard in position.

b What kind of **logic gate** do the valves in the above circuit form? Look back at *An introduction to control logic* (pages 152 to 155) if necessary.

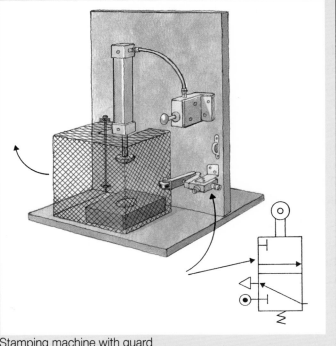

Stamping machine with guard

Dual control

Sometimes it is necessary to be able to operate a machine from more than one position. The circuit shown here works in this way. The single acting cylinder can be activated by pressing either button A *or* B. The circuit, however, must contain a **shuttle valve**. This 'new' component is explained below.

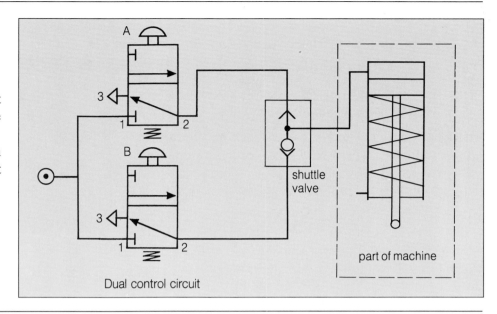

Dual control circuit

part of machine

The shuttle valve explained

A shuttle valve is a very simple component, as you can see.

It has three ports, and contains a small rubber piston which is free to move between A and B within the valve. If air enters port 1A, the piston is pushed into position B. The air therefore, has to flow out of the valve through port 2. Similarly, if air enters the valve through port 1B, the piston is pushed into position A and once again the air can only 'escape' through port 2. If air enters both ports 1A and 1B at the same time, the piston 'floats' between A and B and again the air escapes through port 2.

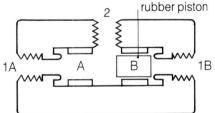

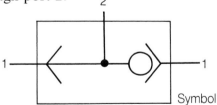

Symbol

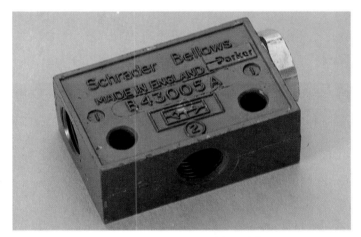

Question

2 The shuttle valve in the 'dual control' circuit is included for a good reason. If it was replaced with a simple 'T' connector, the circuit would not work. Neither valve A nor valve B could be used to activate the cylinder. Explain why.

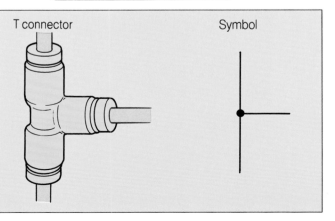

T connector

Symbol

Forces at work

Air under pressure can be released to do useful work, as explained in the introduction, and as we saw in Jo's stamping machine (page 170).

The single acting cylinder in Jo's machine produces a **force** (and does work) because air exerts a **pressure** upon the piston. The force which a piston produces depends on two factors: the **air pressure**, and the **surface area** of the piston.

If the air pressure was 0.5 N/mm² then the air would exert a force of 0.5 newtons on each square millimetre of piston, as you can see on the diagram. So if the piston had a total area of 300 mm², then the total force on the piston would be 0.5 × 300 newtons. Can you see that:

force = pressure × area?

Note   The force produced by a single acting cylinder as it goes negative, does *not* depend upon the air pressure or piston area. The force comes from the spring inside the cylinder.

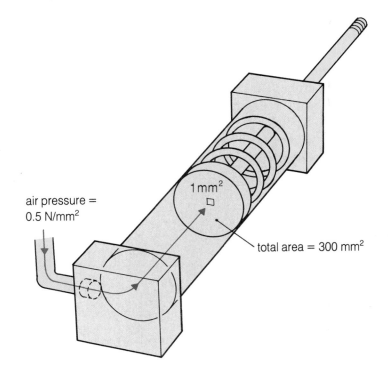

air pressure = 0.5 N/mm²

1 mm²

total area = 300 mm²

Force = pressure × area
Force = 0.5 × 300 (for above example)
      = 150 N

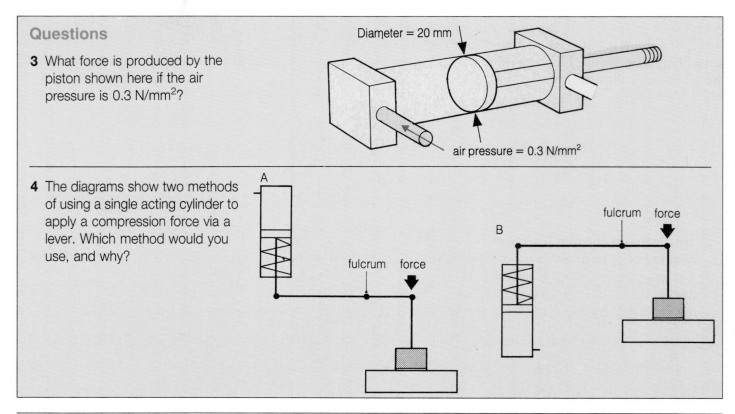

Questions

3 What force is produced by the piston shown here if the air pressure is 0.3 N/mm²?

Diameter = 20 mm

air pressure = 0.3 N/mm²

4 The diagrams show two methods of using a single acting cylinder to apply a compression force via a lever. Which method would you use, and why?

A

fulcrum   force

B

fulcrum   force

The double acting cylinder

A double acting cylinder and its symbol are shown here.

Notice that unlike a single acting cylinder, it does *not* contain a 'return' spring. Its movement *in both directions* is powered by compressed air.

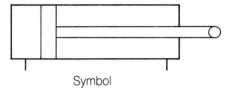

Symbol

Forces in a double acting cylinder

The force produced by a double acting cylinder as it goes positive, is **not** equal to the force it produces when going negative.

This can be explained by looking at the piston in the cylinder, and remembering that

force = pressure × area

Notice that the areas of the 'front' and 'back' faces of the piston are *not* equal. The piston rod reduces the area of the 'back' face. So although the air pressure on either side of the piston may be exactly the same the force produced will be less for a piston going negative.

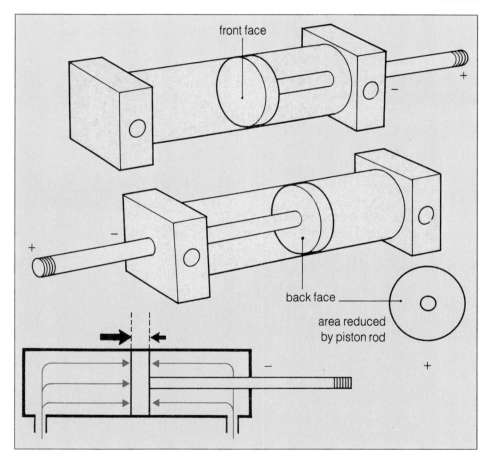

front face

back face

area reduced
by piston rod

Questions

The pressure available to operate the piston shown here is 0.4 N/mm².

5 What force does the positive-going piston produce?

6 What force does the negative-going piston produce?

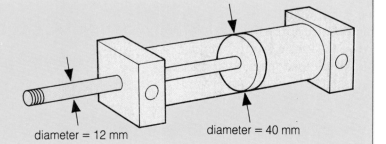

diameter = 12 mm

diameter = 40 mm

Controlling double acting cylinders

One method of controlling a double acting cylinder is illustrated in the project shown here. It was one pupil's solution to the following brief.

Brief   Design a 'pneumatic grab' which can grip a heavy round bar, lift it vertically and drop it when required.

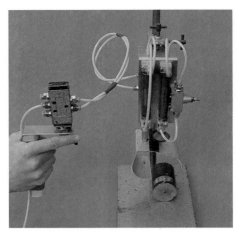

Pneumatic grab project

How the circuit operates

In addition to two double acting cylinders, two 'new' components are used in this project: a **five port valve** and a **flow regulator**.

The five port valve explained

As the name implies, this valve has five ports. This particular one is lever operated.

When the spool is in the position shown in diagram 1, compressed air from the supply passes through the valve between ports 1 and 2, and the air causes the pistons to move 'down'. Air trapped below the pistons is forced down the pipes and through the valve, escaping into the atmosphere through port 5.

When the lever is moved to its other position the spool moves up as shown in diagram 2.

Now follow the air flow on the diagram, and you will see that the pistons are forced to move 'up'. Also note how the trapped air above the pistons is forced out of the system.

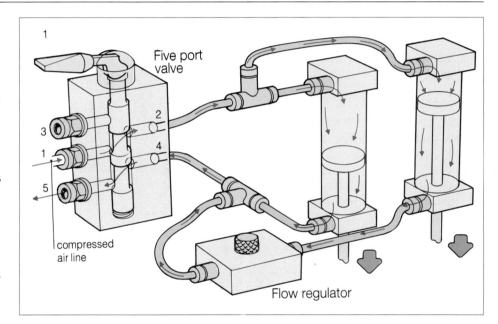

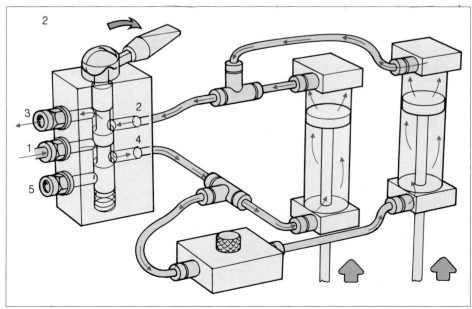

The five port valve symbol explained

Note   Make sure that you understand the three port valve symbol (explained on page 171) before you read the following.

Ignore the top half of the symbol for a moment, The bottom half shows the connections inside the valve when the lever is in one particular position.

Now ignore the bottom half of the symbol, and imagine that when the lever is moved to the other position the top half of the symbol slides over the bottom half. This shows the connections inside the valve now.

Notice that a 'lever' symbol appears on both ends of the five port valve symbol. This is rather confusing – there is, of course, only *one* lever on the real valve.

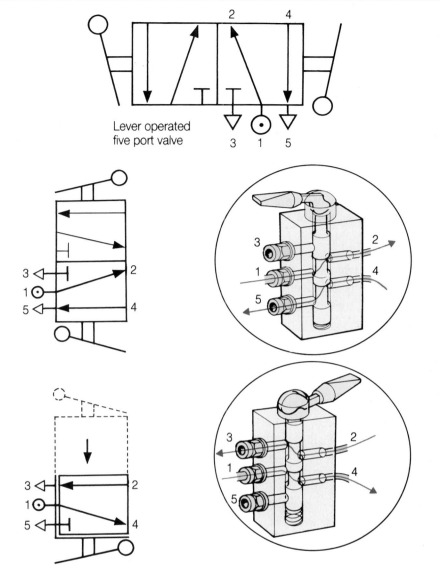

Lever operated five port valve

Piston speed control

It is often necessary to control the *speed* of a piston's movement.

For example, in the pneumatic grab project, piston 2 needs to move more slowly than piston 1.

Piston 1 positions the grab, and a few seconds later, piston 2 closes it as shown in the diagram. In the project a **flow regulator** was used for this purpose.

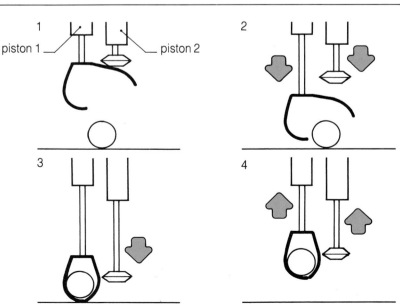

The flow regulator explained

Several different types of flow regulator are available. One example is shown here.

Air can pass through the regulator in either direction. When air enters port 1, however, a rubber piston is pushed into position A so that air can only pass through the regulator down the central pipe. The flow of air through this pipe can be controlled by turning a finger screw.

If air enters the regulator through port 2, however, the piston is pushed into position B and the air can flow through the valve unrestricted.

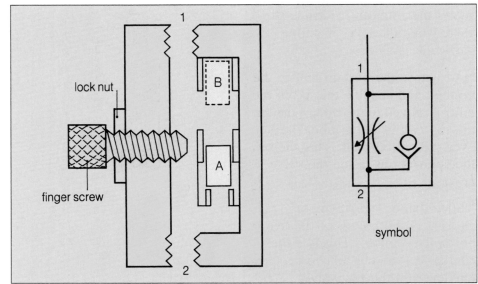

Pneumatic grab circuit

The diagram shows the circuit for the pneumatic grab project illustrated on page 176.

Can you see that the flow regulator makes piston 2 move down more slowly than piston 1? However, when the pistons are rising both pistons move at the same speed.

Note Piston speed control is achieved, in this circuit, by regulating the rate at which **exhausting air** can leave the cylinder. This produces a much smoother control than regulating air flow into a cylinder.

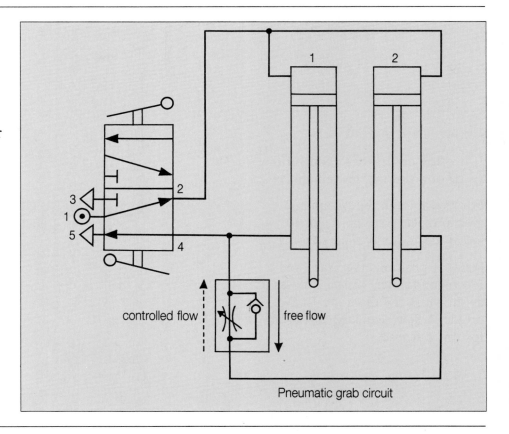

Pneumatic grab circuit

More flow regulator applications

The diagrams show part of a labelling machine and its control circuit.

When button A is pressed, the roller advances *slowly*, and labels the box. When A is released the piston rapidly returns the roller to its rest position.

Note For light applications, regulating air flow into a cylinder is acceptable.

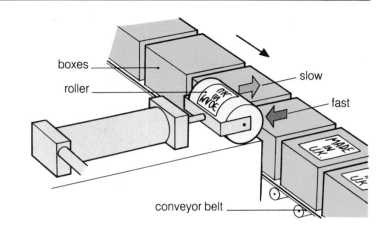

Questions

7 It was found that the rapid return of the label roller often caused the printing on the label to smudge.

Using the same components (but including a second flow regulator) draw a circuit which would control piston speed going both forwards and backwards, for this machine.

8 Wherever it is dangerous to move something at full piston speed, or where a sudden jerky movement could cause damage to a product or device, piston speed must be controlled.

Choose one of the processes pictured here and design a control circuit for its safe operation. You may use any of the pneumatic components described in this chapter so far.

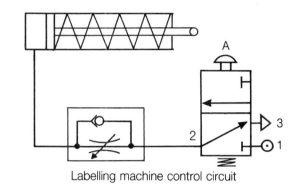

Labelling machine control circuit

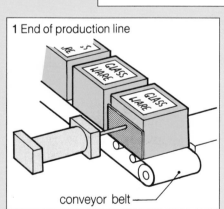

1 End of production line

conveyor belt

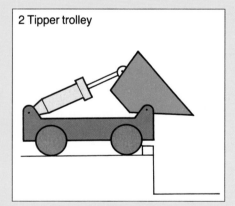

2 Tipper trolley

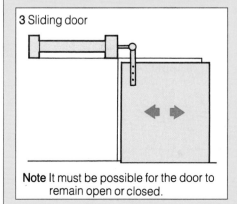

3 Sliding door

Note It must be possible for the door to remain open or closed.

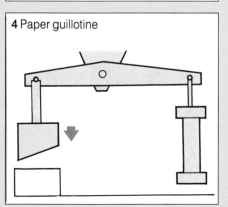

4 Paper guillotine

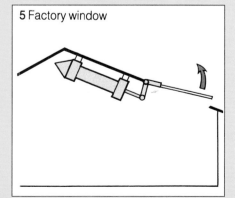

5 Factory window

Air operated valves

In the valves described so far, the spool (which controls the flow of air through the valve) has been moved either by a button or lever. In air operated valves, the spool is moved by air pressure.

Three different air operated valves, and their symbols, are shown here. Notice that **arrow-heads** and **dashed lines** are used to indicate that they are air operated.

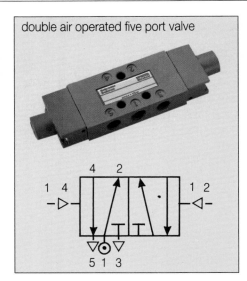
double air operated five port valve

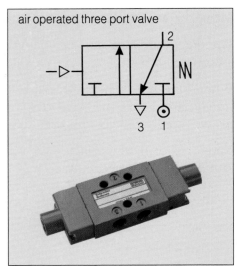
air operated three port valve

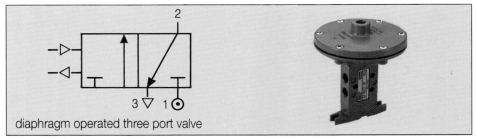
diaphragm operated three port valve

Double air operated five port valve – DAO5PV

One of the dangers associated with pneumatic equipment is the very high pressures which are sometimes used. For example, high pressure air escaping from a loose pipe causes the pipe to 'lash about' violently. This can cause serious injury.

In industry, where high pressure systems are common, it is essential to keep employees well away from danger. The system shown here allows you to do this.

In the circuit, the DAO5PV is being used to control a cylinder at very high pressure. However, the air pressure required to control the valve itself (the signal) only needs to be small. Hence the operator can work in safety.

Notice that the symbol for the pipe supplying the air signals to control the DAO5PV is shown dashed and that the valves used to provide the signal are called **pilot valves**.

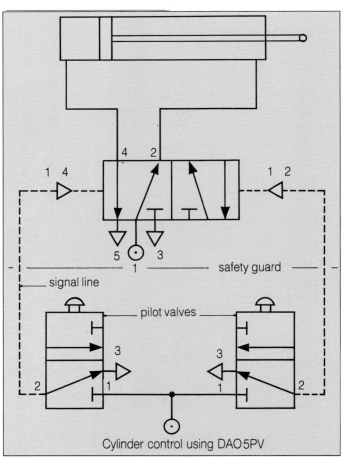
Cylinder control using DAO5PV

The DAO5PV symbol explained

The internal structure of this valve is very similar to the five port valve described on page 176.

When the signal is applied to the DAO5PV as shown here, the spool moves and connects port 1 to port 2 (and 4 to 5). This is why the numbers 1 2 are written on the symbol.

Similarly, when the signal is applied to the valve, as shown here, the spool moves and connects port 1 to port 4 (and 2 to 3). This is why the numbers 1 4 are written on the symbol.

Note   If a DAO5PV receives a signal from both ends (and at the same pressure) the spool does not move.

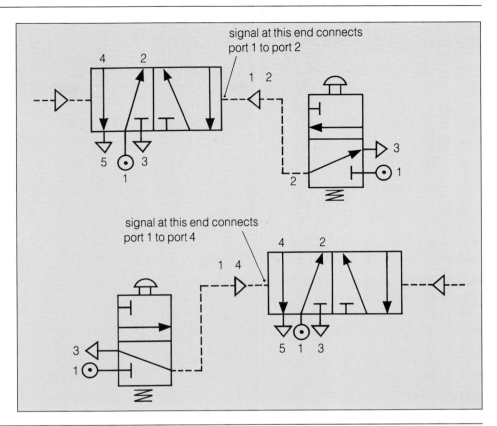

signal at this end connects port 1 to port 2

signal at this end connects port 1 to port 4

Diaphragm operated three port valve

For some applications, it is necessary to use a valve which will operate at *very low* signal pressures. The diaphragm operated valve is designed to do this.

Now **Force = pressure × area**. Therefore, if only a tiny pressure is available to operate a valve, then to provide enough force to move the spool the area upon which the air signal acts must be large. This is the purpose of the diaphragm in this valve.

Note   Sometimes it is necessary to operate a valve by an air signal *below* normal air pressure. For this purpose the signal is connected to the vacuum port on the valve.

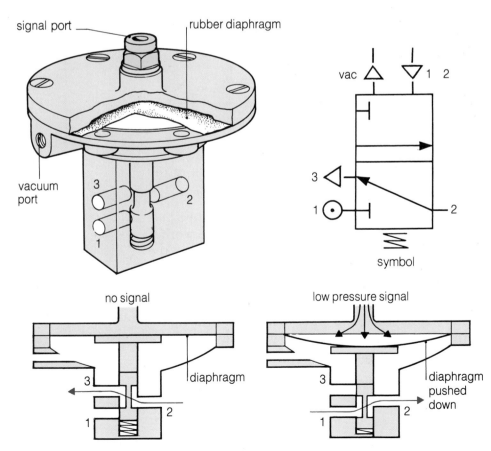

signal port

rubber diaphragm

vacuum port

symbol

no signal

diaphragm

low pressure signal

diaphragm pushed down

Diaphragm operated valve applications

One application of a diaphragm operated valve is shown here. It is a system used in some garages to indicate to the attendant that a vehicle has driven onto the forecourt. It uses what is called an **air bleed circuit**.

How the system operates

Air from the supply is fed into a flow regulator. This emits a controlled flow of air into a T-junction. One pipe from this junction is connected to the diaphragm operated valve and the other is left open to bleed air into the atmosphere. This is why the circuit is called an air bleed circuit.

When the air bleed pipe is 'blocked off' by a vehicle's wheel, pressure builds up in the pipe and the diaphragm operated valve is activated (connecting port 1 to port 2). This allows compressed air to activate the piston, making it go positive and hit the gong.

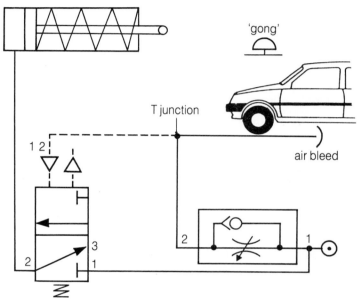

Forecourt alarm – air bleed circuit

Piston position sensor

Another application of the diaphragm operated valve is as a **sensor** to detect when a piston is at the end of its stroke (either fully in or fully out).

Here is an example of its use. This picture shows part of a semi-automatic assembly line. When the worker is ready to receive a component, the worker taps the foot operated valve. This activates a circuit, causing a piston to push the next component to the worker. When the piston reaches the end of its stroke, the circuit detects this, and automatically returns the piston to its rest position ready to supply the next component.

The complete control circuit is described below.

foot
operated valve

Control circuit operation

First notice that the air supply to the diaphragm operated valve is connected in an unusual way. It is connected to port 3 instead of port 1.

Now, when the piston is held negative (by the connection of port 1 to port 2 in the DAO5PV), the pressure at X also supplies an air signal to activate the diaphragm operated valve (connecting port 1 to port 2). In this state, no signal reaches the DAO5PV from this valve.

However, when the button of the foot operated 3 port valve is pressed an air signal is sent to the DAO5PV, the valve is activated, and ports 1 and 4 are connected. So the piston begins to go slowly positive (controlled by the flow regulator) and at the same time the regulator helps to maintain the pressure at X. At the end of the stroke (when all the air is exhausted) the signal pressure to the diaphragm operated valve drops. This valve then returns to its normal off position allowing an air signal to be sent to the DAO5PV. The valve is activated, and ports 1 and 2 are connected, causing the piston to go negative automatically.

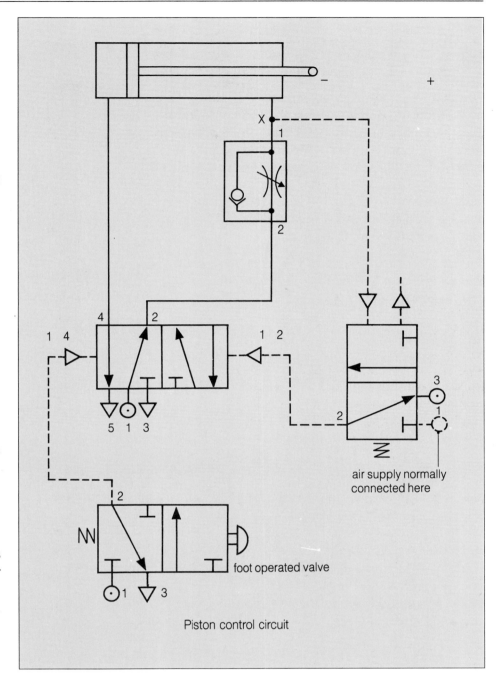

Piston control circuit

Question

9 The diagram shows a junction between two conveyor belts in a factory. Boxes (containing delicate components) are transferred from one belt to the other by the action of a single acting cylinder. An air bleed pipe is used to detect when a box is in position for transfer.

Design a control circuit for this equipment.

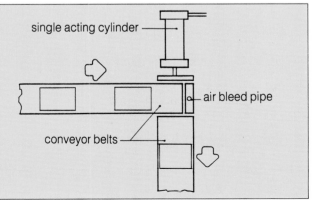

Time delays

Sometimes it is necessary to introduce a **time delay** at some stage in the operation of a pneumatic circuit.

For example, here is a machine used in the production of laminated table mats. The operator loads the machine with a mat base and a decorative surface lamina (both coated with impact adhesive). After the button is pressed momentarily, the piston (and pressure pad) go positive, and the table mat is held under pressure for a few seconds before the piston automatically goes negative again. This allows the impact adhesive *time* to grip.

To produce a time delay of this kind you need to understand another pneumatic component called a **reservoir**, see below.

Time delays explained

Time delays in a pneumatic circuit can be created using the components shown here. The only component new to you is the reservoir. A reservoir is simply a container for air.

A flow of air (controlled by the flow regulator) enters the reservoir, slowly 'filling it up'. When the pressure in the reservoir reaches about 0.2 N/mm^2, the DAO5PV is activated. The delay time depends upon the adjustment of the flow regulator and the **volume** of the reservoir.

The complete circuit diagram for the pneumatic press is shown here.

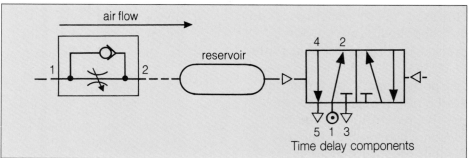

Time delay components

Question

10 Describe the operation of the pneumatic press and its circuit. Begin your description like this. *When the push button is pressed, an air signal is sent to the . . .*

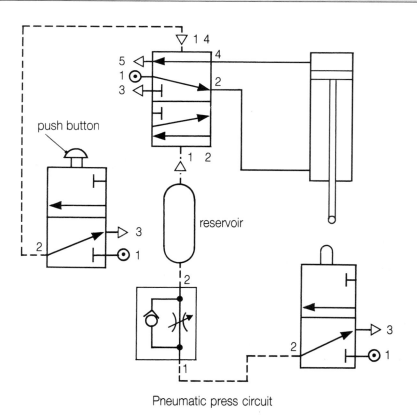

Pneumatic press circuit

Automatic control

All the pneumatic circuits described so far have needed an **input** from the outside world to make them operate: a button being pressed, or a pipe being blocked off, for example. A fully automatic circuit however, controls itself.

The pictures here show a pupil's idea for a technology project which uses a fully automatic circuit.

The brief was to design a moving advertising board to attract attention to a discount tyre centre. A pneumatic system was chosen because compressed air would be readily available.

The piston in this device goes positive–negative, positive–negative continuously (**reciprocates**) and this action is used to drive the mechanism which makes the mechanic's arm move. The control circuit is explained below.

rear view of drive mechanism

The automatic control circuit explained

This circuit works automatically because the piston operates its own control valve (C) by activating pilot valves A and B at each end of its movement.

Look at the circuit and imagine that at this moment the piston is going positive. When fully positive, the piston activates valve A, which sends an air signal to activate valve C (connecting port 1 to port 2). Therefore, the piston immediately begins to go negative until valve B is activated. Valve B then sends an air signal to activate valve C (connecting port 1 to port 4) and the piston begins to go positive again . . . and so the cycle repeats continuously as long as the air supply is maintained.

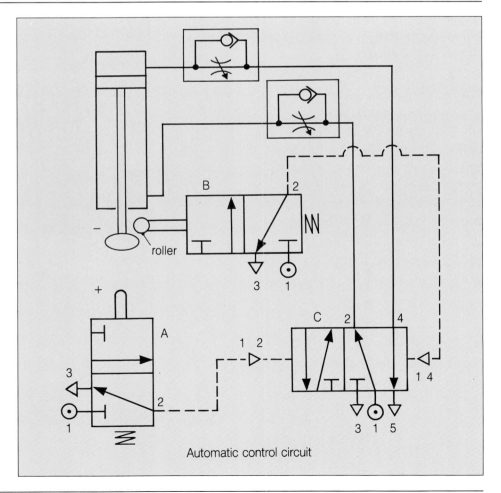

Automatic control circuit

Questions

11 For some industrial applications it is not practicable to control an automatic circuit using mechanical valves (as above); the valves get in the way of the work being done. The circuit shown here, avoids this by using **air bleeds**.

Explain the full operation of this circuit.

12 Sometimes it is necessary for the piston, in an automatic circuit, to return and stop in the negative (or positive) position, when the circuit is switched off.

Where would you connect a valve to make this circuit stop automatically with the piston in the negative position only?

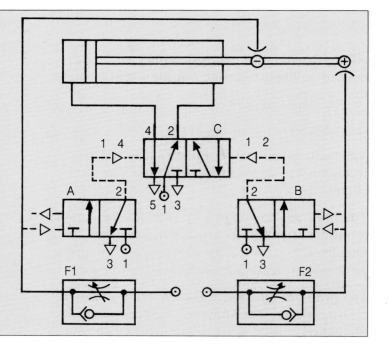

Sequential control

Sometimes, two or more pistons in a pneumatic circuit, are required to operate in a particular order to carry out a job. An example is shown here.

This machine is designed to stamp triangles on to wooden blocks in a continuous process. The blocks are fed into the machine at point X, and are ejected at point Z. To carry out this job, pistons A and B must go positive and negative in a particular sequence.

If you follow the diagrams in order from **1** to **4**, you will see that the sequence is as follows.

1 Piston A goes positive.
2 Piston B goes positive.
3 Piston A goes negative.
4 Piston B goes negative.

The above can be written as

Sequence = A+, B+, A−, B−

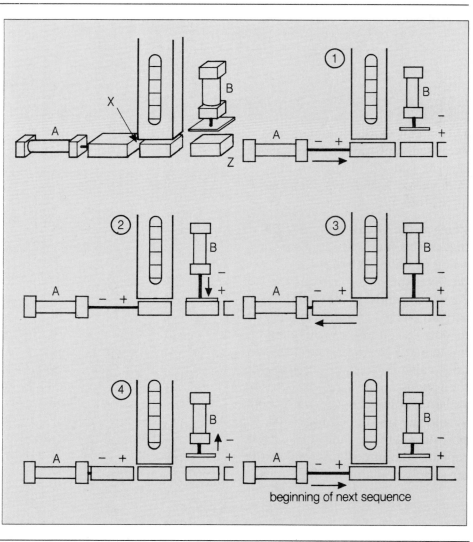

Sequential control circuit explained

Look at the circuit and imagine that at this moment piston A is going positive.

When fully positive, pilot valve A2 is activated. An air signal is therefore sent to control valve C1 (connecting port 1 to port 4).

Therefore, piston B goes positive (and stamps the triangle). When fully positive, piston B activates pilot valve B2. An air signal is therefore sent to control valve C2 (connecting port 1 to port 4).

Therefore, piston A goes negative. When fully negative, piston A activates pilot valve A1. An air signal is therefore sent to control valve C1 (connecting port 1 to port 2).

Therefore, piston B goes negative. When fully negative, piston B activates pilot valve B1. An air signal is therefore sent to control valve C2 (connecting port 1 to port 2) . . . and so the sequence is repeated continuously until the air supply is switched off.

Questions

13 Where would you position an 'on/off' valve in this circuit so that when the circuit was switched off, both pistons would return and stop in their negative positions?

14 Describe how this system could be made to switch off automatically when the supply of wooden blocks runs out.

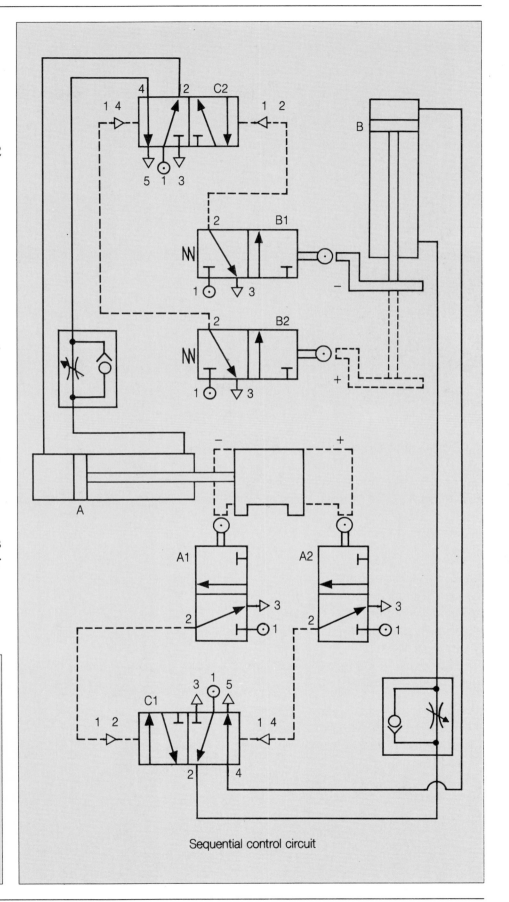

Sequential control circuit

Hydraulics

Look at the pictures of the mechanical digger and the refuse lorry here. Notice that both vehicles have mechanisms which make use of **cylinders**.

You might be surprised to know that the cylinders and pipes on these vehicles do not contain air (as in a pneumatic system) but oil.

In a hydraulic system, oil replaces compressed air as the means of transmitting motion and force.

Refuse lorry

Mechanical digger

Hydraulics explained

A simple hydraulic system is shown here. It consists of two cylinders of different diameters connected together by a pipe and containing oil.

When a force is applied to piston A, oil is forced to move along the pipe and into cylinder B. Piston B therefore rises. The force exerted by piston A creates a pressure which is transmitted through the liquid in all directions.

Pressure is a measure of force over a given area. If the area of piston A is 100 mm², and the force exerted by the piston equals 50 N then the pressure exerted by the piston equals 0.5 N/mm².

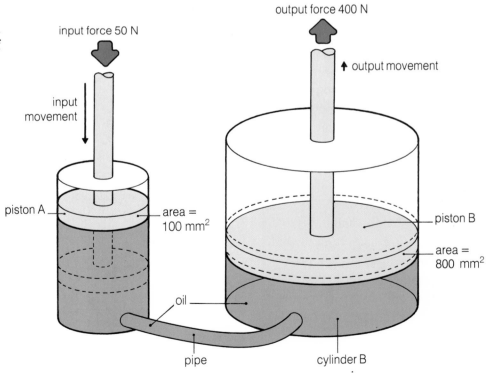

input force 50 N

input movement

output force 400 N

output movement

piston A

area = 100 mm²

piston B

area = 800 mm²

oil

pipe

cylinder B

Force = Pressure × Area (see page 174)

$\therefore$ Pressure $= \dfrac{\text{Force}}{\text{Area}}$

(for above example)

Pressure $= \dfrac{50}{100} = 0.5$ N/mm²

Now, pressure is transmitted through the liquid in all directions, so the pressure exerted on piston B is also 0.5 N/mm^2. However, because the area of piston B is 800 mm^2, the force produced at piston B becomes 400 N – eight times greater than the input force. (See opposite.)

It might appear that you are getting 'something for nothing', but in fact you are not because for each 1 centimetre moved by piston B, piston A has to be moved 8 cm.

Hydraulic jack

Oil has a major advantage over compressed air: *it cannot be compressed*. The hydraulic jack illustrates this advantage.

Because oil cannot be compressed it is possible to jack up a vehicle safely. The large piston can be stopped at any point in its movement and will stay there whatever happens to the load. This is not possible with compressed air.

How the jack works

A piston (connected to the jack handle) moves up and down as the handle is moved up and down. This piston, which has a small diameter, forces oil from a reservoir through a one-way valve into a cylinder of larger diameter. So only a small force is required by the operator to raise the heavy load. To lower the vehicle, the one way valve is released and the vehicle's weight forces the oil back into the reservoir.

Force = Pressure × Area

$$\text{Therefore force on piston B} = 0.5 \times 800$$

$$= 400 \text{ N}$$

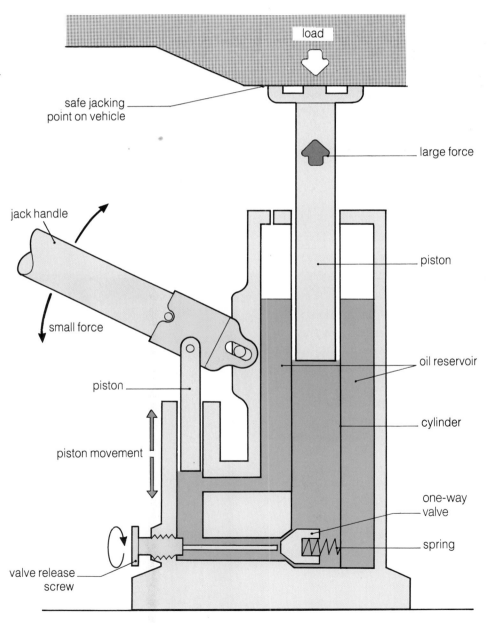

Hydraulic jack

Hydraulic brakes

The brakes on most vehicles today are hydraulically operated. The diagram shows part of a motor car's braking system.

When the brake pedal is pressed, a small piston in the **master cylinder** creates a pressure in the brake fluid which is transmitted to the **wheel cylinders** (at each of the four wheels). The pistons in the wheel cylinders exert a force on the **brake pads** which rub against the rotating **disc**. This slows down, and eventually stops the vehicle.

Although some cars have disc brakes on all four wheels, most use **drum brakes** on the rear (and disc brakes at the front).

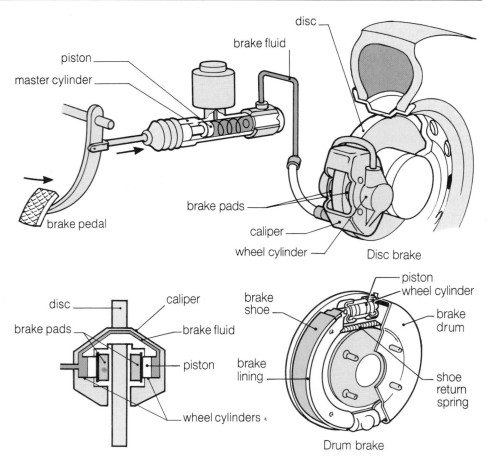

Disc brake

Drum brake

Other hydraulic systems

The jack and the car brakes (described above) rely on the human body to provide the force to create the pressure in the hydraulic system. For most applications however, a **pump** (driven by an electric motor or internal combustion engine) creates the pressure.

The mechanical digger and the refuse lorry (pictured on page 188) and the machines shown here, illustrate just a few of the numerous applications of pump driven hydraulic systems.

Close up of aircraft undercarriage

Bulldozer

Extending mobile crane

Lorry mounted crane

Pump driven hydraulics explained

The diagram shows a basic pump driven hydraulic system for a single **ram**.

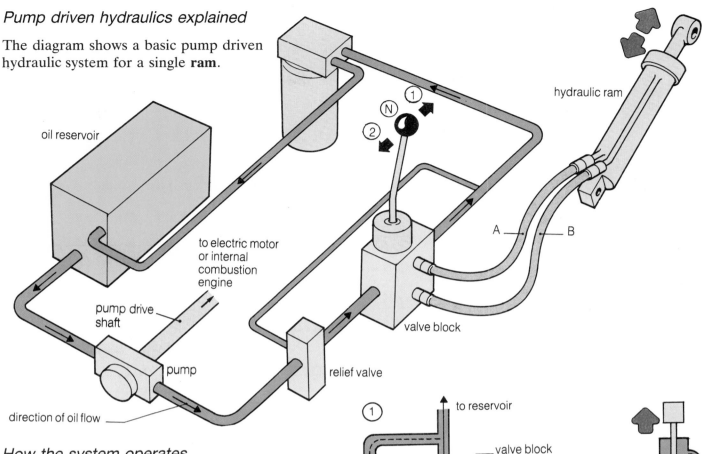

oil reservoir

hydraulic ram

to electric motor or internal combustion engine

pump drive shaft

pump

relief valve

valve block

A — B

direction of oil flow

How the system operates

When the control lever is in the 'neutral' position (diagram 1), oil is pumped straight through the valve block and back to the reservoir.

With the lever in position 1 (diagram 2), a spool (in the valve block) *stops* the oil flowing straight through the valve, and directs it into pipe A – sending the ram positive. Oil on the 'top' side of the piston is forced out of the cylinder, through pipe B and back into the main circuit through the valve block.

When the ram is fully positive, the oil flow to the valve block stops completely, but the **relief valve** opens to allow oil to continue to flow around the main circuit (as in diagram 3).

To drive the ram negative, the lever is moved into position 2 and the valve block redirects the oil accordingly.

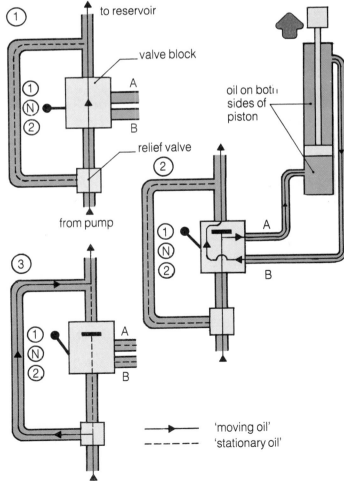

to reservoir

valve block

relief valve

from pump

oil on both sides of piston

→ 'moving oil'

- - - - 'stationary oil'

Projects

A number of project briefs are given below. Follow the design process (outlined in Chapter 1) as you try to satisfy the briefs.

1 Walking machine

The sketches show an idea for a novel 'walking machine'.

Either develop the idea and construct a working model, or design and construct a totally new system.

The machine must walk slowly and safely without falling over. It can be either automatically or manually controlled.

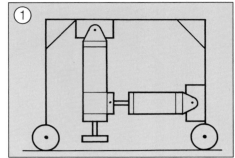
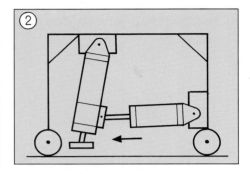
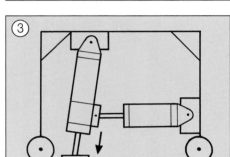
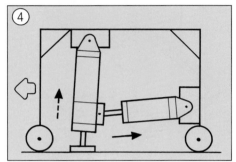

2 Clay extruder

Design and construct a pneumatically operated 'miniature' clay extruder for use in a school ceramics department.

The machine must be capable of producing a range of useful extrusions, and must be very easy to operate and clean.

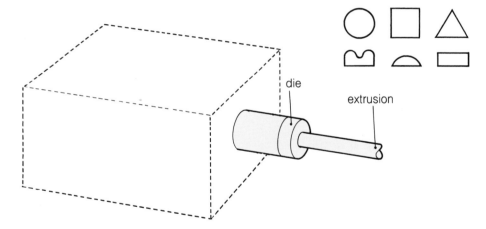

die

extrusion

3 Car park barrier

Design a **coin-operated** car park barrier. The barrier should rise when the correct coinage is deposited, and allow the vehicle to pass through safely before closing automatically.

Note   The information below may be useful for your design.

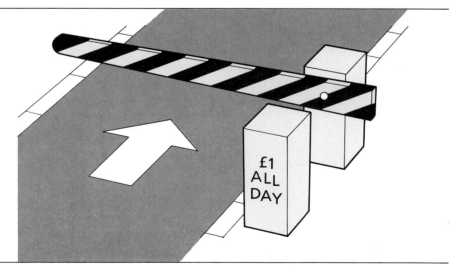

£1 ALL DAY

Information

Sometimes it is necessary to control a pneumatic circuit with an **electrical signal** instead of an air signal. For this purpose a **solenoid-operated valve** may be used.

A solenoid is simply a coil of wire. When an electric current is passed through the wire, it produces a magnetic field around the coil. A piece of soft iron called an armature, placed just inside the coil, will be attracted into the coil whilst the current is flowing. A spring can be used to push the armature out again when the current is switched off.

The diagrams show how these principles are used to operate a pneumatic valve.

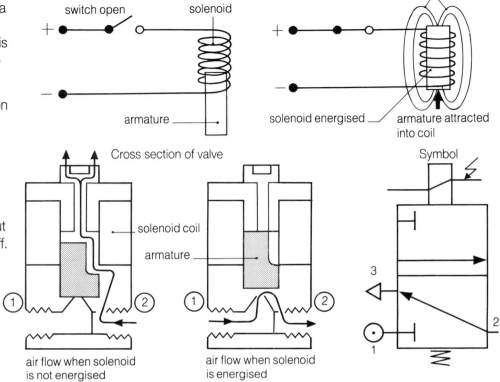

4 Automatic door

To cut down on heating costs, the owners of a large garage wish to install an automatic door to reduce heat loss from the garage workshop area.

Design and construct a model of a working system which makes use of the garage's compressed air supply.

The door should open automatically when a vehicle approaches, and close when the vehicle is safely 'in' or 'out'. The system must be completely safe – it must not be possible for the door to trap or injure any person standing in the doorway or nearby.

Further ideas for project work

- Pneumatic road drill
- Automatic self-levelling suspension for trailer used on very steep farmland

- Labelling machine
- Polishing machine
- Metal bending machine

Examples of school technology projects

Automatic stamping machine
(Andrew Wilson – 5th year)

Brief   To investigate an automatic production process for my project using pneumatic equipment.

I shall try to design and make a model of a machine which stamps triangles onto blocks of wood in a continuous process.

Solution   See photograph and **sequential control** information on pages 186 and 187 of this chapter.

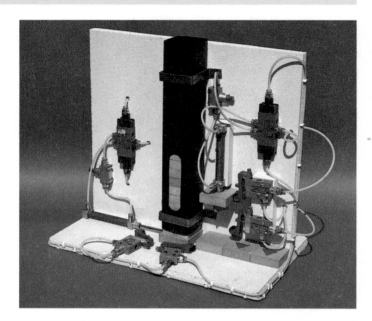

Belt strap manufacturing machine
(John Hollingsworth – 5th year project)

Brief   To design and make a machine which will produce belt straps from a continuous roll of leather. The machine must stamp out the holes, cut the tongue and produce belts of any length.

Solution   See photograph.

Exercise   Design an electro-pneumatic control circuit for this project.

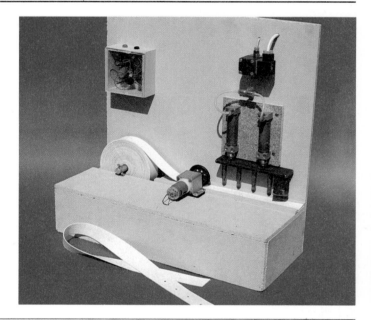

Car park barrier
(Nick Geeson – 5th year)

Brief   To design and make a model of a car park barrier for use in a hospital car park. The barrier will be operated by a car park attendant who will charge patients and visitors for entry but allow hospital staff to enter without paying.

Solution   See photograph.

Bus step aid
(Neal Hillier – 5th year)

Brief   Some buses have high steps which make it difficult for some elderly people, and small children, to get onto the bus. The problem is made worse when the bus parks next to a low kerb, or when there is no kerb at all.

Design and make a model of a pneumatically-operated step which could be moved into position when the bus stops, and be retracted before the bus moves off.

Solution   See photograph.

Exercise   Design a control circuit for this project.

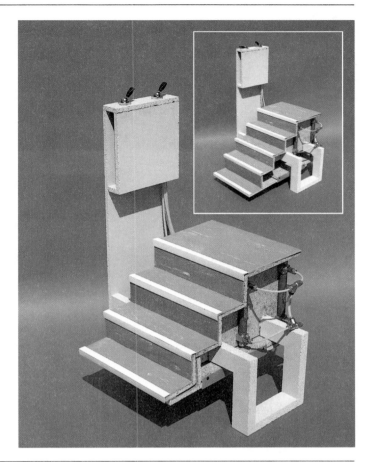

Remote-controlled hoist
(Louise Roe – 5th year)

Brief   When I was on 'work experience' in a factory I saw the need for a simple hoist to raise boxes of fabric from one floor to the next.

Design a safe, remote-controlled hoist, which could make use of the factory's compressed air supply.

Solution   See photograph.

To understand how the hoist operates, you will need to be familiar with a simple 'block and tackle' pulley system. You will then notice that the **effort** force is being applied at the point *where the load normally hangs* and that the load is suspended on the rope where the effort is normally applied. In this way a large lifting movement is produced for a short piston movement.

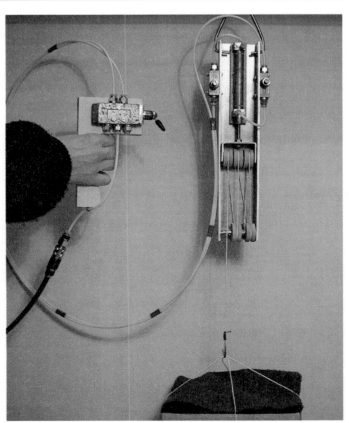

CHAPTER EIGHT

Materials

Think for a moment about all the different kinds of materials which are in use today, and their many different forms. We have an enormous range at our disposal and new materials are being developed all the time.

Anyone involved in designing and making needs to know what materials are available, how they behave, and how to use them. This chapter provides a useful introduction.

Selecting materials

When selecting a material for a particular product, the first question you need to ask is: what materials are **suitable** for the product?

A material which melts at a low temperature, for example, would not be suitable for making a saucepan. Similarly, a material which absorbs water, would be unsuitable for making wellington boots.

It is essential therefore, to choose a material with the appropriate **properties**. In the case of the saucepan body, the material must be capable of withstanding a high temperature, be a good conductor of heat, be light in weight, and so on. In the case of the wellington boots, the material must be waterproof, have good heat insulating properties, and be flexible for example.

The **aesthetic** qualities are important too. These will include colour, surface texture, pattern etc.

The way the product will be made – the **method of construction or manufacture** – is another essential factor in the choice of materials. Some materials can only be 'worked' in a limited number of ways. Others are more versatile. You will need, therefore, to consider the range of tools, equipment and machinery available to you, and the methods of working. Your own skills (or the skills of the workforce in a factory) are essential considerations too.

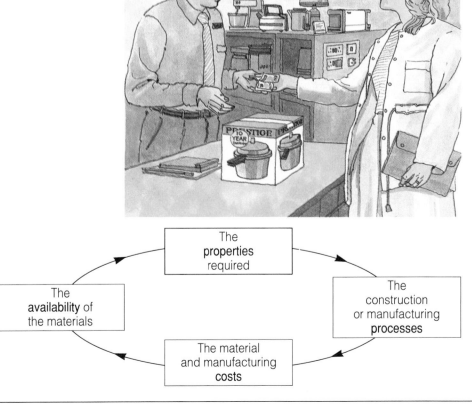

Cost is another vital element. In school the cost of the materials used is your main concern. In industry however, many different factors are involved. For example, quality of product, type of market, projected life etc, will all affect 'spending' on materials. Manufacturing costs are also affected by the chosen material because the material dictates the processes used, which in turn affects profitability.

Finally, both the short and long term **availability** of a material will affect its selection for use. This must be investigated carefully.

In conclusion therefore we can see that there are four **inter-related** factors which affect the choice of material.

The properties required

The construction or manufacturing processes

The material and manufacturing costs

The availability of the materials

The properties of materials

Strength

Strength is a measure of how good a material is at resisting being mis-shapen, or deformed, when acted upon by a force.

Tensile strength

This is the ability of a material to withstand pulling forces or **tension forces**.

A material which deforms easily under tension has a low tensile strength.

Which of these materials has the lowest tensile strength?

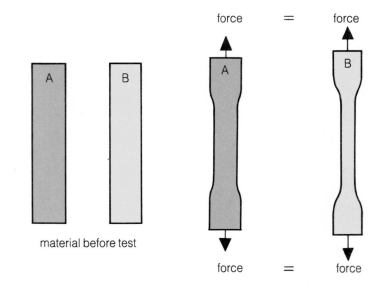

material before test

Compressive strength

This is the ability of a material to withstand 'squeezing' forces or **compression forces**.

A material which can resist a large compression force with little deformation, is said to have a high compressive strength.

Which of these materials has the highest compressive strength?

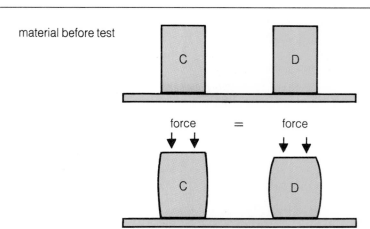

material before test

Torsional properties

Another test of a material's strength is its ability to withstand twisting forces, or **torsion**.

Which of these materials has the highest torsional strength?

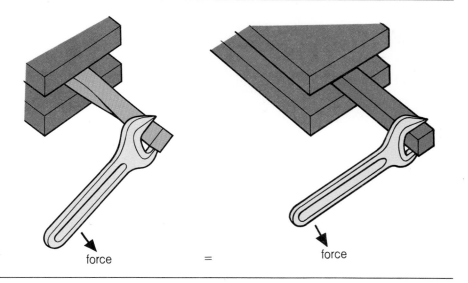

Question

1 For each of the products shown here, state whether the structure indicated needs to be strong in **tension**, **compression** or **torsion**.

Stiffness

Stiffness is the property of a material to resist a bending deformation.

Which is the stiffest material here?

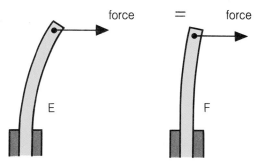

Ductility

This is the property of a material which allows it to be elongated or 'stretched'.

A ductile material will be fairly strong in tension.

material before test

Brittleness

A brittle material is one which fractures with little or no deformation.

A brittle material under tension can break suddenly and without warning. A ductile material always stretches before breaking.

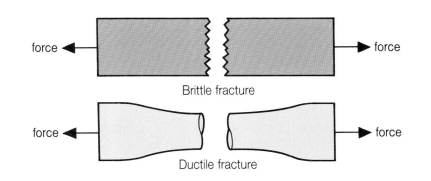

Brittle fracture

Ductile fracture

Question

2 This home-made screwdriver snapped during use. Was the material too ductile or too brittle?

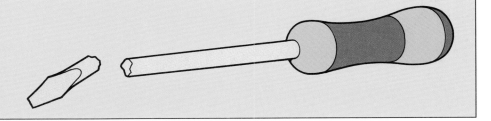

Hardness

The hardness of a material is a measure of its ability to withstand being scratched, cut or dented.

Which of the two materials shown here is the hardest? (Assume that equal pressure was applied to both scribers.)

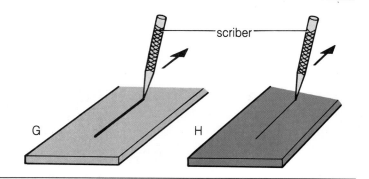

Toughness

This is a measure of **how much energy is required to break a material**. The energy of a 'swinging hammer' can be used to compare the toughness of different materials, as shown here.

Potential energy is given to the hammer as it is raised to position **1** in the diagram.

When the hammer is released, its potential energy is transferred into motion energy or kinetic energy. At position **2**, the hammer has maximum kinetic energy.

If a material is clamped into the vice, the energy of the swinging hammer can be used to break it.

By experimenting with the 'release height', the energy required to break a material can be found.

Which of these materials was the toughest?

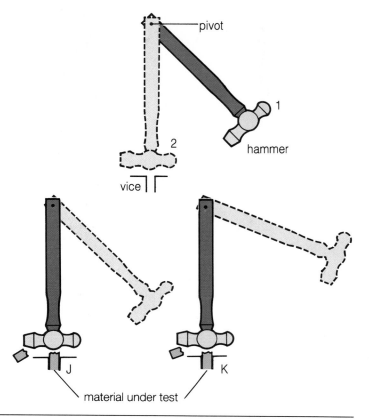

Density

Density is the **mass** of **1 cubic centimetre** of a substance.

Aluminium for example, has a density of 2.7 grams per cubic centimetre (2.7 g/cm³), and lead has a density of 11.3 g/cm³.

To calculate a material's density we use the equation:

$$\text{density} = \frac{\text{mass}}{\text{volume}}$$

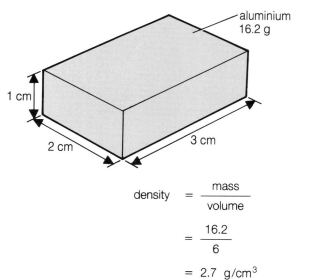

$$\text{density} = \frac{\text{mass}}{\text{volume}}$$

$$= \frac{16.2}{6}$$

$$= 2.7 \ \text{g/cm}^3$$

Questions

3 Bumpers are made from plastic on many modern cars.

Why is it necessary to choose a material which is very tough?

4 State one of the important properties of the material used for the blades of tinsnips.

blade

Thermal conductivity

'Therm' is an ancient Greek word meaning heat. **Thermal conductivity** relates to **how heat travels**, or is **conducted** through a material.

This simple apparatus, can be used to **compare** the thermal conductivity of different materials.

The heat is conducted along the material until it 'reaches' the candle wax. The wax melts and the ballbearing falls off.

Metals are good conductors of heat. Most non-metals have a low thermal conductivity.

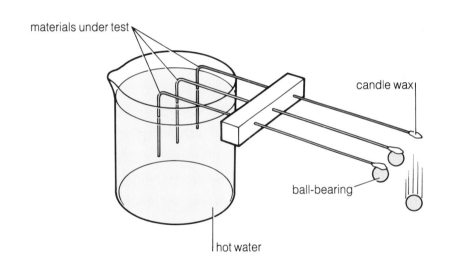

materials under test

candle wax

ball-bearing

hot water

Thermal expansion

Most materials 'get bigger', or **expand** when heated, and 'shrink', or **contract** as they cool down. This property can be demonstrated using the jaws and T-bar apparatus.

When cold, the T-bar will just slide between the metal jaws.

During heating however, the bar **expands** and will no longer fit. Only after the bar has cooled to its original temperature will it again slide between the jaws.

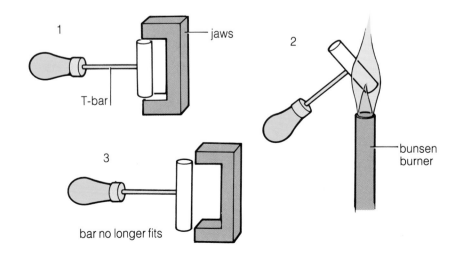

1

jaws

2

T-bar

3

bunsen burner

bar no longer fits

Questions

5 Which part of this saucepan needs to have a low thermal conductivity? Explain your answer.

6 Why is it necessary for the tip of a soldering iron to be a good conductor of heat?

7 One of the components in this automatic electric kettle makes use of the thermal expansion. Try to find out what it is, and what its function is.

Can you think of any other examples of where this property is used to advantage, and where it can be a disadvantage?

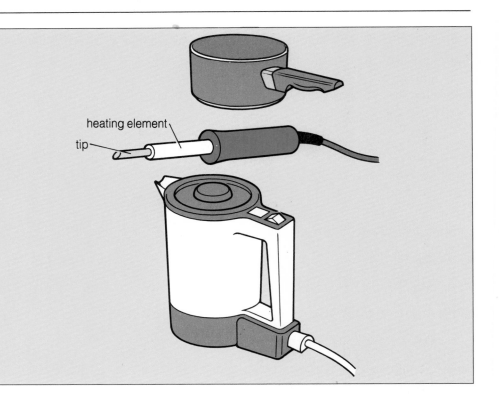

Electrical properties

The best known electrical property is **resistance**. This is what affects a material's ability to **conduct** electricity. A material with a low resistance will conduct electricity well. If it has a high resistance it will be a poor conductor of electricity.

Using a simple battery and bulb circuit the conductivity of materials can be **compared**.

Which material here has the lowest resistance, and which has the highest? Explain your answer.

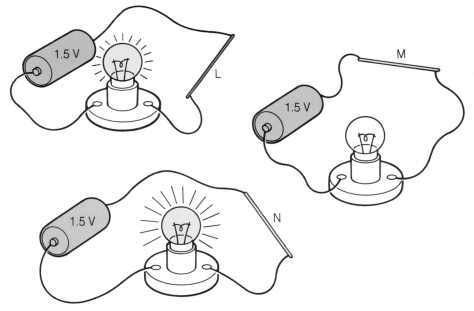

Question

8 Should the body of this electrical plug have a very high or very low resistance? Explain your answer.

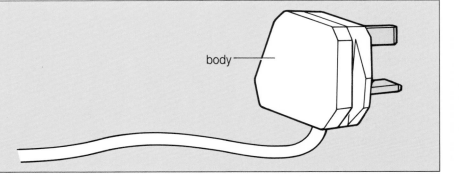

Magnetic properties

Have you ever used a magnet to pick up or attract other materials? It is this ability of a material to **exert a force** upon certain other materials which we call **magnetism**.

Materials which can be attracted by a magnet are those which themselves possess magnetic properties. These include **iron**, (the most magnetic), cobalt, nickel and steel.

The first magnetic material to be used was **magnetite** – a naturally occurring ore known as lodestone. Today, magnets are 'manufactured' using electricity.

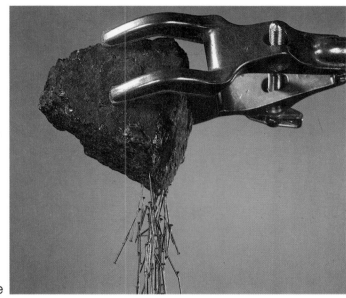

Lodestone

When electricity is passed through a coil of wire, a magnetic field 'appears' around that coil. If a piece of steel is placed inside the coil for a few minutes, it will become magnetised. The 'new' magnet can then be removed, after first switching off the electricity.

If a **soft iron** core is permanently fixed inside the coil we have an **electromagnet** which can be switched on and off. Soft iron is used because it loses most of the induced magnetism when the current is switched off, whereas steel does not.

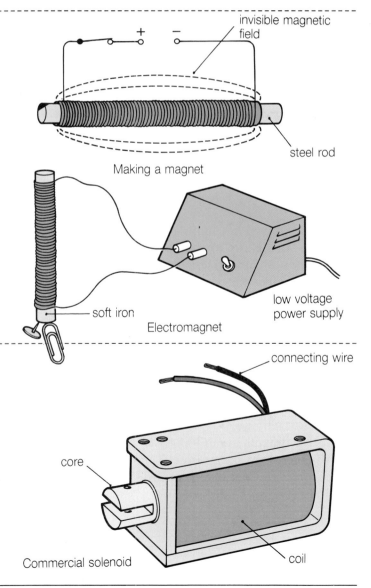

invisible magnetic field

steel rod

Making a magnet

soft iron

Electromagnet

low voltage power supply

Alternatively, if the core is free to move in and out of the coil we have what is called a **solenoid**. A solenoid produces linear motion in the core when electricity is passed through the coil. The core can only be made to 'move in' however – reversing the current will not make it move out.

connecting wire

core

Commercial solenoid

coil

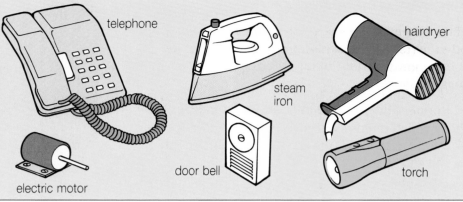

Question

9 Some of the products shown here rely on magnetism for their operation. Which of them do, and which do not? If you're not sure, try to find out.

telephone

steam iron

hairdryer

door bell

torch

electric motor

Optical properties

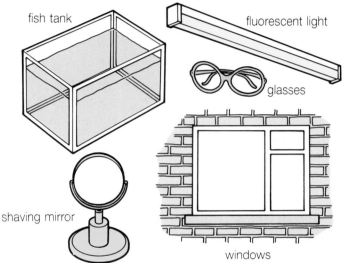

fish tank

fluorescent light

glasses

shaving mirror

windows

The optical properties of a material relate to the way in which it reacts to light.

The most obvious optical property is **transparency**. A transparent material allows light rays to pass through it, which in turn allows us to see images through it. A **translucent** material however, passes some light, but not enough to allow us to see through it.

Some products are shown here which make use of these properties. Can you think of any more?

Reflection

Everyone knows that light 'bounces' off shiny surfaces – this is the property of **reflection**. Whilst some materials have particularly good reflective properties – like the surface of a mirror – **all materials** do of course reflect light. It is the reflection of light from objects which allows us to **see** them.

The **colour** we see is dependent on reflection too. The light from the sun appears to be 'white', but in fact it is made up of the colours of the rainbow – the spectrum.

The reason why grass, for example, looks green, is because it reflects **green** light into our eyes and absorbs the other spectrum colours. Similarly, a **red** object looks red because it reflects red light and absorbs the others, and so on.

Radiation and absorption

The colour of a material also affects its ability to **absorb** (take in) and **radiate** (give out) **heat**. This can be demonstrated with a simple experiment.

In experiment **1**, metal cans containing **cold** water (and thermometers) are placed in direct sunlight.

In experiment **2**, similar cans containing **hot** water (and thermometers) are placed in a cool place.

The results show that a **black** surface not only absorbs heat more readily than a shiny surface, but also radiates heat more readily. In fact, a matt **black** surface is the best absorber and radiator of heat.

1

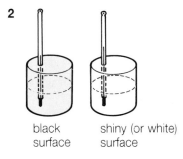
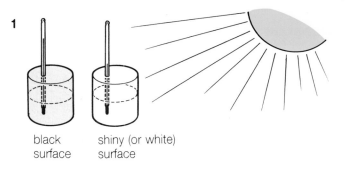

black surface   shiny (or white) surface

2

black surface   shiny (or white) surface

Questions

10 Clothes viewed under artificial light in a shop, appear to have a slightly different colour when viewed outside.

Think about this and try to explain why.

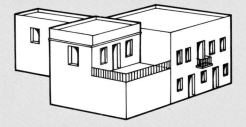

11 Why do you think that houses in very hot countries are often painted white?

12 Solar panels work best when painted one particular colour. What is that colour and why is it the best colour to use?

Metals

Iron ore mining in Western Australia

When the earth was formed the molten mass contained the many different metals which today we extract and use in huge quantities.

Most of the metals combined with rock when molten, to form **metallic ores**. The most common of these are **bauxite**, from which **aluminium** is extracted, and **iron ore** from which **iron** is extracted. More than seventy different metals are extracted and used in the manufacturing industries today. Some,

like copper and lead for example, can be used in their pure state, to take advantage of their natural properties. But often, we combine different metals, or metals with other materials to form **alloys**. By making alloys, we can **change the properties** of a metal to suit our particular needs.

Metals can be divided into two main groups: **ferrous metals** – those which contain **iron**, and **non-ferrous metals** – those which contain **no** iron.

Ferrous metals

Iron

Pure iron is of little use as an engineering material because it is too soft and **ductile**.

When iron cools and changes from a liquid to a solid, most of the atoms in the metal pack tightly together in orderly layers. Some, however, become misaligned, creating areas of weaknesses called **dislocations**.

When a piece of iron is put under stress, layers of atoms in these areas 'slip' over one another and the metal deforms. This begins to explain the ductility of soft iron.

By adding **carbon** to the iron however, we can produce a range of **alloys** with quite different properties. We call these the **carbon steels**.

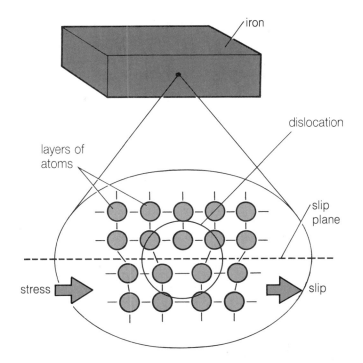

Carbon steels – their properties and uses

Mild steel

Steels produced with a carbon content between 0.1% and 0.3% are classified as mild steels.

When carbon is added to iron in a furnace, the carbon atoms 'enter' the material changing both its structure and properties. The resulting **steel** is much less ductile because the carbon helps to reduce slip between layers of atoms by 'interfering' with the slip planes. It is also harder, and tougher than iron, and has a higher **tensile strength**. Mild steel has a density of 7.8 g/cm^3, and its melting point is around 1600°C. It corrodes by rusting, it can be magnetised, and its colour is grey.

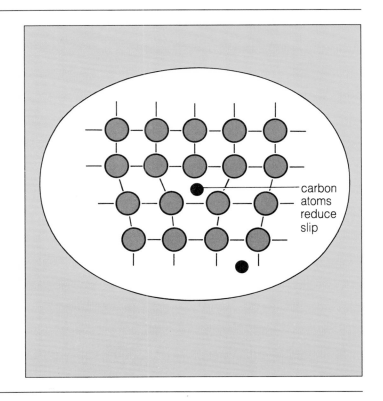

Mild steel is produced in many different forms – some examples of which are shown here. Most will undergo further processing before emerging as products, but some, such as **I** girders and channel for example, are ready for immediate use in buildings, bridges and other structures.

Mild steel can be cut and machined easily, and can be soldered, brazed and welded. The ductility and tensile strength of mild steel allows it to be 'cold' pressed into deep, complex sections. However, pressing and bending changes the 'internal structure' of the steel, making it stronger and harder. This is known as **work hardening**. In many manufacturing processes this effect is welcomed. Work hardened steel however, is less ductile and more brittle. If these properties are not desired, the steel can be returned to its original state by a process known as **annealing**. The metal is heated to red heat, and then allowed to cool down slowly.

Mild steel is the most common type of steel in use today. Some examples of the many products made from this material are shown above.

Medium carbon steel

The medium carbon steels contain between 0.3% and 0.7% carbon. These steels are therefore harder and less ductile than the mild steels. They are very **tough** and have a **high tensile strength**.

Steels with a carbon content of 0.3% and above can be further hardened by **heat treatment**. The medium carbon steels therefore, are more specialised in their use.

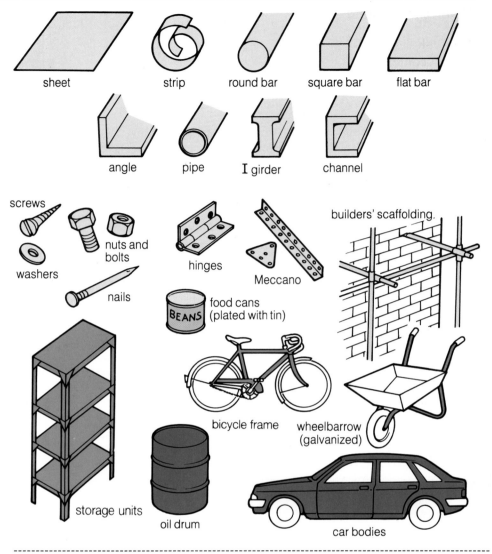

sheet   strip   round bar   square bar   flat bar

angle   pipe   **I** girder   channel

screws
washers
nuts and bolts
nails
hinges
Meccano
builders' scaffolding.
BEANS food cans (plated with tin)
storage units
oil drum
bicycle frame
wheelbarrow (galvanized)
car bodies

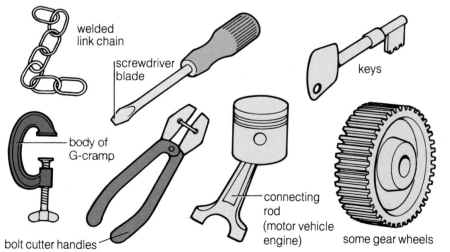

welded link chain
screwdriver blade
keys
body of G-cramp
connecting rod (motor vehicle engine)
some gear wheels
bolt cutter handles

They are used for the manufacture of products which have to be tough and hard wearing.

Some examples of products made from medium carbon steel are shown here.

High carbon steel

The high carbon steels have a carbon content ranging from 0.7% to 1.3%. These are very **hard** and **brittle** materials. The maximum hardness produced by heat treatment is achieved with steels containing about 0.7% carbon.

High carbon steels are used mainly for **cutting** tools and products which have to withstand **wear**. Some examples of such products are shown here.

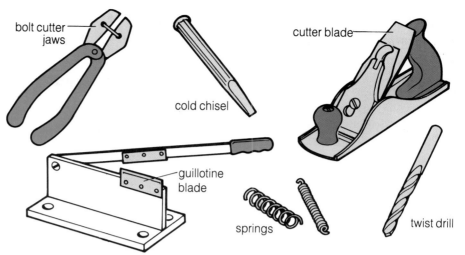

Stainless steel

Stainless steels are **iron/chromium** alloys. A wide range of steels are available with a chromium content between 13% and 27%. Some contain only iron, carbon and chromium, whilst others contain nickel and other alloying elements also.

The effect of the chromium is to create an oxide film which prevents rusting. Paints and other surface treatments are not therefore necessary. The degree of protection depends upon the percentage of chromium present. Other properties such as ductility, hardness and tensile strength are dependent upon the percentage of the other alloying elements.

Stainless steel is a shiny attractive metal (but should not be confused with chromium-plated steel). This, combined with its other properties, makes it a very versatile material.

Some examples of the many products made from stainless steel are shown here.

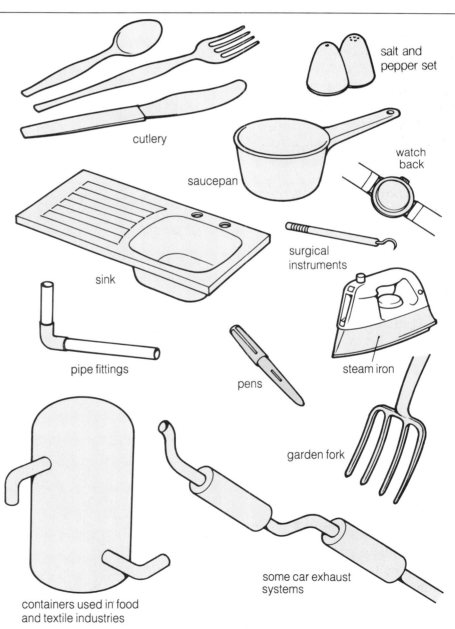

Grey cast iron

Cast iron is an alloy of iron (94%), carbon (3%), silicon (2%) and traces of magnesium, sulphur and phosphorus.

It is a very **brittle** metal with a hard skin. It has a high compressive strength, but low tensile strength, and will fracture if struck with a heavy blow. It corrodes by rusting.

Whilst all metals can be cast (melted and poured into a mould), cast iron is particularly suited to casting – hence its name. It can be poured at a relatively low temperature (between 1400°C and 1500°C) and will cast into complex shapes. After casting, it can be machined easily (if necessary) into the finished article.

Some examples of products made from cast iron are shown here.

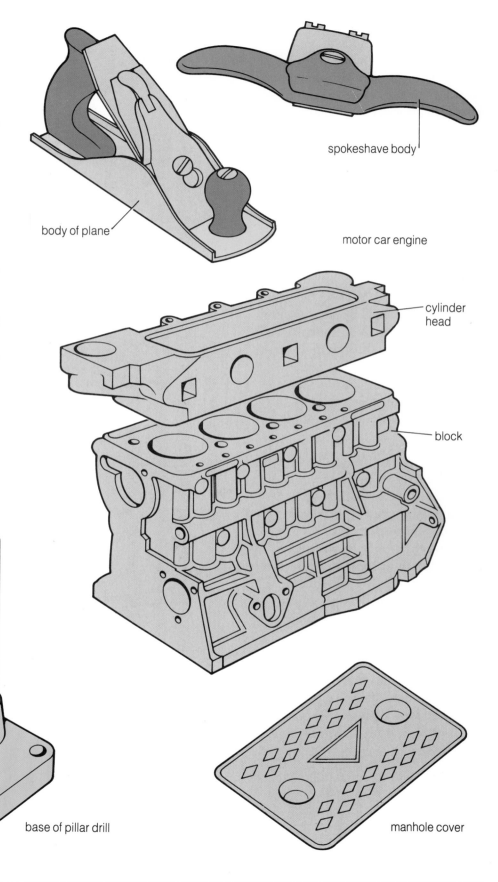

spokeshave body

body of plane

motor car engine

cylinder head

block

base of pillar drill

manhole cover

Non-ferrous metals – their properties and uses

Aluminium

Aluminium is the most abundant metal in the earth's crust and, after steel, is the most widely used of all the metals today.

Pure aluminium is **soft** and **ductile** and has a low tensile strength. Even so, it has a high strength to weight ratio. Its density is 2.7 g/cm^3, ($\frac{1}{3}$ of the density of mild steel). Its melting point is 660°C (compared to 1600°C for steel). It has a shiny silver-grey appearance.

Due to the natural formation of a **surface oxide film**, aluminium has good resistance to corrosion. It is a good conductor of both electricity and heat (next to copper in this respect). It cannot be magnetised. It cuts and machines easily, and can be polished to a bright finish.

Aluminium alloys

Because aluminium is light and resists corrosion, it is an 'attractive' material for engineering purposes. Unfortunately it is soft and has a low tensile strength. To impart hardness and strength and to produce other desirable properties, a wide range of **alloys** are manufactured. The alloying elements include copper, magnesium, chromium, silicon and tin.

Some examples of the numerous products made from aluminium and its alloys are shown here.

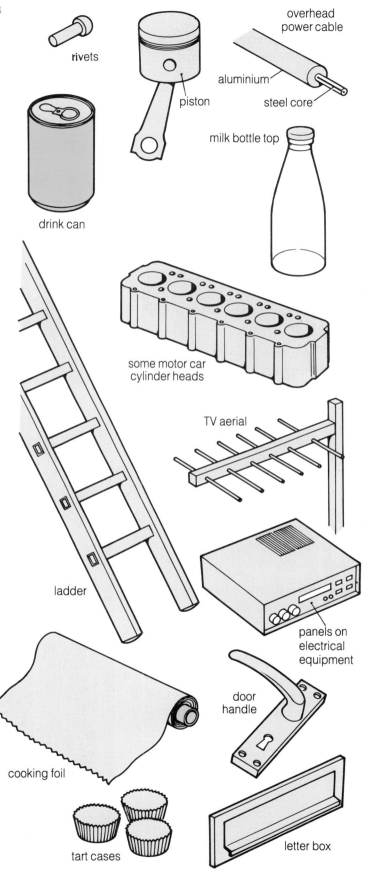

rivets

piston

overhead power cable

aluminium

steel core

drink can

milk bottle top

some motor car cylinder heads

TV aerial

ladder

panels on electrical equipment

cooking foil

door handle

tart cases

letter box

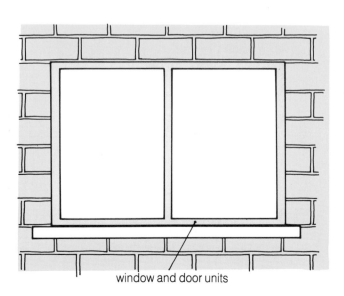

window and door units

Copper

Copper is a **pure metal**. It is the world's third most important metal, in terms of volume of consumption.

It is a fairly **ductile** material and is moderately strong. Its melting point is around 1080°C. It is quite a heavy metal, having a density of 8·9 g/cm³. A naturally forming oxide film (having a greenish colour) gives it good anti-corrosion properties. Copper is a very good conductor of electricity (second only to silver in this respect) and is a good conductor of heat. It cannot be magnetised. It will cut, saw, file and machine easily.

Copper is a reddish-brown metal which will polish to a beautiful deep shine. Some examples of the many products made from copper are shown here.

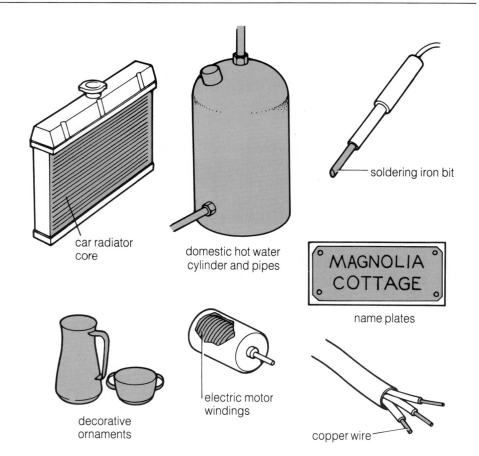

car radiator core

domestic hot water cylinder and pipes

soldering iron bit

MAGNOLIA COTTAGE

name plates

decorative ornaments

electric motor windings

copper wire

Brass

The term 'brass' covers a wide range of **copper–zinc alloys**. The amounts of copper and zinc present are varied to obtain the desired properties.

The melting point of brass is lower than copper, and its density is around 8·4 g/cm³. It has good electrical conductivity (although lower than copper) and good anticorrosive properties. It is gold in colour and, like copper, can be polished to give a deep shine.

Some examples of the many products made from brass are shown here.

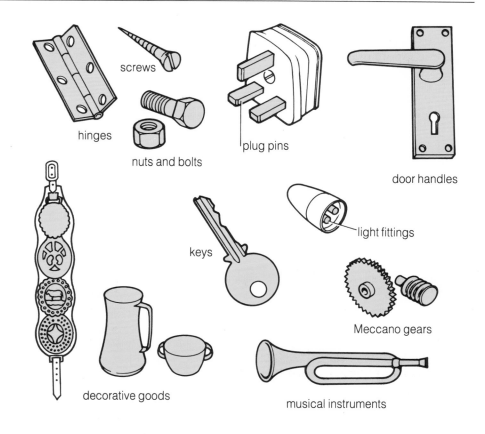

hinges

screws

nuts and bolts

plug pins

door handles

keys

light fittings

Meccano gears

decorative goods

musical instruments

Industrial manufacturing with metals

The manufacture of **metal products**, or **components** for assembly into products, takes many forms. Some of the more common industrial processes are described below.

Blanking

This is one of the simplest 'pressing' operations.

A hardened **punch** is used to stamp sheet metal through a **die**. The metal is stamped **cold**. 'Blanks' of almost any shape can be produced in this way.

Simple components like washers for example, are produced by blanking alone. For many products however, this is just one of a series of production operations. Blanking is often followed by press forming or bending for example.

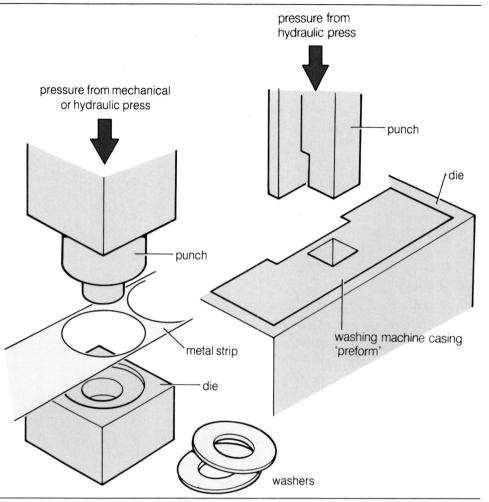

Press forming

This is the shaping of components from **sheet** metal between a punch and a die. The metal blank (or preform) is pressed **cold**. Components made in this way have consistently accurate dimensions and **work hardening** imparts strength and rigidity. The process is also very fast and produces very little waste.

Most sheet metals are suited to this process, but mild steel is the most widely used.

Motor car panels (wings, doors, roofs, etc.) are amongst the numerous components which are press formed.

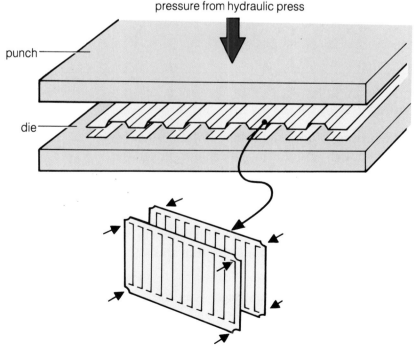

Press-formed panels for domestic radiator

Forging

Forging is the shaping of metal using compression forces. The force may be applied by hammer, press or rollers. The metal is usually **hot**, but some operations are carried out cold. (See cold heading for example.) Forging at temperature increases the plasticity of a metal, and reduces the forces needed to work it. Many different forging operations are carried out, but we will only discuss drop forging here.

Drop forging

This is the forming of a component from a metal bar or billet between two 'half' dies. The **hot** metal is placed on the lower die, and is forced into the cavity between the upper and lower die by the blow of a machine hammer.

Parts made in this way cannot usually be formed by the single hammer blow in a single die. A drop forged component is usually moved from one die impression to the next until the final shape is produced. Forgings can be made to very close tolerances, hence very little **finishing** is required.

Materials used in drop forging include: mild and medium carbon steel, aluminium and copper alloys.

Motor car crankshafts, some G-cramps, and other tools, door handles, and other 'hardware' items are amongst the numerous products which are drop forged.

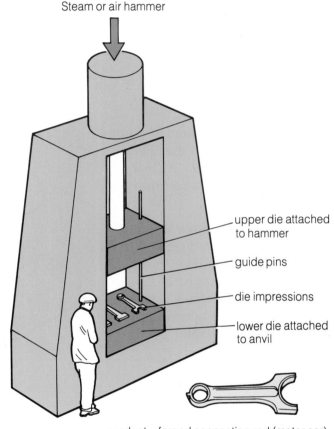

Steam or air hammer

upper die attached to hammer

guide pins

die impressions

lower die attached to anvil

product – forged connecting rod (motor car)

Cold heading (also known as cold upsetting)

This is the process of forming **cold** metal slugs or wire into components by 'squeezing' the metal into a die cavity. This is a quick and cheap method of changing the shape and diameter of a metal bar to produce products.

Brass, stainless steel, mild steel and medium carbon steel are the materials commonly used in this process.

The largest single use of this process is in the manufacture of bolts, screws, rivets and nails.

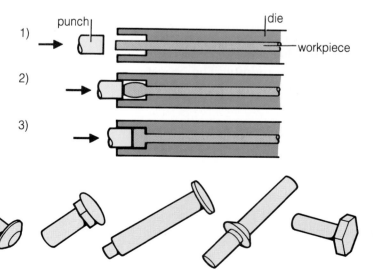

punch   die

1)   workpiece

2)

3)

Examples of cold-headed components

Thread rolling

This is one method of applying a **thread** to machine bolts produced by cold heading. Other parallel-sided components can be threaded in this way too.

Knurled patterns, splines and worm gears are just a few of the many other forms which can be produced by **roll forming**.

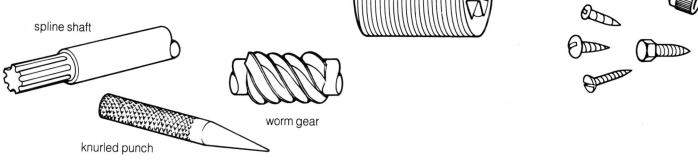

spline shaft

knurled punch

worm gear

rotating cyclindrical dies

workpiece

Examples of roll-formed components

Impact extrusion – forward extrusion

This process consists of forcing a **hot** billet of metal through an extrusion die using a hydraulic ram.

The product is a continuous length of metal whose shape corresponds to the die orifice.

An almost infinite number of solid cross-sections can be produced in this way, as well as tubing. Extrusion produces complex sections which could otherwise only be manufactured by expensive machining operations.

Products made from extruded sections include: door and window frames, hinges, components for locks, edging strips etc.

By far the largest number of sections produced are made from aluminium and brass.

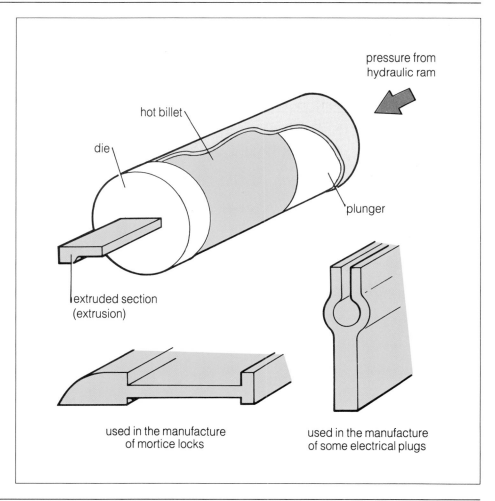

pressure from hydraulic ram

hot billet

die

plunger

extruded section (extrusion)

used in the manufacture of mortice locks

used in the manufacture of some electrical plugs

Sand casting

This is the shaping of metal by 'pouring' **molten** metal into a **mould**. A mould is a cavity which has the shape of the required object.

Sand is a particularly good material for making moulds. It can withstand very high temperatures and can be moulded into complex shapes. It is particularly suitable for the high melting point metals.

Sand casting is a quick method of producing complex shapes, but a new mould is required for each new casting. The more common casting metals include: cast iron, steel, aluminium alloys, and brass.

Motor car engine blocks and cylinder heads, bases for heavy machinery, manhole covers, and the body of a mechanic's vice (found in the school workshops) are examples of sand cast products.

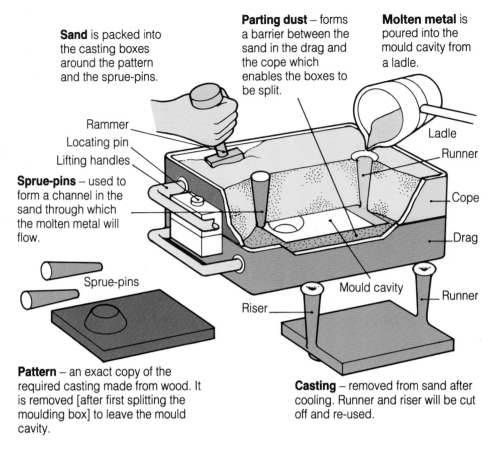

Sand is packed into the casting boxes around the pattern and the sprue-pins.

Parting dust – forms a barrier between the sand in the drag and the cope which enables the boxes to be split.

Molten metal is poured into the mould cavity from a ladle.

Rammer
Locating pin
Lifting handles

Sprue-pins – used to form a channel in the sand through which the molten metal will flow.

Sprue-pins

Ladle
Runner
Cope
Drag
Mould cavity
Runner
Riser

Pattern – an exact copy of the required casting made from wood. It is removed [after first splitting the moulding box] to leave the mould cavity.

Casting – removed from sand after cooling. Runner and riser will be cut off and re-used.

Die casting

Where many items of the same form are to be manufactured, die casting is employed. In this process, molten metal is forced into the cavity between dies under high pressure. After the metal has been injected, the pressure is held for a short time whilst the metal solidifies. The die blocks are then opened and the casting is ejected automatically.

Die casting is a very fast production method which can produce extremely complex precision parts due to the injection of metal under pressure. The products have a high quality surface requiring very little secondary finishing.

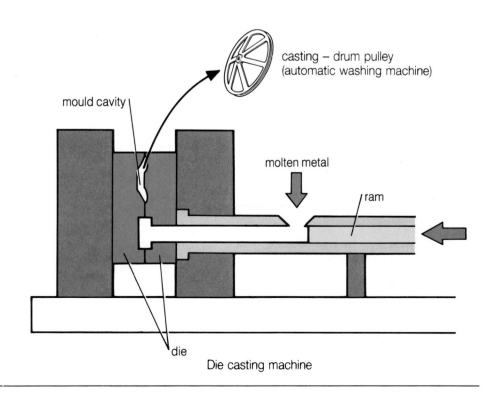

casting – drum pulley (automatic washing machine)

mould cavity

molten metal

ram

die

Die casting machine

Many thousands of different die cast products are manufactured. These include: the cases of some electric hand tools (drills, jig-saws, sanders, etc.), chassis for record players, tape decks and other similar products, component parts for washing machines, food mixers and lawn mowers, and, not least, many motor car components including, fuel pump and carburettor parts, fans and grills, body trim and door handles.

Die casting is limited to non-ferrous metals whose molten temperatures will not damage the dies.

Machining

Some components can be shaped into their final form in just one operation, such as in die casting. Many however, have to be **machined** into their final form. The machining processes which include **drilling**, **cutting** and **grinding** are carried out on **machine-tools**. Some of the more common machining operations are described below.

Lathework

Turning is the most basic operation to be carried out on a lathe. The metal workpiece is shaped as it is rotated in contact with a cutting tool.

The tool (which will be shaped according to its purpose), can be moved across, along, and at an angle to the workpiece. (See diagrams **1**, **2** and **3**.)

Other lathe operations include drilling, thread cutting, and boring. (See diagrams **4**, **5** and **6**.)

The centre lathe is only suitable for 'one off' or short production runs. By replacing the tailstock with a **turret** however, and automating the lathe feed mechanisms, mass production can be achieved.

The **CNC** (**c**omputer **n**umerically **c**ontrolled lathe) can be programmed for fully automatic production.

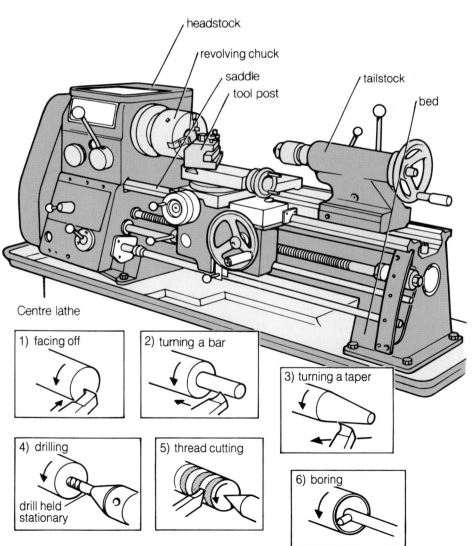

headstock
revolving chuck
saddle
tool post
tailstock
bed

Centre lathe

1) facing off
2) turning a bar
3) turning a taper
4) drilling — drill held stationary
5) thread cutting
6) boring

Milling

Milling is the use of a rotating cutter to shape a metal workpiece. The workpiece is fixed to a table which can be moved in relation to the cutter.

Just a few of the numerous types of milling cutters are shown in operation here

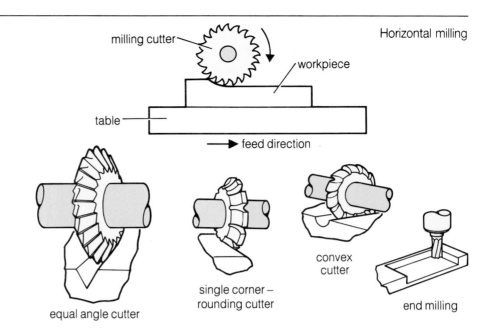

Horizontal milling

milling cutter
workpiece
table
feed direction

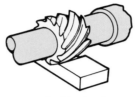

cylindrical cutter

equal angle cutter

single corner – rounding cutter

convex cutter

end milling

Grinding

This is the process in which metal is removed by the 'rubbing' contact of an abrasive material such as **carborundum**. Most grinding operations are carried out using grinding **wheels**, but rotating belts and other machines are also used.

Unlike 'heavy' cutting with a metal tool, grinding applies only a tiny force to the workpiece. As a result there is very little deformation of the workpiece and an accurate and very smooth finish can be obtained.

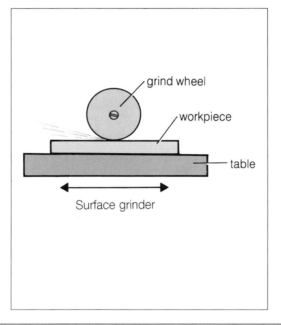

grind wheel
workpiece
table

Surface grinder

Pedestal grinder

Drilling

Drilling a circular hole is one of the most common metal cutting operations. The cutting tool is usually a twist drill.

In industry, multi-head drilling machines are common. The photograph shows part of an adjustable multi-head machine.

Question

13 To choose the most suitable material for a particular product requires you to have a good knowledge of materials. See how much you know about **metals** by using the chart below. **Copy it** on to a piece of paper and 'fill in' the empty boxes (and also add to the other boxes if you can). Some of the information you require can be found in this chapter. For more detailed information you will need to use a more specialist book.

Material	Ferrous	Non-ferrous	Composition	Colour	Properties	Common uses
mild steel	✓		iron + 0.1% to 0.3% carbon		fairly high tensile strength heavy metal (density = 7.8 g/km³ high melting point (1600°C) corrodes by rusting	
		✓			soft and ductile low tensile strength lightweight (density = 2.7 g/km³) melting point 660°C	milk bottle tops cooking foil ladders door and window frames
			iron + 0.3% to 0.7% carbon	siver-grey		
			pure metal	reddish-brown	heavy metal (density = 8.9 g/cm³) good conductor of electricity and heat cannot be magnetised	
	✓				properties vary depending upon percentage of chromium	
	✓				brittle high compressive strength low tensile strength corrodes by rusting	machine bases manhole covers motor car engine blocks
			copper-zinc	yellow		

14 Hammer heads need to be hard-wearing and very tough. They are manufactured by forging. Which of the materials, mild steel or medium carbon steel, do you think, is used for their manufacture?

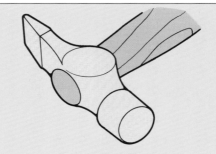

15 The frame of this pushchair was fabricated from **stainless steel** tubing.
   a What properties make stainless steel particularly suitable for this product?
   b Why was tubing used rather than solid bar?
   c What would be the disadvantages of using mild steel for this product?
   d Some pushchairs are made from aluminium. State one advantage and one disadvantage of using aluminium for this product.

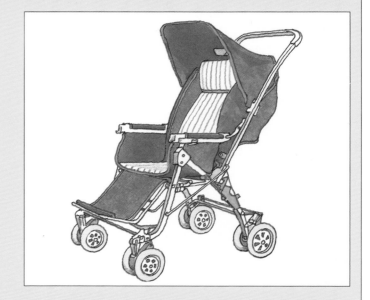

16 Some door hinges and bolts are made from extruded brass.

   a What machining process might be carried out on the extrusions to complete the production of these products?
   b What other material is commonly used for making extruded door bolts?

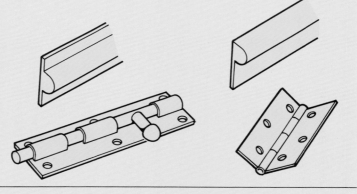

17 The road wheels on some motor cars are fabricated from mild steel pressings. Others are cast in aluminium alloys. Steel has a density of 7.8 g/cm^3, aluminium alloys around 2.7 g/cm^3. Steel is cheaper than aluminium.
   a State three reasons for choosing to make car wheels from aluminium.
   b Why are the wheels on most small cars made from steel pressings?

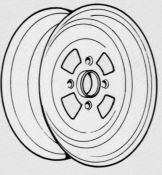

pressed steel

alloy casting

18 This mortice key was fabricated from three components: the shank, bit and bow. The shank was manufactured on an automatic lathe.

  a How do you think the bow was manufactured?

  b What materials would be suitable for this product?

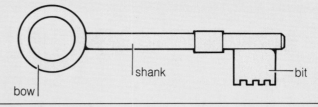

19 The door handles shown were pressure die cast.

  a What materials are suited to this method of production, and why?

  b Why is pressure die casting unlikely to be used for short production runs?

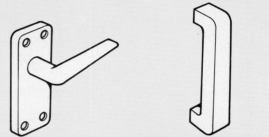

20 The 'high tensile' bolt cutters shown here were assembled from several component parts.

  a Which parts do you think were drop forged?

  b Which components would be made from high carbon steel, and why?

  c Why might an engineer smear oil on the jaws?

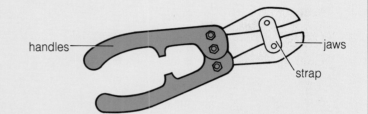

21 Some greenhouse frames are assembled from complex aluminium sections.

  a What method of manufacture do you think was used to produce these sections?

  b What property of aluminium makes it unnecessary for the frame to be painted?

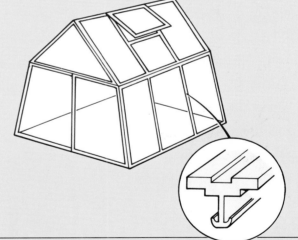

22 Domestic washing machines and refrigerators are usually housed in steel casings. These are fabricated from mild steel pressings.

What is the name of the 'effect', produced by pressing, which imparts hardness to the steel and helps to add rigidity to the product?

Wood

Wood collection in Finnish forest

For thousands of years, **trees** have provided us with a wide range of products including food stuffs, medicines, paper and fuel. Not least, they have provided one of the most versatile construction materials – **wood**.

Large areas of the earth, including much of Britain, were once covered with forests. Today however, Britain produces only limited amounts of timber, most of our wood is imported.

Although there are hundreds of different kinds of trees, there are just two types: deciduous trees and conifers.

Deciduous trees

Deciduous trees have broad leaves which they shed in winter. They grow mainly in the warmer temperate regions of the earth and produce the timber known as **hardwood**.

Conifers

Conifers are usually 'evergreen' with needle-like leaves. They grow mainly in the cooler regions of the earth and produce the timber known as **softwood**.

The structure of wood

Trees are living structures. They grow by producing hollow tube-like cells composed mainly of cellulose.

During the growing season (from spring through to autumn) a tree increases its girth by producing new cells in the cambium layer. In some trees, the cells produced in spring and summer are quite different in diameter. It is this difference which shows up as the 'annual rings' at the end of a sawn log. In other trees, the difference between spring and summer growth is not obvious. Even so, in most trees the cells produced during the drier summer months have thicker cell walls. It is this summer growth which is responsible for much of the mechanical strength in wood.

Softwoods are composed almost entirely of tube-like cells, but hardwoods have a more complex structure. Some contain a great deal of fibrous material which adds mechanical strength to the wood and also makes it harder.

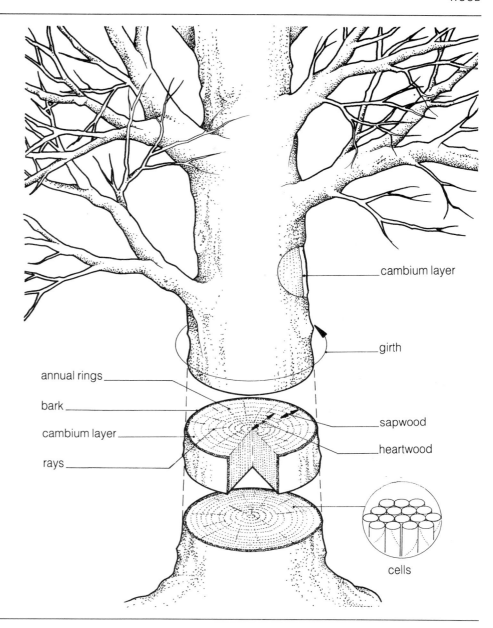

The properties of wood

From an engineering point of view, all wood can be thought of as bundles of parallel tubes, rather like bundles of drinking straws. Further, in all wood these tubes are made essentially from the same material, but with varying wall thicknesses. As you might imagine therefore, the **denser** the wood, the stronger the wood. (See density page 200.)

However, it is important to remember that wood is a **natural** material and that climate and soil conditions will affect its growth. We can only therefore describe the general properties of wood, since even pieces of wood from the same tree will have different characteristics.

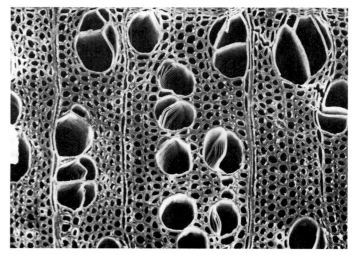

Magnified section of wood – tube cells

The strength of wood

A bundle of drinking straws, glued together, will demonstrate fairly accurately the mechanical properties of wood.

The tensile strength of wood is in general fairly high. Some woods have a tensile strength greater than that of mild steel (weight for weight).

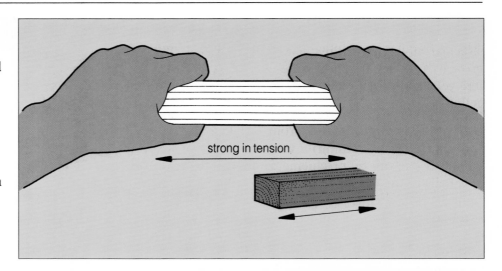

strong in tension

The compressive strength of wood however, is much lower. Wood is also very weak in both tension and compression across the grain.

Hardwoods tend to be **stiffer** than the softwoods and because of their fibre content are usually harder. Even so, it is important to realise that the terms 'hardwood' and 'softwood' are botanical classifications – they are **not** descriptions of the mechanical properties of wood. As you will discover with use, some hardwoods are very soft and easy to work whilst some softwoods are tough and difficult to work. Balsa wood and jelutong are notable examples. They are both hardwoods and yet are soft and can be worked easily. Most softwoods cut easily, but the majority of hardwoods will machine better. The **decorative finish** of most hardwoods is also superior to the softwoods.

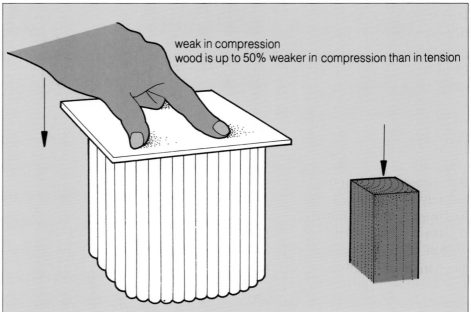

weak in compression
wood is up to 50% weaker in compression than in tension

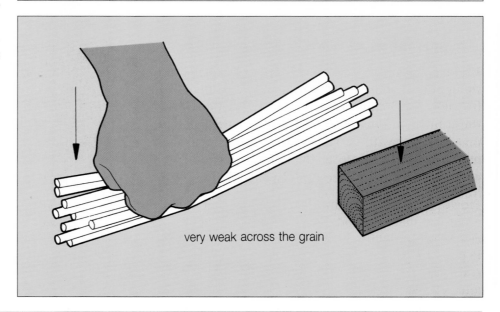

very weak across the grain

The conversion of timber

After a tree has been felled, its logs are sawn up into boards or planks. This is known as **conversion**.

There are two general methods of doing this: **plain sawing** (sometimes known as through and through) and **quarter sawing** (or radial sawing).

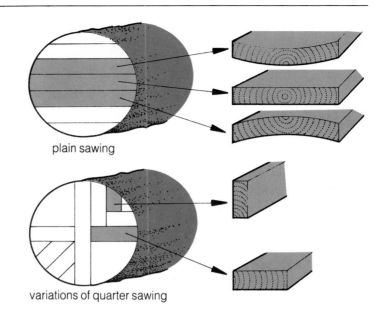

plain sawing

variations of quarter sawing

Often a combination of the two methods is used to avoid waste and therefore provide the most **economical** conversion.

Plain sawing is the cheapest way of converting a log but the outer planks or boards tend to warp. Quarter sawing is far more expensive because it requires more time and labour, and produces more waste. However, quarter sawn logs are far more **stable** (less likely to warp).

The effects of water content on wood

Timber contains a great deal of moisture when felled, which makes it almost impossible to work. It also shrinks as it dries out and often cracks. To reduce these problems, the wood must be **seasoned**. Seasoning involves stacking the wood for long periods in dry air to allow the moisture to evaporate. Alternatively the wood can be dried under controlled conditions in a kiln.

Even after seasoning however, wood can still **warp** and **twist** when in use. This happens because wood is **hygroscopic** – that is, it absorbs water from a moist atmosphere (causing it to expand) and loses water in a dry atmosphere (causing it to contract). A timber which is prone to this problem is said to be **unstable**. Paints and other surface treatment reduce this effect, but do not eliminate it.

A low water content is also important for durability. Dry wood resists decay, and is less likely to be infested by woodworm and beetle.

Wood drying kiln

Some examples of softwoods

Pine (Red Baltic pine, Scots pine)

Pine, which is commonly known as **deal**, is probably the most common softwood and is one of the most durable. Its colour varies from a pale yellowy cream to reddy brown. It is grown in the USSR, Scandinavia and the British Isles.

The best quality pine is almost knot free. The lower quality materials, whilst containing some knots, will contain mainly 'live' or sound knots which do not fall out after shrinking.

When dry, pine can be cut and machined easily, and planed to a bright shiny finish. Whilst it contains some resinous material, it can be glued without difficulty. It can be nailed without splitting and takes screws well.

Pine is a fairly hard, durable material and is quite stable. It is often used unprotected indoors, but is commonly painted or varnished.

Some examples of its uses are shown here.

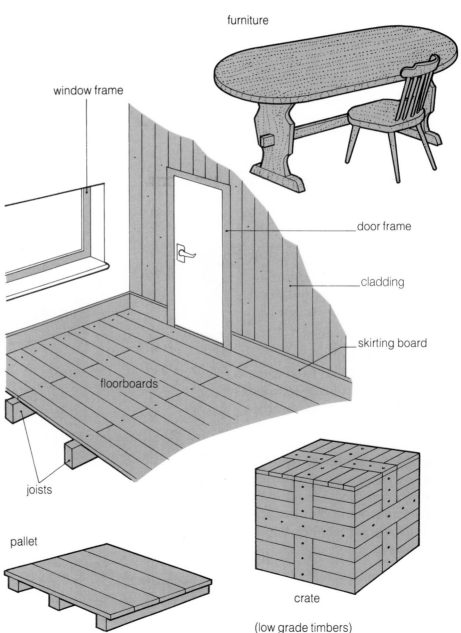

furniture

window frame

door frame

cladding

skirting board

floorboards

joists

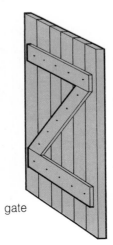

gate

pallet

crate

(low grade timbers)

Spruce

Spruce, which is commonly known as whitewood, has a similar colour to deal but never quite as dark. It grows in Canada and the British Isles.

Unlike deal, it contains a lot of very hard 'dead' knots which often fall out. Resin pockets may also be present – these should be cut out before use.

Spruce is a very tough material, and is fairly hard and durable. Even so, it is not very stable and therefore is not suitable for outdoor use.

Some examples of its uses are shown here.

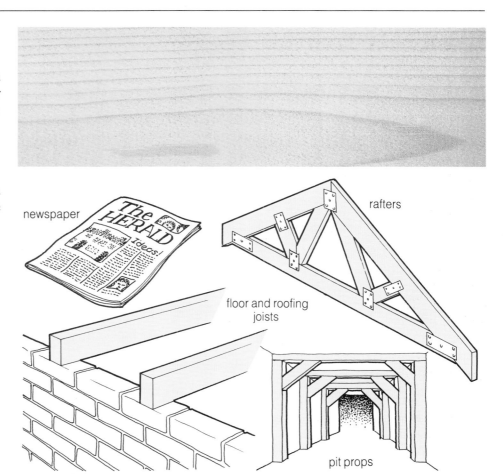

newspaper

rafters

floor and roofing joists

pit props

Parana pine

Parana pine has a fine even texture, and is a pale creamy brown colour. It is available in long wide boards and often without knots. It grows mainly in South America.

It is a fairly heavy, tough timber which is very prone to twisting. For this reason it is commonly used for structures which are securely jointed, or where it can be securely fixed to battens. It is most commonly used for staircases and window boards (sills).

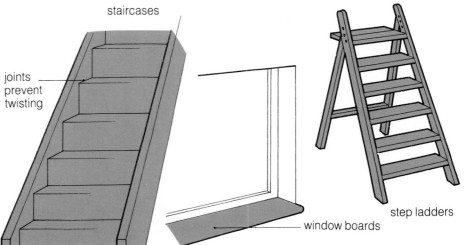

staircases

joints prevent twisting

step ladders

window boards

Some examples of hardwoods

Ash (European)

The colour of ash varies from creamy white to light brown.

It is a long-grained timber which is tough and **flexible**. It also has good resistance to shock – hence its use in sports equipment.

Ash is a stable timber, and therefore can be used outdoors.

Some examples of products made from ash are shown here.

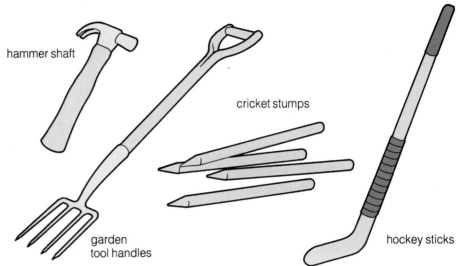

hammer shaft

cricket stumps

garden tool handles

hockey sticks

Beech (European)

Beech is a very light brown wood with very characteristic 'speckles'.

It has a close even grain and is very tough. It is a fairly heavy wood and is quite hard.

It is **not** prone to splitting, and it has no taste or odour. These properties make it particularly suitable for childrens toys and kitchen utensils.

Some examples of the many products made from beech are shown here.

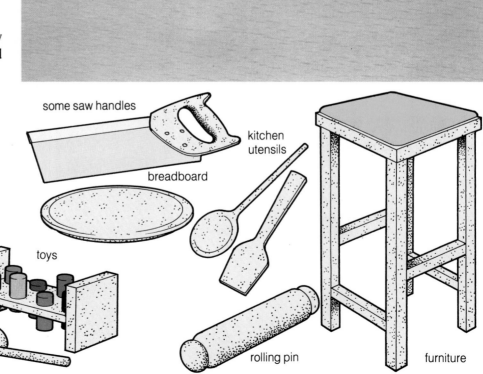

some saw handles

kitchen utensils

breadboard

toys

rolling pin

furniture

Mahogany

Mahogany is the name used to describe a number of reddish-brown timbers whose properties can be quite different. Gaboon, sapele and utile are three common examples. These all grow in Africa.

Sapele is well known for its attractive striped grain, which has made it popular for furniture making. It is a strong, medium weight timber but the nature of its grain makes it difficult to work. The alternate grain stripes 'lift' when it is planed. Ideally it should be finished by machine sanding.

Utile is a denser timber than sapele but it is easier to work. It is a particularly stable and durable timber.

Gaboon is a lightweight timber of fairly low strength. It has little decorative character and because it is fairly cheap is used in the making of plywood.

For many applications, mahogany veneers (thin layers of wood) are applied to a base material (often chipboard or plywood) to make maximum use of the timber.

Some examples of products made from mahogany are shown here.

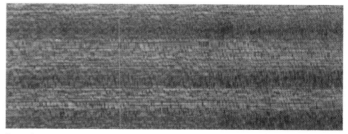
Sapele

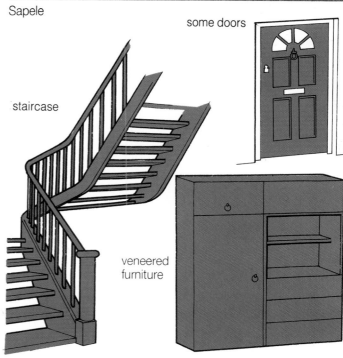
some doors

staircase

veneered furniture

Oak (English)

Freshly planed oak has a beige-brown colour which changes to a rich deep brown with time.

Quarter sawn oak is noted for its decorative **figuring** which shows a silver fleck effect.

It is a very hard, strong and durable timber and is quite heavy. Trees which have grown quickly tend to produce long straight-grained timber which is ideal for furniture making. The harder short-grained timbers from slow growing trees are more suitable for outdoor use.

Some examples of products made from oak are shown here.

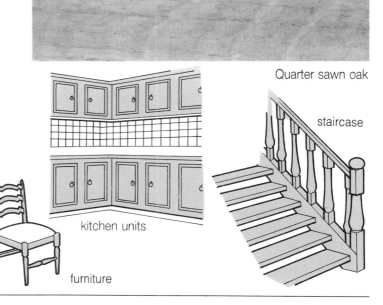
Quarter sawn oak

staircase

kitchen units

furniture

Manufactured boards

Some of the disadvantages of natural wood can be overcome by using manufactured boards. These include: plywood, chipboard and hardboard. These are essentially **sheet** materials.

Plywood and its properties

Plywood is made up of three or more thin layers (or veneers) of wood, glued together. The veneers are arranged so that their grains run in alternate directions. Since wood is much stronger along the grain than across it, this gives the material **uniform strength**. This can be demonstrated with a straw model.

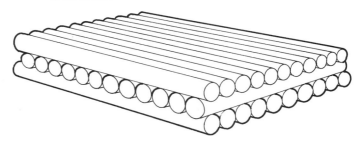

Veneer being cut (rotary method)

straw model

Because of this construction, plywood is less likely to warp or split than natural woods. It is always made with an odd number of veneers 3, 5, 7 etc. The greater the number, the stronger the plywood.

Although very 'stable', plywood is not immune to warping, since the tensions in the veneers are never equal. Further, if one side of the board gets wet, or is heated, the board will warp as the outer veneers expand or contract.

A major advantage of plywood over natural timber is that it is relatively cheap and is available in much larger sheets than natural woods, and in a wide range of thicknesses. Decorative hardwood veneers can also be attached to a cheaper core or base material. This allows for the economic use of rare woods, and provides wide boards which otherwise might not be available. Plastic coatings are also used to provide water-resistant surfaces. Another advantage of plywood is that it is flexible and can be 'formed' into curves.

If individual veneers are glued together between formers a **permanent** curved shape can be produced. These are known as **laminated forms**.

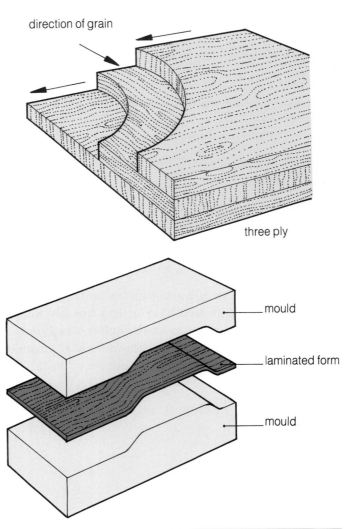

Types of plywood

A range of plywoods is available, made from different woods, and each having its own particular properties. Birch ply for example, is one of the strongest and most rigid plywoods. It will cut easily, and its edge can be planed to a good quality finish. Douglas fir however, is a much coarser grained plywood. It snags badly when sawn, and is difficult to plane to a good finish.

The type of **glue** used in the manufacture of the plywood will determine its use. Plywood suitable for exterior use or boat building must have waterproof glue.

Some examples of products made from plywood are shown here.

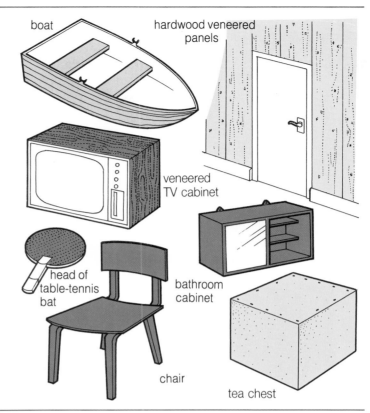

boat

hardwood veneered panels

veneered TV cabinet

head of table-tennis bat

bathroom cabinet

chair

tea chest

Chipboard (particle board)

Chipboard is made from chips (or particles) of wood, mixed with a synthetic glue. The mixture is squeezed between rollers and then dried between metal plates under high pressure and heat.

Because the particles criss-cross, chipboard has similar strength properties in both directions. Even so, it is a relatively weak material and will break under fairly low bending forces. However, the material is given considerable strength when its surface is covered with a veneer. Hardwood veneers and plastic coatings are common.

Chipboard will cut and machine easily, but it wears saw teeth and cutters quickly because of the high glue content. It can be jointed similarly to natural wood, but fixings should not be made into the edge – they will pull out easily. A hardwood edging strip (or lipping) should be fitted before attaching hinges and other fittings.

Some examples of products made from chipboard are shown here.

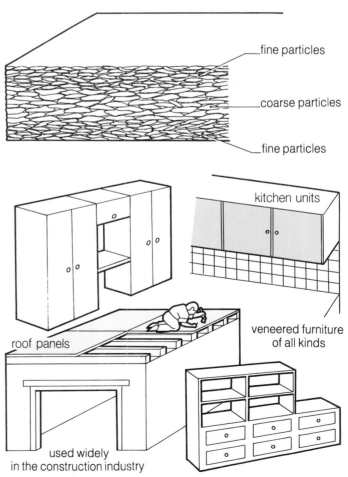

fine particles

coarse particles

fine particles

kitchen units

veneered furniture of all kinds

roof panels

used widely in the construction industry

Hardboard and its properties

Hardboard is made from softwood pulp which is formed into sheets under high pressure. **Standard hardboard** is smooth on one face whilst the reverse side has a rough mesh-like texture.

A variety of other forms are available including: double faced (smooth on both faces), perforated (pegboard for example), embossed (having a raised patterned surface) and so on. **Medium hardboard** (of which Sundeala is a well known example) is a softer and thicker board.

Although hardboard is a versatile sheet material, it has very little rigidity and must therefore be fixed to battens, or a solid surface, to prevent buckling. Untreated hardboard absorbs water readily, and is particularly susceptible to buckling.

Some examples of products made from hardboard are shown here.

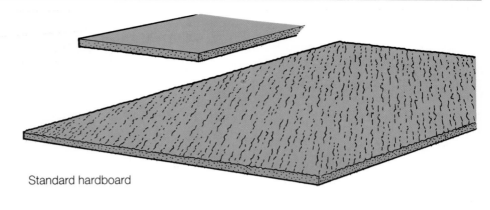

Standard hardboard

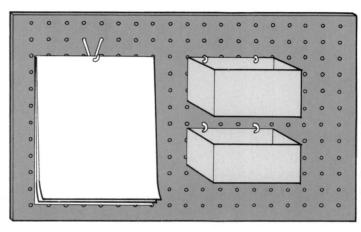

pegboard storage rack

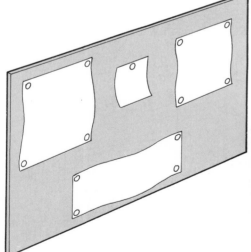

'Sundeala' noticeboard.

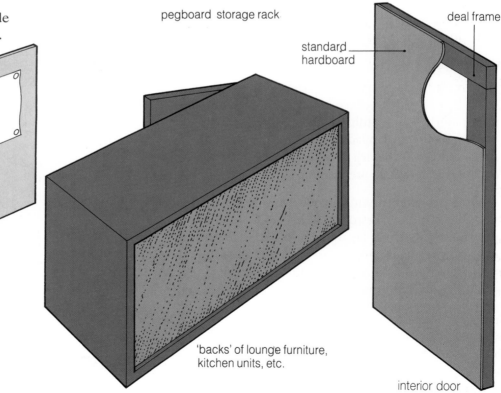

'backs' of lounge furniture, kitchen units, etc.

standard hardboard

deal frame

interior door

Industrial manufacturing with wood

Of all the construction materials, wood is the one most commonly used by the home DIY enthusiast. This is because wood can be worked and formed using relatively simple, inexpensive tools. In mass production however, most of the hand tool operations are carried out on specialist machines. Some of the more common industrial wood working processes are described below.

Sawing

Nearly every woodwork job begins with sawing. After sawing, some timbers are ready for assembly into finished products. Most however, are passed on for further processing on other machines.

Circular saws are used for 'through cutting', 'cross cutting' and 'trenching' for example.

Band saws are used mainly for 'through' and 'cross cutting'.

circular saw

fence

through cutting

adjustable tilting angles

bevel cross cutting

cross cut and trenching machine

Band saw

Planing

Planing is the process which most often follows sawing. Planing reduces the wood to **exact dimensions** leaving it flat and smooth.

Surface planers are used to prepare the 'face side' and 'face edges' of the timber. Thicknessers can then be used to plane the timber to an exact thickness. After planing, the next stage of production is often **moulding** or **joint cutting**.

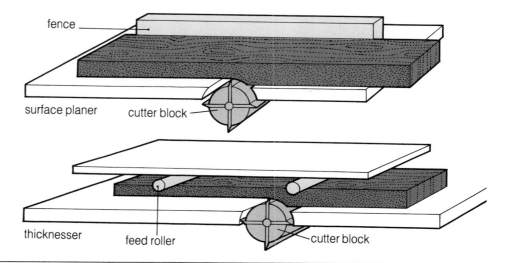

fence

surface planer   cutter block

thicknesser   feed roller   cutter block

Moulding

Moulding machines are used to produce a wide range of 'shaped' timbers called **mouldings**. These are then used in the manufacture of numerous other products.

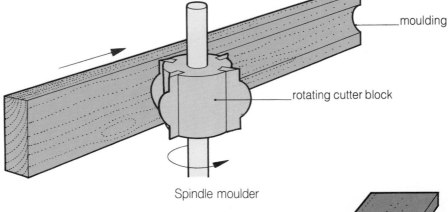

window sill   dowel   picture frame   staircase hand rail

Some common mouldings

Spindle moulders   These are used to machine a single face or edge on a previously planed timber.

Planer moulders   These machines first plane, and then produce a moulding in **one** through cutting operation. All four surfaces can be machined in one pass. Although moulding machines are very expensive, the products (the moulding) can be produced very rapidly and to very close tolerances. Further, a moulded section (such as a window sill) is a much more stable and durable product compared to a 'constructed' section.

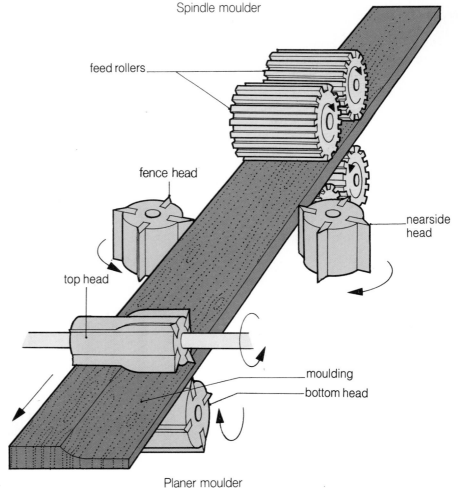

moulding

rotating cutter block

Spindle moulder

feed rollers

fence head

nearside head

top head

moulding

bottom head

Planer moulder

Joint cutting

The construction of a product from wood nearly always involves some form of jointing.

Many different types of joint are used which fall into the categories: **T** joints, **L** joints and **+** joints. The choice of joint will be dependent upon:
1 the task which the joint has to fulfil,
2 the nature of the material,
3 the appearance of the joint.

Some joint cutting machinery is shown here.

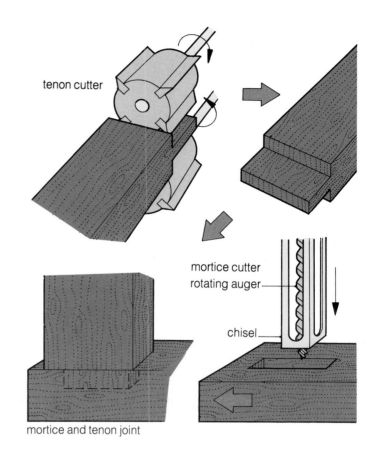

tenon cutter

mortice cutter
rotating auger

chisel

mortice and tenon joint

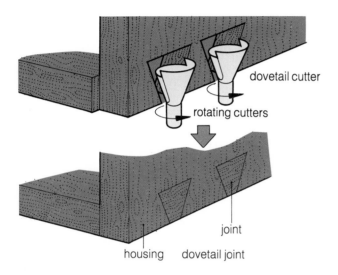

dovetail cutter

rotating cutters

joint

housing   dovetail joint

Routers

A router is a cutting tool whose operation can best be understood by looking at some of the many forms which can be manufactured.

A router's cutting tool (or profile cutter), is 'guided' (on the latest machines), by a computer.

CNC or **Computer Numerical Controlled** machines can be fully automated. This increases both the speed of production and the accuracy of the product.

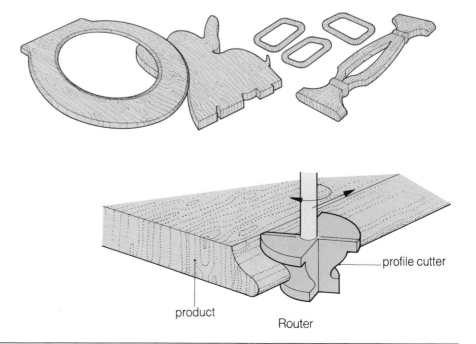

profile cutter

product

Router

Sanding

After assembly, most products are 'cleaned up' and given a very smooth surface by sanding. Disc, bobbin and belt sanders are all used for this purpose.

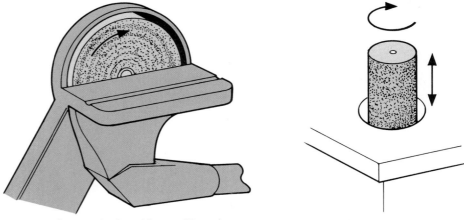

disc sander (used for small items)   bobbin sander (used for curved edges)

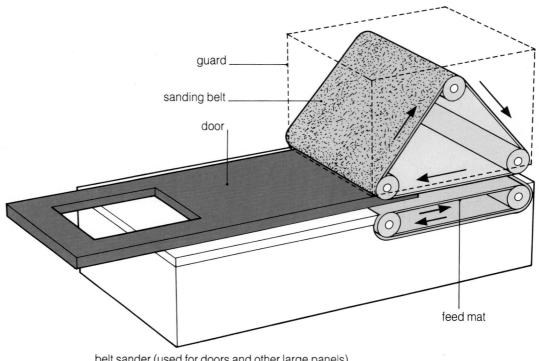

guard

sanding belt

door

feed mat

belt sander (used for doors and other large panels)

Finishing

After sanding the product may be 'finished' with a surface coating. The type of finish will depend upon: the type of wood, the required effect, and the function of the product.

Oil, varnish, paint and wax polish are some of the many types of finishes used on wood.

23 To choose the most suitable material for a particular product requires you to have a good knowledge of materials. See how much you know about **wood** by using the chart below. **Copy it** on to a piece of paper and 'fill in' the empty boxes (and also add to the other boxes if you can). Some of the information you require can be found in this chapter. For more detailed information you will need to use a more specialist book.

Name	Natural	Manu-factured	Colour	Properties	Common uses
pine (deal)	✔			fairly hard durable and quite stable cuts and machines easily finishes well	
			creamy white to light brown		hockey sticks garden tool handles hammer shafts
				fine even texture tough prone to twisting	staircases window boards step ladders
beech				close even grain very tough quite heavy and hard doesn't split easily no taste and odour	
			reddish-brown		veneered furniture solid furniture window and door frames
				some very stable available in large sheets of various thicknesses	cabinets small boats wall panels tea chests
			creamy and 'speckled'		roofing and flooring base material for knock down furniture

Questions

24 This 'peg basher' toy is made from **beech.**

What properties make beech particularly suitable for this product?

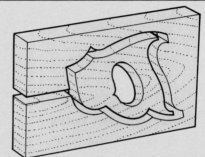

25 Some saw handles are made from **ash**.
   a What method of manufacture do you think was used to produce this handle?
   b What other wood might be suitable for making saw handles?

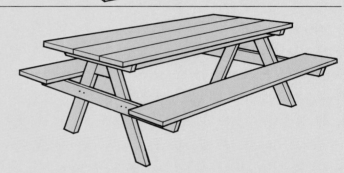

26 This picnic bench is made from **Scotch pine**. Would quarter sawn or plain sawn timbers be more suitable for this product? Explain your answer.

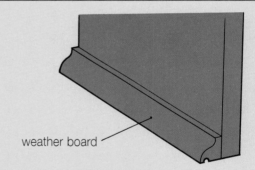

27 This exterior door is fitted with a weather board. How do you think this product was manufactured?

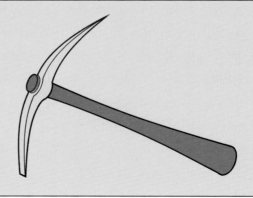

weather board

28 a What kind of wood might this pick-axe handle be made of?
   b What properties make your chosen material particularly suitable for this product?

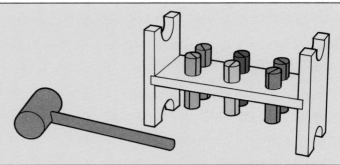

29 This gate is made from **red baltic pine**.
Why is parana pine unsuitable for this product?

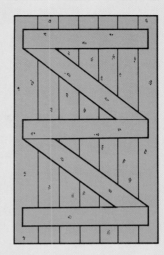

30 a What would be a suitable wood from which to
make these kitchen utensils?
b What properties make your chosen material
particularly suitable for these products?

Salad servers

31 Half of the world's tropical
rainforests have been destroyed
in the past 40 years. As well as
timber, the rainforests are the
main sources of chemical
compounds for medicines and
are home to half of the world's
species. Britain is the largest
European importer of tropical
timber, of which 5% is from well-
managed forests, where the
amount of timber felled is
carefully controlled. Uses of
tropical hardwoods include
some chipboards and plywoods,
veneers, doors, furniture,
window frames, coffins and
salad bowls.

As a consumer, what steps can
you take to preserve the tropical
rainforests?

Amazon rain forest

Plastics

ICI plastics division, Wilton, Cleveland

'Plastic-like' materials were first used thousands of years ago. These were the plastics which occurred in nature. **Amber** for example (a resinous substance from trees), was used by the Egyptians and other civilisations to make jewellery. Similarly, the **horns** of animals were used to make drinking vessels and simple instruments.

Today of course, numerous different plastics are available. Some are still made from natural materials (such as cellulose from plants), but most are made entirely from chemicals obtained from crude **oil** and, to a much lesser extent, coal.

It is the job of the plastics manufacturer to convert these chemicals into plastics. Product manufacturers then use these materials to produce goods.

The structure of plastics

One of the chemicals obtained from crude oil is the gas **ethene**. This can be used to make the well known plastic **polythene**.

If we look at how polythene is made, we can learn about the general structure of plastics and begin to understand their properties.

A simple explanation must begin with the understanding that all substances are made up of tiny units called **molecules**, and that each molecule is made up of minute particles called **atoms**. The ethene molecule is described here.

The ethene molecule

Molecules of course are invisible to the naked eye, but we can build models or make drawings to represent them.

A scientist might draw an ethene molecule like this. Notice that it is made up of two **carbon** atoms and four **hydrogen** atoms. In the drawing the lines (——) represent the chemical bonds which hold the atoms of the molecule together.

Ethene gas is made up of millions of these molecules which 'move around' quite freely, and with very little attraction for one another.

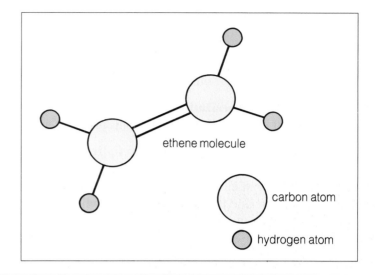

ethene molecule

carbon atom

hydrogen atom

How polythene is made

Polythene is made, by 'persuading' the free roaming ethene gas molecules to join together to form long chain polythene molecules. The persuasion is provided by chemicals known as **catalysts** or **initiators**. During the process many thousands of ethene molecules join together to form each molecule of polythene.

Now, although ethene gas molecules have very little attraction for one another, the newly formed polythene molecules **do attract one another** and become tangled and twisted together to form the **solid** – high density **polythene**.

Small molecules such as ethene, which can link together in this way, are called **monomers**. The process of joining molecules is called **polymerization**, and the products of polymerization – such as polythene – are called **polymers**.

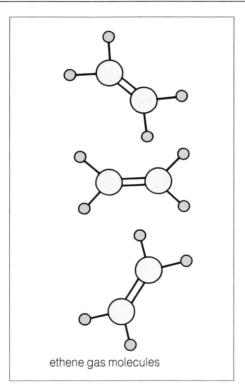

ethene gas molecules

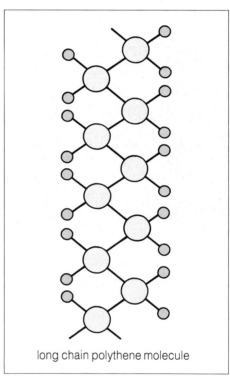

long chain polythene molecule

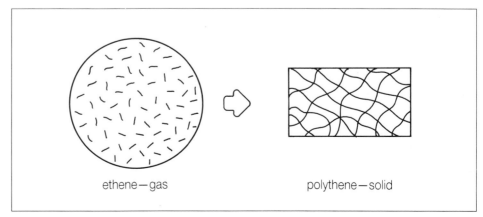

ethene – gas

polythene – solid

Types of polymerization

When a polymer is made as described above, the process is known as **addition polymerization** because molecules of the monomer 'join together' to form the long chain molecules.

Condensation polymerization is a different process which usually involves the joining of two different kinds of monomers.

By starting with different **monomers** therefore, and using different polymerization processes, a whole range of polymers (plastics) can be made. Even so, in each case the polymer formed will be made up of **long chain molecules**, and it is these molecules which give plastics the properties which we find so useful.

Plastics and their properties

The name 'plastic' describes a material which, at some point in its manufacture, behaves in a plastic or putty-like way. In other words, it will deform under pressure, and retain the 'new shape' when the pressure is removed.

Although there are many different kinds of plastic, there are just two main types: **thermoplastics** and **thermosetting plastics**.

Thermoplastics

Polythene, PVC and polystyrene are examples of thermoplastics. They soften on heating and can be moulded into shape. On cooling they harden again.

On heating, the molecules are given the energy to move apart. As a result the forces between the molecules become weaker. This allows them the freedom to slip over one another to form a new shape when under pressure. This process of softening and hardening can be repeated over and over again because the molecules in a thermoplastic are always free to behave in this way.

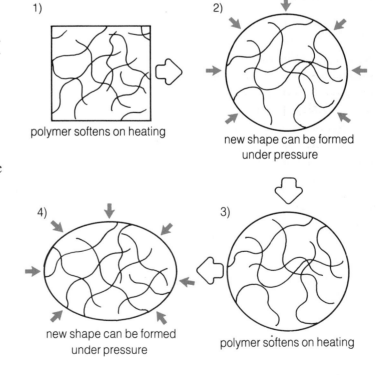

1) polymer softens on heating

2) new shape can be formed under pressure

3) polymer softens on heating

4) new shape can be formed under pressure

Thermosetting plastics

Phenol formaldehyde (Bakelite) and urea formaldehyde are examples of **thermosetting** plastics. These behave quite differently to the thermoplastics.

On first heating, the polymer softens and can be moulded into shape under pressure. However, the heat triggers a **chemical reaction** in which the molecules become permanently locked together. The reaction is known as **cross linking**. As a result the polymer becomes permanently 'set' and cannot be softened again by heating.

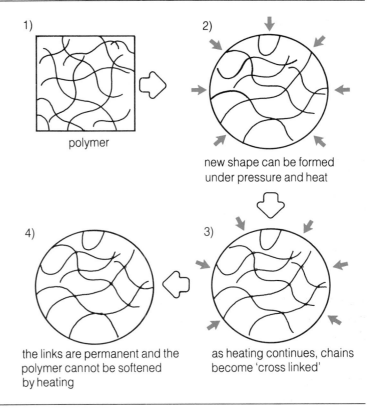

1) polymer

2) new shape can be formed under pressure and heat

3) as heating continues, chains become 'cross linked'

4) the links are permanent and the polymer cannot be softened by heating

Some examples of thermoplastics

Polythene (high density)

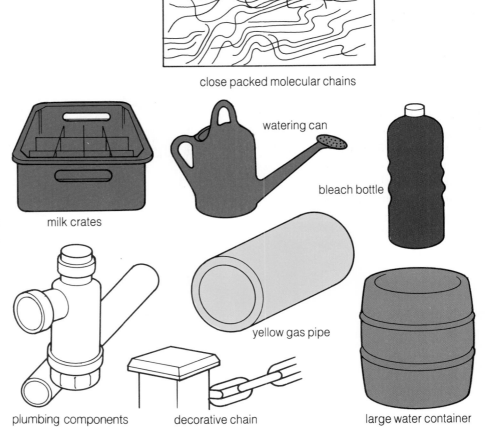

close packed molecular chains

High density polythene is made in such a way that the chains are 'straight'. This allows the molecules to **pack close together** to produce a high density material. (See density, page 200). Because the chains lie close together, they attract one another firmly and have less freedom to move.

The result is a fairly stiff, strong plastic which is also quite tough. It softens at a fairly high temperature (around 120–130°C), and is resistant to chemical attack.

Some examples of the many products made from high density polythene are shown here.

milk crates

watering can

bleach bottle

plumbing components

decorative chain

yellow gas pipe

large water container

Polythene (low density)

Low density polythene is made by a process which produces **side branches** on the chains. These branches prevent the chains from packing close together. As a result, they are less firmly attracted to one another, and the polymer is weaker, softer and more flexible than high density polythene. Less energy is required to separate the chains and therefore the polymer softens at a lower temperature (around 85°C). The polymer can be transparent or opaque. It is a very good electrical insulator.

We 'consume' more low density polythene than any other polymer.

Some of its many uses are shown here.

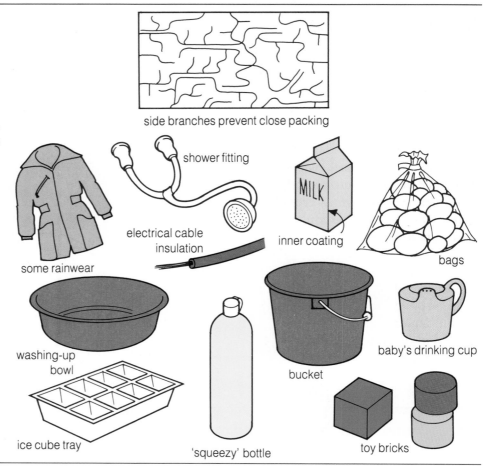

side branches prevent close packing

shower fitting

electrical cable insulation

some rainwear

inner coating

MILK

bags

washing-up bowl

bucket

baby's drinking cup

ice cube tray

'squeezy' bottle

toy bricks

Polypropylene

Polypropylene belongs to the same family of plastics as the polythenes. It is tougher however, and more rigid than high density polythene. It also has a greater resistance to heat – it softens at around 150°C. Polypropylene has the lowest density of the thermoplastics, and yet it has a very high impact strength. Its ability to be flexed many thousands of times without breaking is another valuable characteristic.

Some examples of the many products made from polypropylene are shown here.

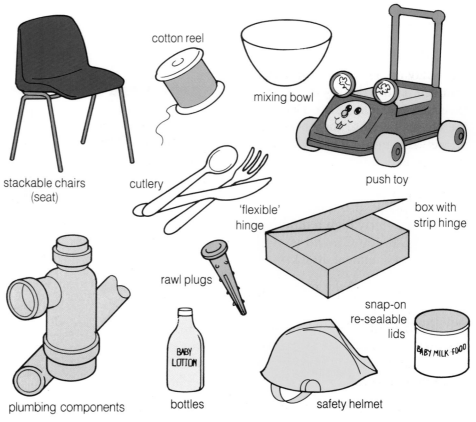

cotton reel

mixing bowl

stackable chairs (seat)

cutlery

push toy

'flexible' hinge

box with strip hinge

rawl plugs

snap-on re-sealable lids

plumbing components

BABY LOTION

bottles

safety helmet

BABY MILK FOOD

Polyvinyl chloride (PVC)

PVC can be produced to give a range of properties. The stiff, hard wearing PVC used to make drain pipes and guttering is one example. A more flexible and rubbery material can be produced by adding a **plasticiser** to the PVC.

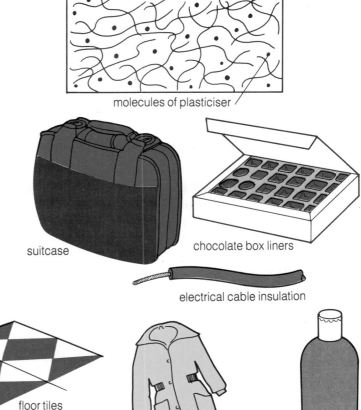

molecules of plasticiser

The plasticiser chemical has molecules which are much smaller than those of the polymer. Their effect is to **separate the polymer chains** making them attract each other less strongly. As a result they slide more easily over one another and the polymer becomes more soft and pliable. PVC is used in its softer forms as an insulator for electrical cables, and in the manufacture of some rainwear. PVC containing a higher proportion of plasticiser is used to coat cloth in the production of 'leathercloth'. This tough, flexible material is used to cover some motor car seats, and in the manufacture of furniture and handbags for example.

suitcase

chocolate box liners

electrical cable insulation

garden hose pipe

floor tiles

waterproof clothing

bottles

Acrylics

Probably the most familiar acrylic plastic is the sheet material known by its trade name **Perspex**. The polymer is called polymethyl methacrylate. It can have a glass-like transparency or be opaque. Both forms can be coloured with pigments. It is fairly hard wearing and will not shatter. However, it can crack and is fairly easily scratched. It can be formed, bent and twisted when heated to temperatures between 165 and 175°C. In its cold state Perspex is quite brittle and care must be taken to avoid cracking when it is cut or drilled.

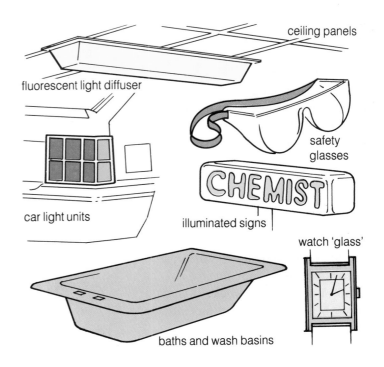

ceiling panels

fluorescent light diffuser

car light units

safety glasses

CHEMIST

illuminated signs

watch 'glass'

baths and wash basins

Acrylic is also produced in granule form for use in injection moulding machines. (See page 250.) For this purpose the methyl methacrylate is polymerized in a different way from that used for Perspex. The polymer obtained softens more readily, and in this form is known as **acrylic moulding powder**.

Some examples of the uses of acrylic are shown here.

Nylon

Many different types of nylon are produced, which are identified with a number: type 6.6 and type 6.10 for example.

Nylon is probably best known in the form of a **fibre** and is widely used in the manufacture of clothing, carpets and brushes for example. It is a fairly hard material with a good resistance to wear and a high degree of resistance to chemical attack.

'Solid' nylon is widely used for engineering purposes. It is particularly useful for making fast moving parts such as gears and bearings. It wears well, has low frictional properties, and has a fairly high melting point. In this form it is usually a creamy white colour.

Some examples of the many products made from nylon are shown here.

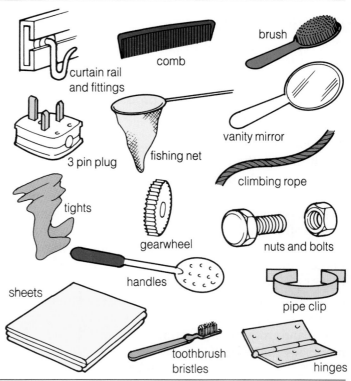

curtain rail and fittings
comb
brush
3 pin plug
fishing net
vanity mirror
climbing rope
tights
gearwheel
nuts and bolts
handles
sheets
pipe clip
toothbrush bristles
hinges

Polystyrene

Polystyrene is available in several forms but is most common as a crystal clear solid, and a 'foamed' plastic known as expanded polystyrene.

In its 'solid' form it is very brittle and can be identified by the metallic ring it makes when dropped. In this form it is used to make a wide range of products, including containers and packaging.

Expanded polystyrene is soft and spongy. During manufacture a gas is produced which becomes trapped within its honeycomb structure. This gives the material good heat insulating properties. It is a very low density material, and because of its spongy nature is very good at absorbing shock. It is used a great deal in the building trade as an insulating material, and is widely used in packaging.

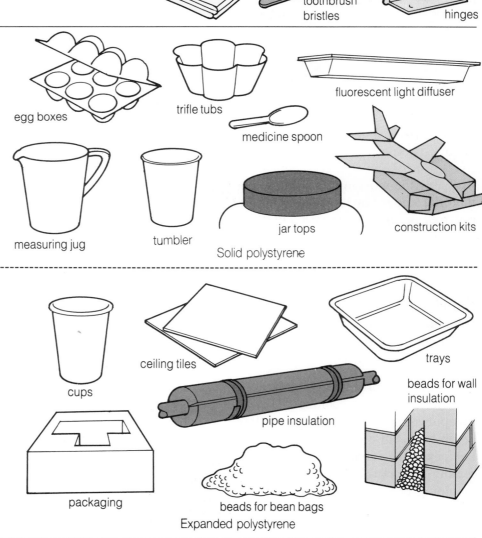

egg boxes
trifle tubs
fluorescent light diffuser
medicine spoon
measuring jug
tumbler
jar tops
construction kits
Solid polystyrene

cups
ceiling tiles
trays
beads for wall insulation
pipe insulation
packaging
beads for bean bags
Expanded polystyrene

Some thermosetting plastics

Phenol formaldehyde (Bakelite)

The first plastic to be made artificially from chemicals was **Bakelite** (named after the man who first made it in 1909 – Leo Baekeland).

It is a hard, brittle plastic with a natural **dark** glossy colour. As it is a 'thermoset' plastic it resists heat without softening (see page 243) and is a good thermal insulator. However, at very high temperatures it will char and decompose. Bakelite is a good electrical insulator.

Despite its dark colour, it has many applications. Some examples are shown here.

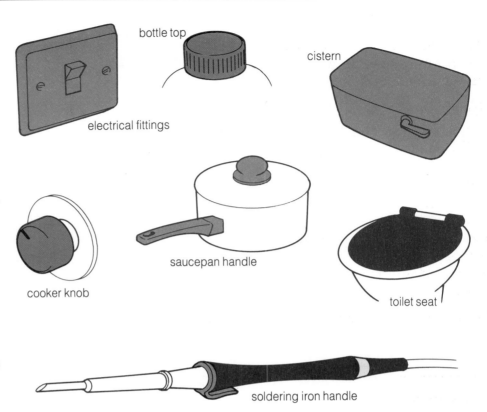

Urea formaldehyde

Unlike Bakelite, urea formaldehyde is a colourless polymer. It can therefore be coloured artificially with pigments to produce articles in a wide range of colours. It is harder than Bakelite and has no taste or odour. It is a good thermal and electrical insulator.

Some examples of products made from this material are shown here.

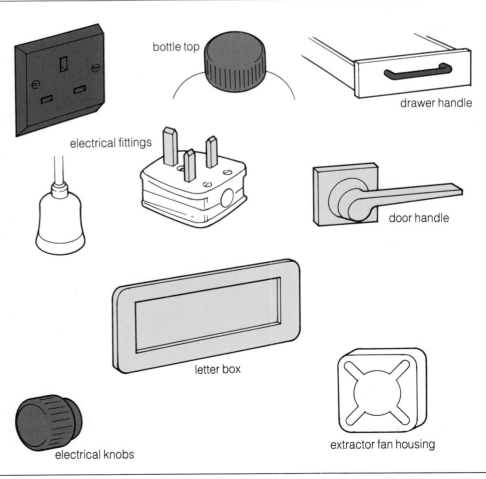

Melamine formaldehyde

This polymer has similar properties to urea formaldehyde and is used in the manufacture of high quality tableware. Its heat resistant properties make it particularly suitable for the surfaces of laminated kitchen worktops.

unbreakable tableware

handles

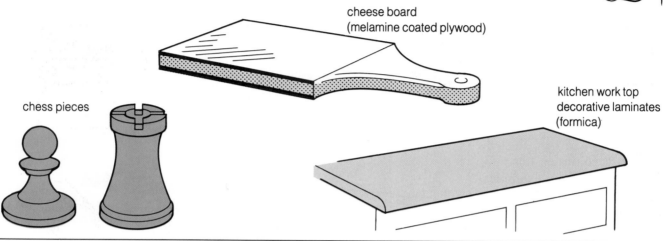

cheese board
(melamine coated plywood)

chess pieces

kitchen work top
decorative laminates
(formica)

Polyester resin

Polyester resin is one example of a thermosetting plastic which **polymerizes at room temperature**.

The resin, (a treacle-like substance) and a chemical known as a hardener, are mixed just before use. When set the plastic is stiff, hard and brittle. To add strength and bulk, it is often reinforced with **glass fibre** to make glass reinforced plastic (GRP).

Some examples of its uses are shown here.

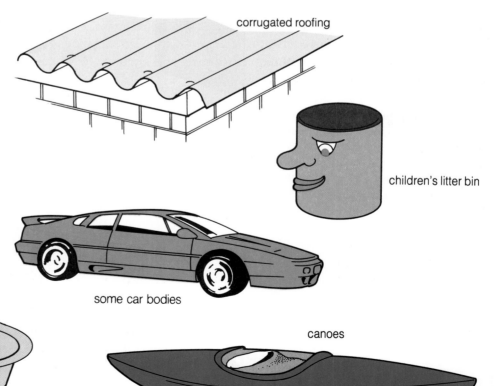

corrugated roofing

children's litter bin

some car bodies

canoes

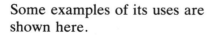

garden ponds and swimming pools

Manufacturing with plastics

Plastic raw materials are available in a variety of forms including powders, viscous fluids, pellets and granules. Product manufacturers use a wide range of processing machinery to convert these materials into components and products. Some of this machinery is described below.

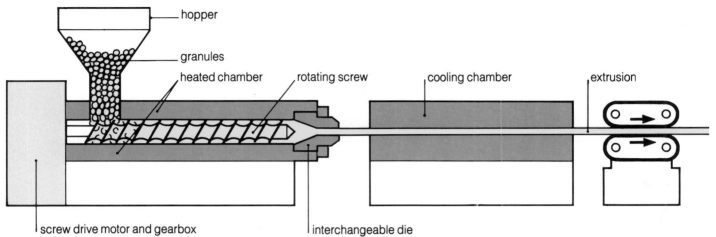

Extrusion

This is the process used to make 'long' products like drain-pipes and curtain rails. Plastic granules are fed from a hopper on to a rotating screw. The screw forces the plastic through a heated tube where it becomes molten before being forced under pressure through a die. The die contains a hole whose shape corresponds to that of the required article. As it leaves the die, the 'extrusion' is cooled in a water bath or in jets of air. The hardened extrusion is then cut into lengths or coiled, depending on the product. Thermoplastics such as polythene, PVC and nylon are commonly used in extrusion.

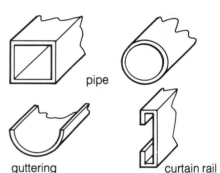

Some common extrusions

Extrusion blow-moulding

This process is used for making articles like bottles and hollow toys.

Air is blown into a section of extruded plastic tube, causing it to expand and take up the shape of the mould. The mould is then opened and the product removed.

PVC, polythene and polypropylene are common blow-moulding materials.

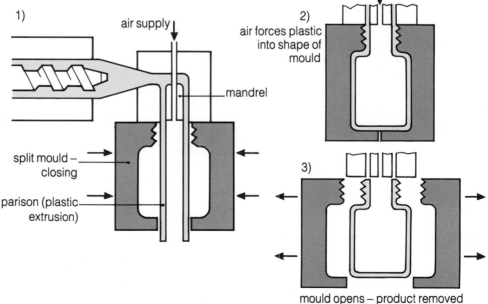

Injection moulding

This is the process of forming articles by injecting **molten** plastic into a mould. An injection moulding machine is similar to that used for extrusion, the difference being that the feed screw (in addition to feeding plastic from the hopper) is used as a ram. The screw is moved backwards, as it rotates, until a measured quantity of plastic is at position **A** in the diagram. The screw is then driven forwards by a hydraulic ram, forcing the molten plastic into the mould.

The mould consists of two or more parts which fit together forming a cavity of the required shape. Cold water is circulated through the body of the mould to reduce the cooling time of the moulding. After a short time the mould can be opened and the moulding removed. The complete cycle can then be repeated.

Injection moulding produces components and products which have consistently accurate dimensions and a high quality finish. A wide range of complex forms can be produced which could otherwise only be manufactured by expensive machining processes. Production is fast and the process produces very little waste.

An enormous range of products are manufactured in this way. These include:

- kitchenware – pedal bins, bowls, buckets, jugs, cutlery and containers;
- cases for electrical appliances – hairdryers, vacuum cleaners, food mixers etc;
- toys and games;
- products for the car industry;
- component parts for many other products.

Polythene, polystyrene, polypropylene and nylon are typical injection moulding materials.

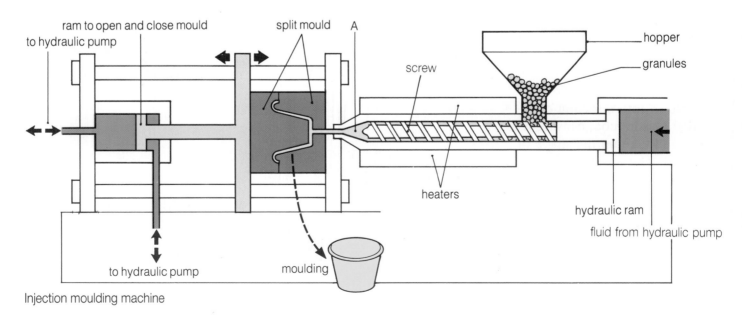

Injection moulding machine

Compression moulding

In compression moulding, huge forces are used to squeeze a measured quantity of polymer into shape between **heated** moulds.

The polymer can be in the form of a powder or 'slug'. A slug is simply powder which has been compressed into a cube shape. Slugs can be handled more easily than powder, and can be pre-heated in a high frequency oven. This reduces the 'cycle time' in the moulding machine.

Compression moulding is used for **thermosetting** plastics. The heat from the mould triggers the chemical reaction known as 'cross-linking' (see page 243).

After a short period of time (known as the curing time), the cross-linking is complete and the mould can be opened and the moulding removed. The mouldings have a high quality finish requiring only the removal of 'flash'.

Electrical fittings (plugs and sockets for example), saucepan and cutlery handles, bottle tops and toilet seats are just a few of the many products which are manufactured in this way.

Phenol, urea, and melamine formaldehyde are typical compression moulding materials.

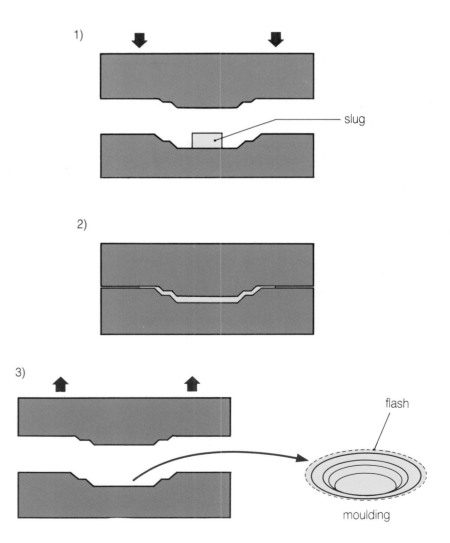

Vacuum forming

This is one of the processes used to make articles from **thermoplastic sheet**. The sheet is first cut to size and clamped above a mould. A heater then raises the temperature of the sheet until it becomes soft and rubbery.

Finally, air is evacuated from beneath the sheet. This allows the normal 'outside' air pressure to push down on the softened sheet, forcing it to take up the shape of the mould.

After a suitable cooling period, the hardened moulding can be removed from the mould.

The process described above is used mainly for shallow products made from thin sheet. When large or complex mouldings are produced using thicker sheet, a pressure chamber may also be used above the sheet. Vacuum forming enables **large** irregular shaped mouldings to be produced which could not be manufactured by any other plastic forming process. Further, the equipment is relatively cheap and requires the use of only one mould.

Products manufactured in this way include

- egg boxes, chocolate box liners and numerous other food and confectionery packaging
- seed trays
- shop signs and fittings
- some motor car dashboards
- wash basins and baths.

Acrylic, polystyrene, and PVC are typical vacuum forming materials.

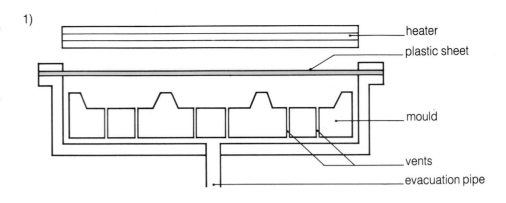

1)

heater
plastic sheet
mould
vents
evacuation pipe

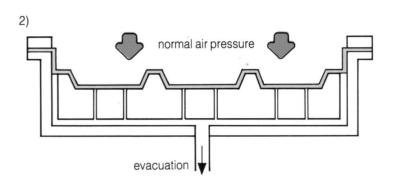

2)

normal air pressure

evacuation

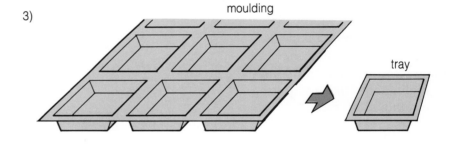

3)

moulding

tray

32 To choose the most suitable material for a particular product requires you to
have a good knowledge of materials. See how much you know about **plastics**
by using the chart below. **Copy it** on to a piece of paper and 'fill in' the empty
boxes (and also add to the other boxes if you can). Some of the information
you require can be found in this chapter. For more detailed information you will
need to use a more specialist book.

Name	Thermo-plastic	Thermo-setting plastic	Properties	Common uses
high density polythene	✔		hard and stiff quite tough softens at around 120–130°C	
				garden hose electrical cable insulation waterproof clothing floor tiles door and window frames
		✔	very hard and brittle good thermal insulator dark glossy colour	
			rigid high impact strength softens at around 150°C has the lowest density of the thermoplastics can be flexed many times without breaking	
	✔			plastic bags and sheets squeezy bottles hollow toys buckets and bowls
	✔		available in fibre and 'solid' form hard and tough good resistance to chemical attack low frictional properties hard wearing	
acrylic				
			stiff, hard and brittle	(when reinforced with glass fibre) canoes, garden ponds some car bodies

Questions

33 Fish and chips are often served on expanded polystyrene trays. Hot water pipes are sometimes enclosed in expanded polystyrene 'sleeves'.

What property makes this material particularly suitable for these applications?

34 Some car bumpers are injection moulded in **polypropylene**.

a What properties make this material particularly suitable for this product?

b Why is injection moulding unlikely to be used for short production runs?

35 This garden hose is made of PVC.

What method of manufacture would have been used to make it?

36 The handle of this saucepan was compression moulded in **urea formaldehyde**.

Why is this material particularly well suited to this application?

37 Electrical cable is made by extruding a plastic coat on to copper wire.

Name two plastics which are used for this purpose.

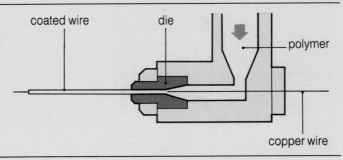

coated wire   die   polymer

copper wire

38 The body of the 3 pin plug labelled **A** is made of **nylon 6.6**. Plug **B** is made of **phenol formaldehyde**.

What method of manufacture would have been used for each of these products?

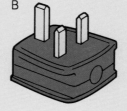
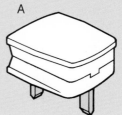

B   A

39 This washing-up bowl is made of **low density polythene**.

How do you think it was manufactured?

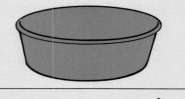

---

40 This 'squeezy' tomato ketchup bottle is made of **polythene**.

  a From which kind of polythene would it be made?
  b What method of manufacture do you think was used to produce this product?

---

41 This patio door unit was fabricated from a very stiff **PVC** called uPVC. A cross section of part of the door unit is shown inset.

  a What do you think the 'u' stands for?
  b What method of manufacture do you think was used to produce the plastic members?

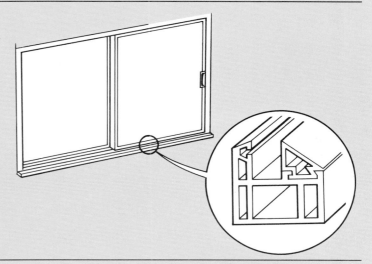

---

42 When **expanded polystyrene** is destroyed it releases chlorofluorocarbon gases (CFCs). Evidence suggests that these CFCs (which are also used as propellent gases in some aerosol cans) damage the ozone layer – a layer of ozone gas in the earth's atmosphere which soaks up ultra violet rays from the sun and prevents lethal levels of radiation from reaching the earth.

Below are some common uses for expanded polystyrene.

  a Lagging for hot water pipes.
  b Take-away food boxes and trays.
  c Packaging for electrical equipment.
  d Egg boxes.

Can you think of an alternative material which could be used successfully in each of these cases?

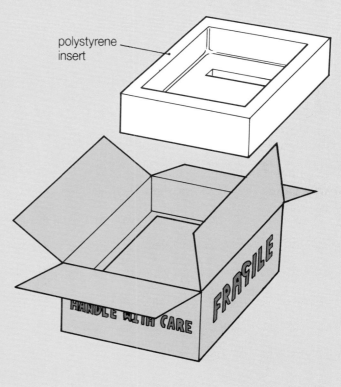

polystyrene insert

Working with materials at school

Marking out

When you have decided which material, or materials to use for a particular 'job', those materials will need **marking out**.

Accurate marking out is very important. It helps to ensure that the different parts fit together correctly and that the final product looks good.

Refer to your working drawings when marking out

Straight edges

Marking out usually starts from a straight edge.

If the material doesn't have one, you will need to make one using a file, plane or disc sander for example.

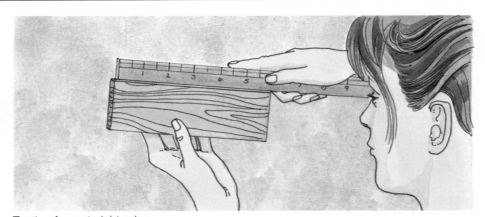

Testing for a straight edge

Right angles and parallel lines

Lines which need to be at 90° to the straight edge can be marked out using a **try square** and a scriber, marking knife or pencil.

Parallel lines can be made using a **marking gauge** on wood and with **odd leg callipers** on metal and plastic.

use a marking knife on wood

try square
scriber

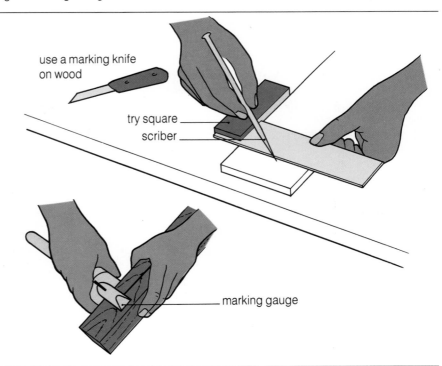

odd leg callipers

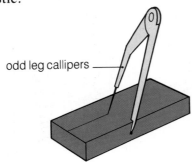

marking gauge

Circles

Circles, or parts of circles can be marked out using a pair of **compasses** or **dividers**.

To prevent the dividers slipping on metal and plastics, a small dent should be made at the 'centre' of the curve using a centre punch.

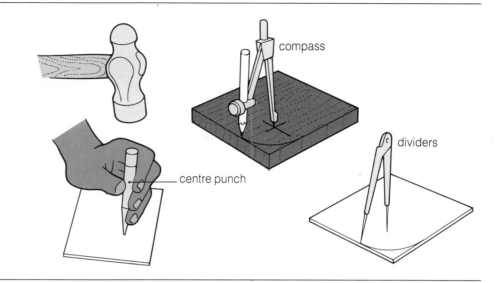

centre punch

compass

dividers

Centres

When preparing to drill a hole, you will need to mark out the hole's centre using a ruler.

The centre of the end of a round bar can be found using a **centre square**. On the end of a square or rectangular bar the centre can be found using diagonal lines.

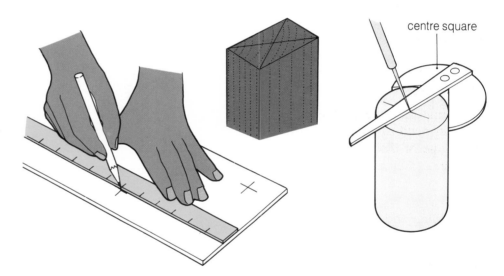

centre square

Irregular shapes

When you need to mark out an irregular shape, it is sometimes useful to use a **template**.

A template can be made from cardboard for example, around which you can **draw** the shape. Alternatively a paper template can be 'stuck' onto the material to act as the guide when cutting.

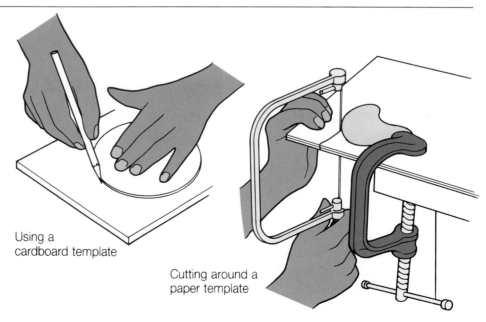

Using a cardboard template

Cutting around a paper template

Shaping materials

Shaping metal

Sawing

This is often the first process to be used when shaping metal. A **hacksaw** with the appropriate number of teeth on its blade should be selected. (See diagrams.)

For very fine work a **junior hacksaw** can be used. **Abrafiles** are used for cutting curves. The blade is actually a very fine round file.

Always hold the material firmly in a vice (or using a G cramp) and position it so that you cut as close to the vice as possible. This reduces vibration.

Sawing produces a rough surface, so cut on the waste side of the line and finally smooth down to the line by filing.

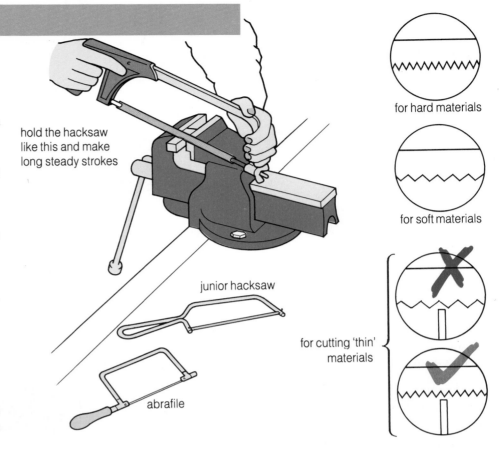

hold the hacksaw like this and make long steady strokes

junior hacksaw

abrafile

for hard materials

for soft materials

for cutting 'thin' materials

Filing

Cross-filing and **draw-filing** are the two basic operations used to produce a straight edge on a piece of metal.

Cross-filing is used to remove waste material. Draw-filing produces a final smooth finish.

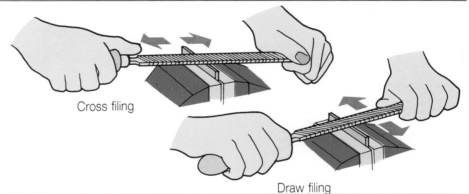

Cross filing

Draw filing

Types of files and their uses

A range of different files are available. Some of the more common types are shown here.

You should always select the most suitable file for the job. For example, when removing a lot of waste material use a coarse file (a file with large teeth). Use a fine file for smoothing and finishing. When filing a long edge, use a broad file, and so on. Small shapes can be produced using a round, square, or 'triangular' file as required.

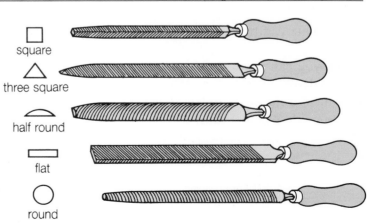

square

three square

half round

flat

round

Shearing

Shears (or tinsnips) can be used for cutting and shaping thin metals.

Note   Take care – sheared metals can be very sharp. They usually require finishing by filing.

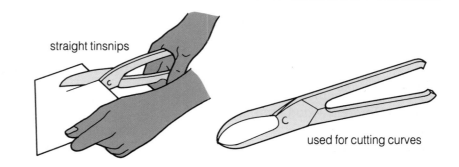

straight tinsnips

used for cutting curves

Bending

After marking out, sheet metal can be shaped by folding. This can be done using a special folding bar (or alternatively, pieces of strong metal) clamped in a vice.

The bending force can be applied using a heavy mallet. To prevent damage to the metal, use a piece of scrap wood as shown.

Note   If a piece of metal is to be bent in several places, the **order** in which the bends are made is often important – so check!

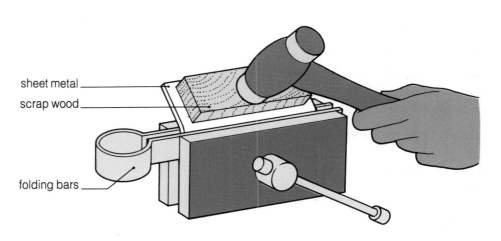

sheet metal

scrap wood

folding bars

Drilling

Drills are used to produce round holes in a material. After marking out the hole's centre, use a centre punch to make a small dent in the metal – this will prevent the drill from slipping.

Whether using a drilling machine or hand drill, always clamp work securely using a hand vice, machine vice or G cramp.

Safety note   If you fail to do this, and the drill jams (when using a drilling machine), the metal will spin and this could cause you serious injury.

Other metal shaping and forming operations include **lathework** (see page 217) and **casting** (see page 216).

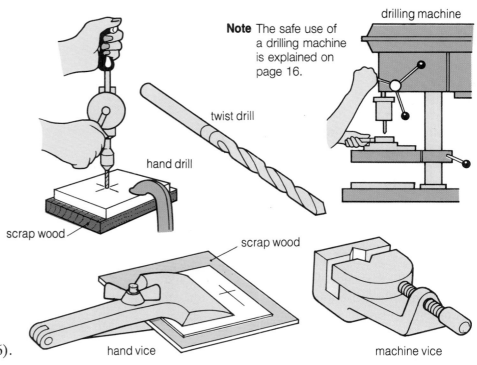

hand drill

scrap wood

twist drill

Note The safe use of a drilling machine is explained on page 16.

drilling machine

scrap wood

hand vice

machine vice

Shaping wood

Sawing

This is usually the first process to be used when shaping wood. A range of different wood cutting saws are available.

A **tenon** saw is used for making short straight cuts – it has a stiff metal back which holds the blade straight and firm.

Hand saws are used for cutting long lengths or sheets of wood. Small curves can be cut with a **coping saw** whose blade can be turned in the frame to allow access to awkward places.

Always hold the work firmly using a vice, bench hook, or G cramp.

Sawing always produces a rough surface, so cut on the waste side of the line and, where required, plane to a smooth finish.

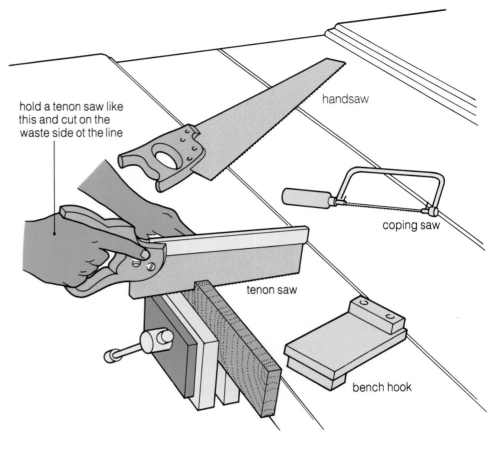

hold a tenon saw like this and cut on the waste side of the line

handsaw

coping saw

tenon saw

bench hook

Planing

Planing is carried out to remove excess wood and to produce a smooth surface finish.

The two most common planes are shown here.

The **jack plane** is heavier and longer than the smoothing plane. It is used for removing excess wood and for producing a smooth surface on **longer** pieces of timber. The **smoothing** plane is a general purpose plane and, as its name suggests, is used for smoothing – particularly on smaller pieces of work.

jack plane

smoothing plane

press

push

at the end of the cut, raise the plane like this whilst holding the back pressed down

Use a plane like this

Useful tips for planing

1 The surface of some types of wood 'roughs up' when planing. When this happens, try planing in the opposite direction.

2 Planing **end grain** often causes the wood to split (as shown). To prevent this, either plane from both ends towards the centre, or clamp pieces of scrap wood to the work as shown.

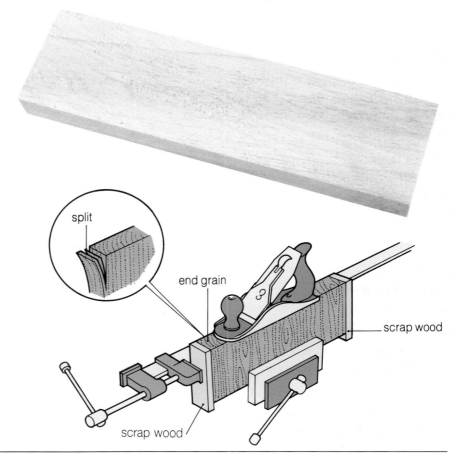

split

end grain

scrap wood

scrap wood

Chisels and their uses

Chisels are used for removing small amounts of wood, often between saw cuts. A chisel can be 'pushed' by hand for fine controlled chiselling, or hit with a wooden mallet.

Two basic types of chisel are used, the **firmer chisel** and the **bevel-edged chisel**. The bevel-edged chisel is the weaker of the two, but its shape allows it to be used in difficult corners.

Safety note   Keep both hands *behind* the chisel's cutting edge at all times.

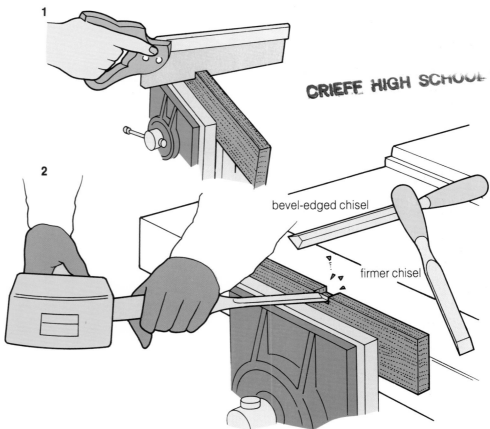

1

2

CRIEFF HIGH SCHOOL

bevel-edged chisel

firmer chisel

261

Shaping plastics

Sawing

Acrylic (e.g. Perspex) is probably the most common plastic used in schools, although nylon and other plastics find many uses.

Any of the saws shown here can be used for cutting acrylic. To prevent breaking however, it is important to hold the material firmly, and to regularly move the work so that it is always being gripped in the area of cutting.

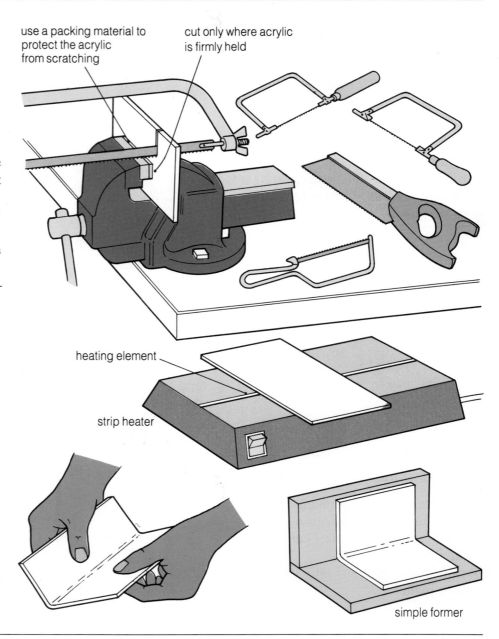

use a packing material to protect the acrylic from scratching

cut only where acrylic is firmly held

heating element

strip heater

simple former

Bending

Acrylic sheet is ideally suited to bending because it is a thermoplastic and softens on heating.

After marking out, acrylic can be prepared for bending using a strip heater. This consists of an electric heating element mounted below a narrow opening in a heat resistant material.

The plastic should be turned frequently to ensure even heating and to prevent burning. When the plastic is soft enough it can be bent into the required shape 'freehand' or using a former.

Vacuum forming

This is a common industrial process which can be carried out in school using relatively inexpensive equipment. The process is used to produce 'hollow' shapes from sheet plastic (see page 252).

School vacuum-forming machine

Fabrication

Fabrication is the 'putting together' of materials and components to make structures or products.

There are basically three different types of **joint** used for 'fixing' things together. These are **permanent joints, temporary joints** and **moveable joints**.

Some examples of each are shown here.

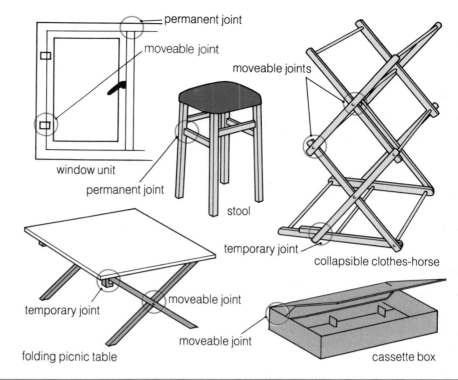

permanent joint

moveable joint

window unit

permanent joint

moveable joints

stool

temporary joint

collapsible clothes-horse

temporary joint

moveable joint

folding picnic table

moveable joint

cassette box

Permanent joints in wood

Many products made from wood are in the form of a **box** structure. These include book cases, drawer units, wardrobes, cabinets etc.

Some examples of the **joints** used in box structures are shown here.

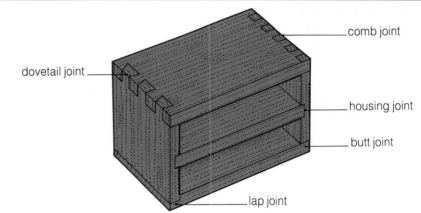

comb joint

dovetail joint

housing joint

butt joint

lap joint

Other products such as chairs, doors, step ladders, stools etc, are examples of **frame** structures.

The diagram shows some examples of frame joints.

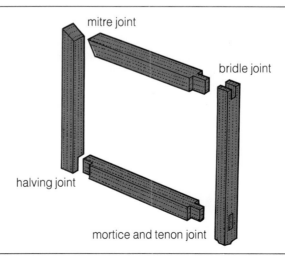

mitre joint

bridle joint

halving joint

mortice and tenon joint

Gluing wood

Most wooden joints are assembled with glue. Glue of course produces a **permanent joint**.

Some joints rely on glue alone and these must be held together firmly until the glue has set.

Other joints are a combination of glue and nails or screws. These do not require clamping but must be left undisturbed until the glue has set.

Nails are produced in many shapes and sizes and are usually made from mild steel. Some examples are shown here.

Screws produce a stronger joint than nails because they 'pull' the joint together. They all have the same basic shape but have different heads. They are most commonly available in mild steel and brass (which may be plated).

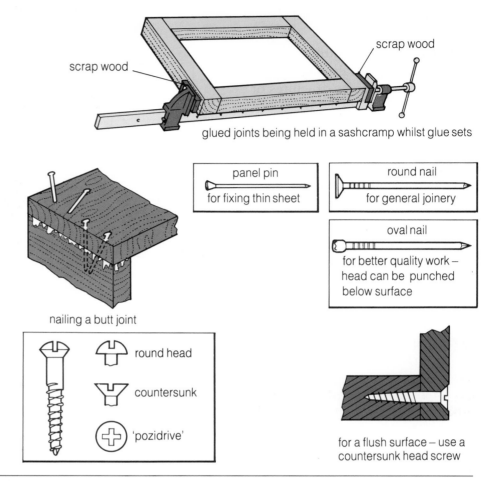

glued joints being held in a sashcramp whilst glue sets

scrap wood

scrap wood

nailing a butt joint

panel pin
for fixing thin sheet

round nail
for general joinery

oval nail
for better quality work – head can be punched below surface

round head

countersunk

'pozidrive'

for a flush surface – use a countersunk head screw

Wood glues

PVA (polyvinylacetate) is a very convenient wood glue. It can be used straight out of the container, but requires 3 to 4 hours to dry. The 'original' PVA is not waterproof and therefore cannot be used for products which come into contact with water. However, a waterproof PVA is now available.

Cascamite is a long established waterproof glue. It is a synthetic resin used where greater strength and water resistance are required. However, it is less convenient to use – it requires mixing with water, but dries within 1 to 2 hours.

Hot glue, delivered by an electrically heated glue gun, is a useful adhesive although not terribly strong. The glue sets very quickly and therefore is only practical for small areas.

PVA

CASCAMITE

mix to a thick paste

gluestick

gluegun

Permanent joints in metal

Soldering

This is the joining of metals with melted solder. A permanent joint is formed on cooling – the strength of the joint being determined by the type of solder used.

Soft soldering

Soft solders are tin–lead alloys. A general purpose solder for use in a school metalwork shop would have a melting point around 230°C. Being a relatively soft substance, it is used mainly for joining thin metals and only produces a relatively weak joint. Most metals can be soldered – but not aluminium.

It is essential that the materials to be joined are thoroughly cleaned. A flux is then applied to keep the materials clean and to help the solder flow into the joint. The complete soldering process (using a gas torch) is illustrated here. For very thin metals a process using a soldering bit would be used.

1 Clean the surfaces to be joined with wire wool or emery cloth.

2 Apply flux to the cleaned surfaces.

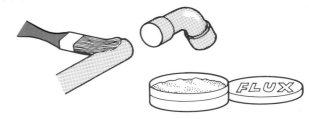

3 Heat the joint. When the metal is hot enough, the solder can be touched on to the joint where it will melt and flow on to the fluxed metal.

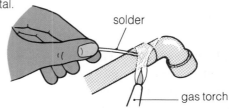

solder

gas torch

4 Allow the joint to cool.

Soft soldering a pipe fitting

Silver soldering and brazing

Silver solders are alloys of copper, zinc and silver having a melting point between 600 and 800°C. They are used for producing strong, ductile joints in copper, brass and in jewellery work.

Brazing (or hard soldering) makes use of copper–zinc alloys. They are melted at temperatures between 850 and 900°C and produce very strong joints. The process is usually confined to ferrous metals in school but can be successfully used for copper.

Both the above processes follow the stages described opposite.

1 Make sure that the surfaces to be joined are a good fit and are clean.
2 Apply a suitable flux.
3 Where necessary, 'wire' materials together to prevent movement.
4 Position the job on a brazing hearth surrounded by bricks.
5 Bring the joint quickly up to red heat, after first warming up the surrounding metal.
6 Apply solder or brazing rod until the joint is made.
7 Allow the job to cool – then dip into cold water.

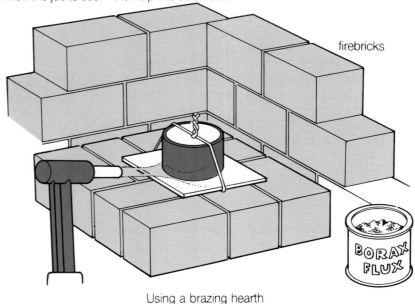

firebricks

BORAX FLUX

Using a brazing hearth

Welding

When metals are welded, the pieces to be joined are raised to a high temperature and are **fused** together.

Oxyacetylene welding uses burning gases to produce the heat needed for welding. A mixture of acetylene and oxygen in equal quantities produces a temperature around 3150°C. Welding rod is used to provide the extra metal needed to produce a good joint.

In **arc welding** an electric current is made to 'jump' a gap between an **electrode** and the metal being welded, producing a temperature in the region of 3600°C. The heat of the arc melts the electrode and droplets of metal are forced across the arc and onto the metal, forming a weld.

Safety note   When welding, special goggles, or masks (having 'coloured' glass) *must be worn* to protect the eyes from the glare from the flame or arc. A leather apron and gloves should also be worn to protect against molten metal and flying sparks.

Gas welding

Arc welding

Riveting

Although large scale riveting has been replaced by welding in industry, riveting is still a useful fabrication technique for some school work.

Riveting involves 'trapping together' the pieces of metal to be joined, using metal rivets of the same material.

Countersunk riveting is used when a flush surface is required. The riveting process is illustrated here.

Round or **'snap' head riveting** produces a stronger join than countersunk, but has the disadvantage of leaving the heads protruding above the work surface. Additional simple tools are also required for this process.

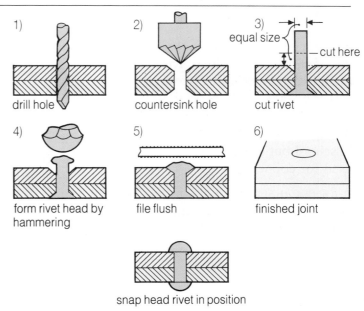

1) drill hole

2) countersink hole

3) equal size — cut here — cut rivet

4) form rivet head by hammering

5) file flush

6) finished joint

snap head rivet in position

Pop riveting is a much quicker and easier process than normal riveting. It uses a special riveting tool and rivets. The resulting joint however, is weaker and less neat.

The riveting process is illustrated here.

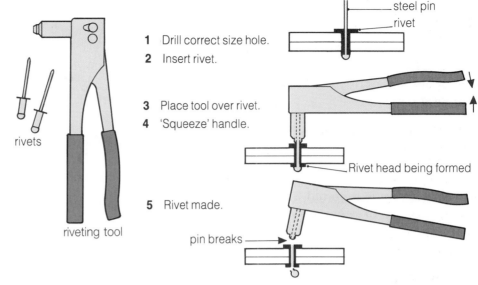

rivets

riveting tool

1 Drill correct size hole.
2 Insert rivet.

3 Place tool over rivet.
4 'Squeeze' handle.

5 Rivet made.

steel pin
rivet

Rivet head being formed

pin breaks

Gluing

Glues are used when other joining methods cannot be used, for example when different kinds of metals are to be joined or when heat would distort the metal, or rivets would spoil the appearance etc. The epoxy resin *Araldite* can be used successfully for joining metals if the surfaces are first roughened using sandpaper.

Rapid Araldite sets in ten minutes, and is quite hard within an hour. 'Standard' *Araldite* requires at least 16 hours to harden.

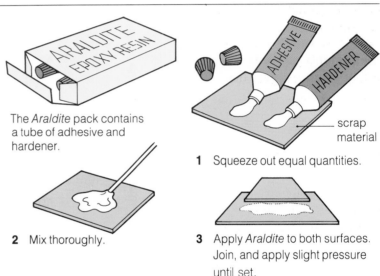

The *Araldite* pack contains a tube of adhesive and hardener.

scrap material

1 Squeeze out equal quantities.

2 Mix thoroughly.

3 Apply *Araldite* to both surfaces. Join, and apply slight pressure until set.

Permanent joints in plastic

Gluing

The most common method (in schools) of producing a permanent joint in plastic is the use of adhesives. If you use the wrong glue for a particular plastic however, it is likely that the plastic will 'break down' or melt.

For acrylic, although *Araldite* can be used successfully, special acrylic glues are better. *Tensol cement* (the trade name of acrylic cements manufactured by ICI) is probably the best known.

To produce a successful joint follow the stages described opposite.

For good results:
1 the joint must be a good fit.
2 the surfaces of the joint must be clean.
3 only use just enough cement for the job.
4 hold the joint securely, applying slight pressure until the cement has set.

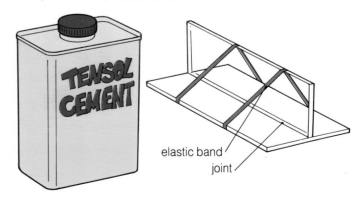

elastic band
joint

Caution Always work in a well ventilated space and avoid inhaling fumes.

Temporary joints

Joints which have to be disconnected, or 'undone' at some time, can be described as **temporary joints**.

Temporary joints are used, for example:

- on devices which have to be erected and dismantled;
- where access is required for maintenance or repair or simply access;
- where a temporary connection has to be made, and so on.

Although '**nuts and bolts**' are widely used in temporary fixings, numerous other devices and components are utilised. Some examples are shown here.

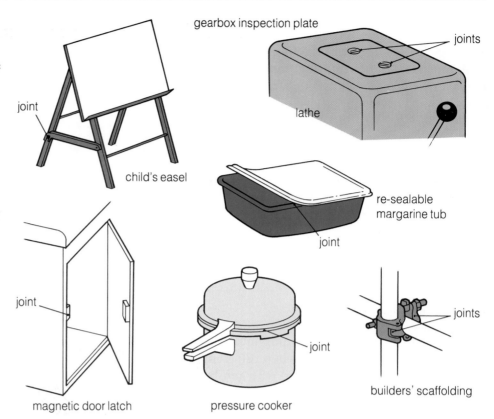

joint

child's easel

gearbox inspection plate

joints

lathe

re-sealable margarine tub

joint

joint

magnetic door latch

joint

pressure cooker

joints

builders' scaffolding

Construction kits

For school technology, a variety of construction kits are available for the temporary assembly of entire projects. These kits of course contain numerous components specially made to form **temporary joints**.

Components from these kits may also be used in conjunction with 'real' materials to manufacture projects.

Legotechnic

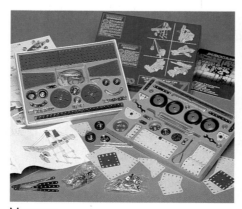

Meccano

Fisher technic

Moveable joints

Many devices rely for their operation on moveable joints. The movement may be linear (in a straight line) or rotary (round and round).

Many types of joint rely simply on one material sliding or rotating in contact with another. Others make use of a material's flexibility, and some rely on one material rolling in contact with another. Where prolonged movement is experienced (as in a bearing) lubrication may be required.

Some examples of moveable joints are shown here.

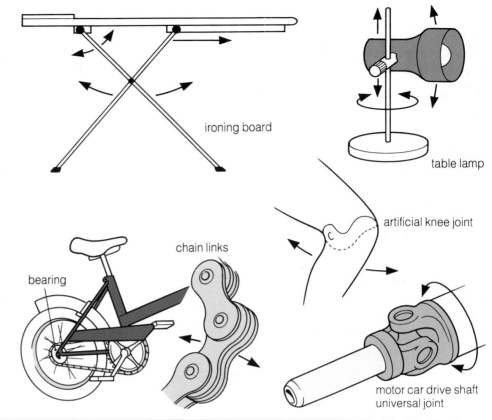

ironing board

table lamp

chain links

artificial knee joint

bearing

motor car drive shaft universal joint

School project work

Construction kits contain a range of specialist moveable joints.

In addition however, ordinary materials and components can be used in all sorts of different ways to form moveable joints in project work.

Some examples are shown here.

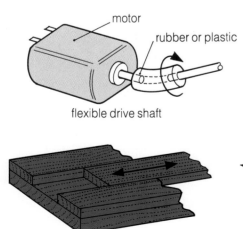

motor

rubber or plastic

flexible drive shaft

slider mechanism

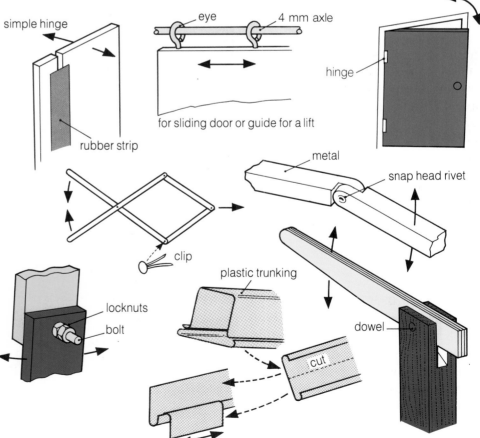

simple hinge

eye

4 mm axle

hinge

rubber strip

for sliding door or guide for a lift

metal

snap head rivet

clip

plastic trunking

locknuts

bolt

cut

dowel

Finishing materials

Surface finishes are used to **protect** a material and to improve or change the way it looks and even the way it feels.

Finishing metals

Some metals need to be protected against the effects of moisture. Ferrous metals, like the carbon steels for example, **rust** if unprotected. Non-ferrous metals however, including copper, brass, and aluminium, do not. Even so, if unprotected these materials eventually lose their shine.

Some common finishes

Oil is sometimes used to provide a temporary protection against rusting.

Paint provides a long term protection providing the surface is well prepared. Cellulose and 'hammer finish' paints are just two types suitable for metals – but don't use emulsion paints on ferrous metals – they contain water. **Always read the instructions** on the tin or can before you begin.

Lacquer can be used on copper and brass for example, to prevent tarnishing. Several different types are available. Cellulose lacquer is just one example – it can be applied successfully using a soft brush whilst working in a warm, dust-free atmosphere.

A **plastic** coat can be applied to a metal to protect it, change its appearance and change the way it feels to the touch. The metal (which must first be heated) is coated by being dipped into a fluidised plastic powder. Many schools have dip coating equipment.

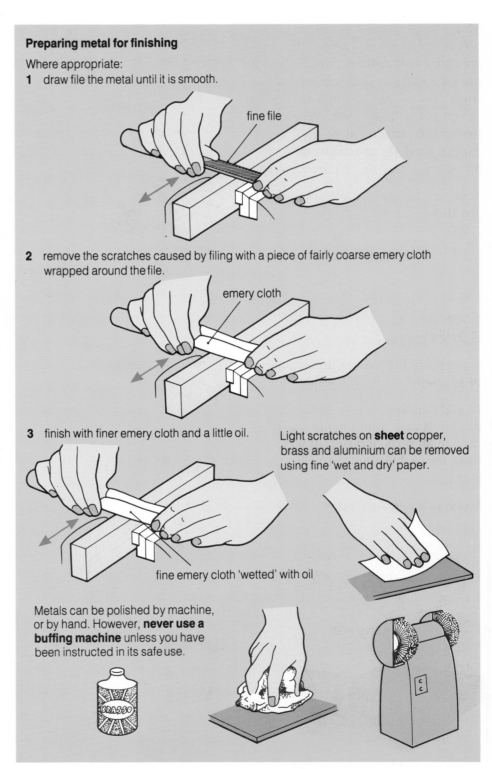

Preparing metal for finishing

Where appropriate:

1 draw file the metal until it is smooth.

fine file

2 remove the scratches caused by filing with a piece of fairly coarse emery cloth wrapped around the file.

emery cloth

3 finish with finer emery cloth and a little oil.

fine emery cloth 'wetted' with oil

Light scratches on **sheet** copper, brass and aluminium can be removed using fine 'wet and dry' paper.

Metals can be polished by machine, or by hand. However, **never use a buffing machine** unless you have been instructed in its safe use.

Finishing wood

Most types of wood require a surface finish to protect them from the effects of moisture (see page 225). In some cases, the finish may also be used to enhance the natural beauty of the wood. Alternatively, a less attractive wood can have its appearance changed by the application of a surface finish.

Some common finishes

Stains are used to change the colour of wood whilst leaving the grain still visible. Numerous different colours and shades are available, but stains **do not** protect the wood against moisture.

Oil finishes (of which linseed is one of the best known) provide a water-resistant, non-gloss finish. All types darken the wood, but leave the grain visible. A liberal quantity should be applied across the grain, left to soak in for an hour or so, and then the surplus wiped off with a soft non-fluffy cloth.

Varnish provides a clear tough surface and can provide a high degree of protection against moisture. Various types and finishes are available. If varnish is applied by brush, first brush across the grain, but finish off by brushing out along the grain.

Paints are used to apply surface colour and to protect against moisture, but they also, of course, provide a different surface texture. Polyurethane gloss paint for example, produces a very smooth shiny surface on wood. Brushing techniques vary for different paints and surfaces – these will be learnt with experience.

To prepare wood for finishing, follow the stages described opposite.

Preparing wood for finishing

1 Sanding should be kept to a minimum (especially on hardwoods) so plane to the best possible finish before sanding.

2 Sand with moderate pressure and always in the direction of the grain. One scratch across the grain takes 'a lot of getting out'.

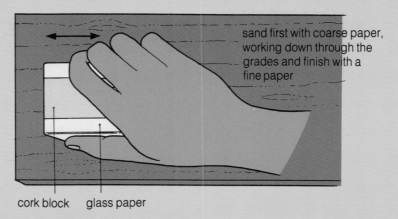

sand first with coarse paper, working down through the grades and finish with a fine paper

cork block   glass paper

3 Use a fine brush to remove dust after sanding – always brush in the direction of the grain.

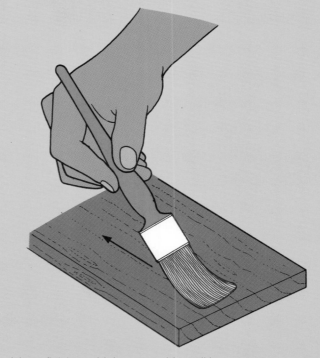

4 When applying a finish, avoid damp or cold conditions.

Finishing plastics

The manufacturing process leaves most plastics with a high quality surface which does not require any kind of surface finish. After cutting and shaping however, the edges (of acrylic for example) will require smoothing. See the illustration opposite.

Some plastics, including acrylic, are supplied with a protective paper covering. This should be 'kept on' for as long as possible during working.

Finishing an edge on acrylic

1   Draw file the edge whilst holding the work firmly in a vice – using a suitable material to protect the surfaces.

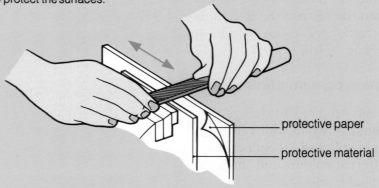

protective paper

protective material

2   Carefully smooth the edge using 'wet and dry' – keep the paper moist with clean water.

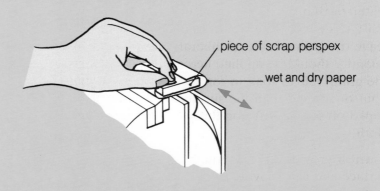

piece of scrap perspex

wet and dry paper

3   Finally, polish the edge using a special acrylic polish or Brasso.

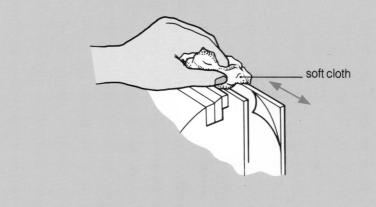

soft cloth

CHAPTER NINE

Energy

What is energy?

Energy is all around us and in many different forms. You cannot see it however, nor can you touch it, but you can be sure that *whenever anything happens*, energy is responsible. Indeed, energy is often defined as **the ability to make things happen**. If you remember this as you read this chapter you will begin to understand what energy is. (See 'Forms of energy' page 274.)

Where does energy come from?

Quite simply, most of the energy available on earth comes from (or came from) the **sun**. At first you might find this difficult to accept. However, it can be explained through the knowledge that energy can be **transferred** from one form into another. Plants are particularly good at transferring the sun's energy to suit their needs, and we humans have become experts at inventing devices for doing useful **work** by converting one form of energy into another. (See 'Energy from the sun' page 276.)

What is energy used for?

Britain is an industrial nation which uses vast quantities of energy. We use energy in the home for cooking, heating and lighting and when we 'plug in' any appliance to an electric socket. We use energy in our transport systems which enable us to travel at home and abroad, and to transport the goods we manufacture. We use energy in industry in the processing of food and in the manufacture of every kind of product. In fact, whenever 'anything happens' **energy** is used. Unfortunately, whenever we use energy, we always waste some of it.

A few years ago, when energy was plentiful, people didn't worry too much about wasting it. Today however, energy is very expensive, and is likely to become much more expensive in the future. If we are to avoid a bleak and uncomfortable future therefore, we must learn to make better use of energy and to avoid waste. (See 'How we use energy' page 278.)

Electrical energy

Electricity provides one of the most convenient and useful forms of energy. Unfortunately, it is very expensive to produce. Power stations use vast quantities of coal and other fuels of which we have only limited supplies left. Further, most power stations produce damaging pollution, and nuclear power stations pose the risk of catastrophic environmental pollution, as the 1986 Chernobyl accident demonstrated. (See 'Electricity' page 288.)

Alternative energy sources

Civilizations developed as humans discovered and learnt how to use different forms of energy. With the discovery of fire our ancestors were able to burn wood, allowing the sun's energy – stored by the tree – to be released in the form of heat. Later they learnt to harness the energy of animals to drive simple machines, and eventually to use the effects of the weather to drive water wheels and windmills. With the discovery of coal, oil and gas, access was gained to unimaginable quantities of energy. Finally came the discovery of nuclear energy and the ability to release energy from within the atom itself. As the reserves of coal, oil and gas decline however, and the worries about nuclear energy grow, the need to develop alternative energy sources increases. The production of electricity from the so-called 'renewable' energy sources is one important area of investigation. (See 'Alternative energy sources' page 292.)

Measuring energy

We can gain a better understanding of energy, and learn to use it more efficiently, if we learn how to measure it. Although energy exists in different forms, all energy is measured in **joules**. (See 'Measuring energy' page 302.)

Forms of energy

Chemical energy

This is the energy stored within chemicals. You can't see it of course, but when 'released' the effects can be dramatic. For example, when a firework is 'let off', chemical energy changes into heat energy, light energy, sound and movement energy in a spectacular way.

Less dramatic, but very much more important, is the energy which can be released from **food** and **fuels**. The energy of food is released by chemical changes in our bodies. Fuels like coal, oil and gas release their energy when they are **burnt** – the chemical energy being changed mainly into **heat**. Heat energy is a very important form of energy. Not least it is used to produce electrical energy in our power stations.

Heat energy

Every substance is made up of molecules. For simplicity you can imagine that these molecules are like tiny spheres which are in constant motion. The **hotter** something is, the **faster** the molecules move. Heat energy then, is really the effect of moving molecules.

In a steam engine, the rapidly moving 'steam molecules' are used to exert a force on the piston causing it to move.

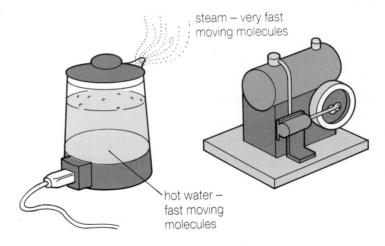

steam – very fast moving molecules

hot water – fast moving molecules

Light energy

Light energy is one of the most important forms of energy. It is the energy carried by light waves. Plants need it to grow and without it there would be no life on earth. Light energy allows us to see, as objects are only visible because they reflect light into our eyes.

sun – light energy

Sound energy

This is the energy carried by sound waves. We can talk to one another and listen to music because of sound energy. Sound energy is really the effect of moving molecules. When we speak we cause air molecules to vibrate. It is the effect of the vibrating molecules on our ear drums which enables us to hear.

Electrical energy

This is the energy carried by an electric current. It is a particularly useful form of energy because it can easily be transferred into other forms of energy to suit our particular needs.

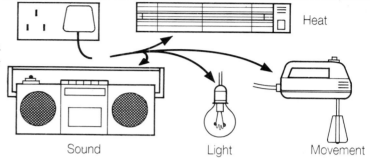

Mechanical energy

There are two types of mechanical energy: kinetic energy and potential energy.

Kinetic energy is the energy something has because it is **moving**. Moving air, for example, has the energy to turn a windmill. The air exerts a force on the blades causing them to rotate.

All moving objects possess kinetic energy. The faster they move, the more kinetic energy they possess.

Potential energy is sometimes called stored energy. In a cuckoo clock, for example, the weights possess stored energy. The energy is slowly released as they move downwards, causing the clock's mechanism to rotate. This kind of energy is called **gravitational potential energy**. Any object which is free to fall has gravitational potential energy.

'Strain energy' is another form of potential energy. It is stored in anything which is stretched, compressed or twisted.

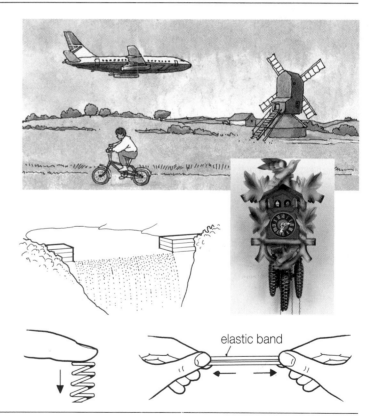

Nuclear energy

This is the energy stored within the nucleus, or centre, of the atom itself. In addition to the enormous destructive power of nuclear energy, it can of course be used in power stations to produce electricity, and is in fact the source of the sun's energy.

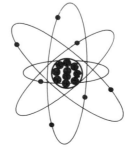

Energy from the sun

1 The sun is a vast powerhouse of energy. It showers the earth continuously with both heat and light. About 99% of the earth's energy comes directly from the sun.

2 Green plants are living things which could not exist without the sun. They use **light** energy to make food (or chemical energy), which is stored in their tissues. Plants use this energy to grow and reproduce.

condensation

3 Animals cannot obtain energy directly from the sun. They rely on eating plants in which chemical energy is stored. Alternatively, some animals eat other animals which have eaten plants. Animals use this energy to move, grow and reproduce.

4 We humans obtain the energy needed for movement, growth and reproduction, from the food we eat. We eat plants, or animals which have eaten plants.

5 **Coal**, and the massive stores of energy which it contains, exists only because of the sun and plants. Coal was formed by the decomposition of vegetation and its compression under the ground over a very long period of time.

6 **Oil** and **natural gas** are invaluable stores of chemical energy which again owe their existence to the sun and plants. Most crude oil (and gas) was formed by the decomposition and compression of sea creatures whose 'food chain' begins with microscopic plants called plant plankton.

7 The sun, therefore, not only supplies all living things with energy but also has been responsible for the massive stores of chemical energy which lie under the ground in the form of coal, oil and natural gas. Today, these energy sources are essential to our modern technological society. Not only do they fuel our industries, power stations, transport systems, etc., but they also provide the raw materials for the manufacture of a wide range of products.

8 The **heat** energy from the sun is essential for the germination and growth of plants, as well as keeping all living creatures warm and comfortable. It also controls the weather. The heat from the sun causes water to **evaporate** and form water vapour, which is carried by the wind, rises, condenses and forms clouds. Some falls as rain on the land to swell the rivers and fill the lakes.

9 The water which becomes trapped in mountain lakes (or purpose-built reservoirs) has **potential energy.** Today, we make use of this energy for the generation of electricity.

10 The sun's heat also causes **convection currents** in the atmosphere. Warm air rises and cold air moves in to take its place. We notice this movement of air as the blowing of the wind. Wind has **kinetic energy** which has long been used to drive ships and windmills. We are now beginning to use this energy to generate electricity using aerogenerators.

11 The wind also causes waves in water. The wind transfers energy to the water producing waves which contain huge quantities of **kinetic energy.** This has enormous potential for the generation of electricity in the future. Small scale equipment is already in use.

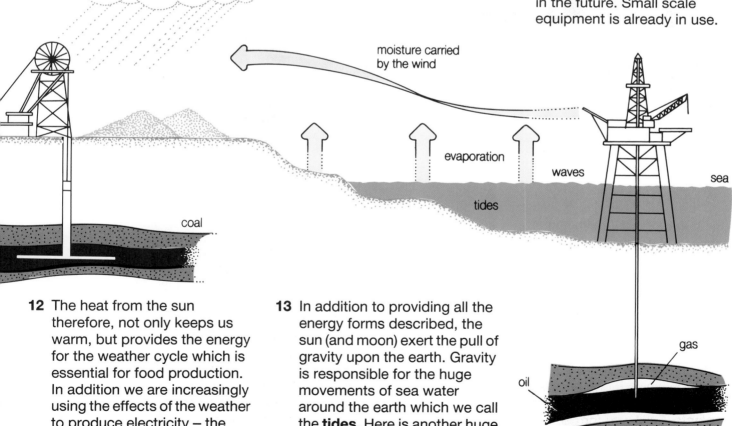

condensation

moisture carried by the wind

evaporation

waves

sea

tides

coal

oil

gas

12 The heat from the sun therefore, not only keeps us warm, but provides the energy for the weather cycle which is essential for food production. In addition we are increasingly using the effects of the weather to produce electricity – the most versatile energy form we have today.

13 In addition to providing all the energy forms described, the sun (and moon) exert the pull of gravity upon the earth. Gravity is responsible for the huge movements of sea water around the earth which we call the **tides.** Here is another huge source of energy which is just beginning to be used for the generation of electricity.

How we use energy

The human body

When we eat, we take in and store **chemical energy** within our bodies. We use this energy to maintain our bodily functions (breathing, circulation of blood etc.) and to do **work**. Work is done whenever we exert a force over a distance, and is calculated using:

work = force × distance moved

(See page 302.)

A weightlifter works very hard when performing a 'lift', and uses a lot of energy during training. The amount of energy people use in a day depends upon their activities and the kind of work they do. To a large extent, this determines the amount of food they require.

Much of the chemical energy we take in as food is itself 'expensive' to produce in terms of energy. The food industries consume huge quantities of energy, and a lot of it is used in the production of non-essential foodstuffs, e.g. sweets and crisps. Even so, food energy accounts for only a small fraction of the total energy used by an individual in a high technology society.

Using energy in the home

About 29% of all the energy we use in Britain is used in the home. Space heating and water heating uses most of this energy (83%), the remainder being used for cooking, lighting and small appliances. Unfortunately, a lot of this energy is wasted.

Energy saving in the home

Energy is wasted in the home in several ways. It can be wasted due to:

1 Bad habits

Leaving doors open, and leaving lights, TVs and radios etc. switched on when they are not needed, wastes energy.

2 Poorly designed equipment

Old equipment and appliances waste energy. Modern fridges and cookers for example, use much better insulation materials than older models, and modern heating systems are much more efficient and have better controls. Careful design of equipment, and the use of new materials in the future therefore, should ensure a lower energy consumption in the home.

3 Poor insulation

Heat energy escapes from our homes mainly by conduction, and convection, and a large proportion of energy wasted in the home is due to poor insulation. Some measures for reducing this energy loss are described below.

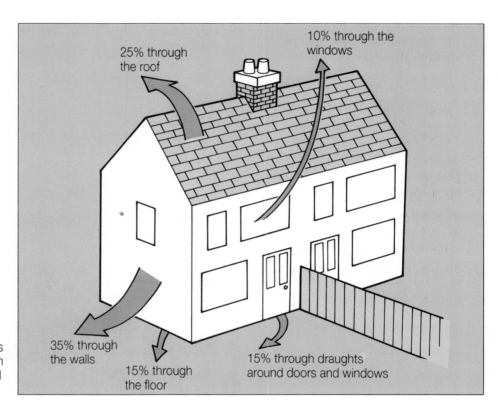

How heat is lost from an uninsulated house

25% through the roof

10% through the windows

35% through the walls

15% through the floor

15% through draughts around doors and windows

a *Roof insulation*

Warm air rises and cold air falls to take its place. This is what is meant by **convection**.

Warm air in our homes rises until it reaches the ceiling. Here, heat is taken away from the air by **conduction**. The heat from the air is conducted through the ceiling and is lost to the air above the joists.

Up to 25% of the energy lost from an uninsulated house escapes in this way. By installing glass fibre between the joists, more than 60% of this heat loss can be stopped. Glass fibre insulation material contains air pockets. Air is a poor conductor of heat and therefore heat loss due to conduction is reduced.

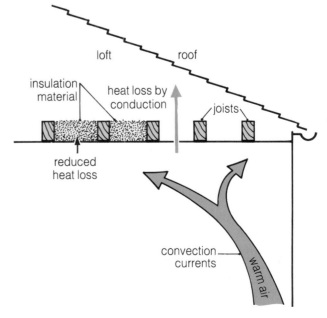

loft

roof

insulation material

heat loss by conduction

joists

reduced heat loss

convection currents

warm air

b **Wall insulation** Modern houses are built with cavity walls. Air trapped within the cavity reduces heat loss by conduction. However, heat energy can still travel from the inner to the outer wall by convection.

Up to 30% of the heat lost from an uninsulated house escapes through the walls.

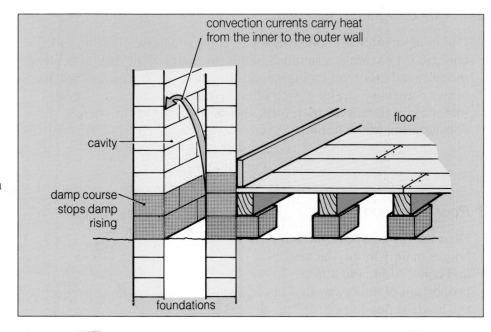

convection currents carry heat from the inner to the outer wall

floor

cavity

damp course stops damp rising

foundations

c **Cavity wall insulation** By filling the cavities in the walls with a special foam or glass fibre, more than 60% of this heat loss can be stopped. It is very important however, not to use a material which allows moisture to rise, causing damp.

d **Double glazing** Glass is not a particularly good conductor of heat. Even so, up to 10% of the heat energy which is lost from an uninsulated house, escapes by conduction through the windows.

A double glazed window has two panes of glass between which a layer of air is trapped. This can reduce heat loss by up to 50%, as the air acts as an insulator.

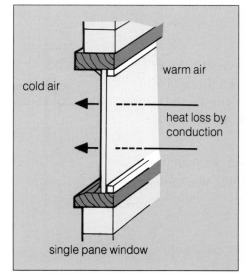

cold air

warm air

heat loss by conduction

single pane window

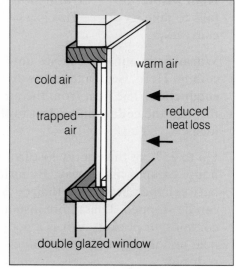

cold air

warm air

trapped air

reduced heat loss

double glazed window

e **Draught-proofing**   Draughts are responsible for up to 15% of the heat lost from an uninsulated house. This loss can be reduced by fitting draught excluders to doors and windows. However, if the house is heated by fuel-burning appliances (gas, oil, coal or paraffin) it is essential to provide adequate ventilation, as these fuels need oxygen to burn. Draught excluders should never be fitted in bathrooms or kitchens as ventilation is required here to prevent condensation and mould growth.

f **Lagging**   Domestic hot water, heated by a boiler or immersion heater, is stored in the hot water tank until it is needed. In an uninsulated tank the water quickly cools down as heat is conducted through the copper tank to the surrounding air. To reduce this heat loss, tanks (and pipes) should be **lagged**.

Modern tanks are lagged during manufacture, with polyurethane foam. Old tanks can be lagged using a fibre-glass lagging jacket.

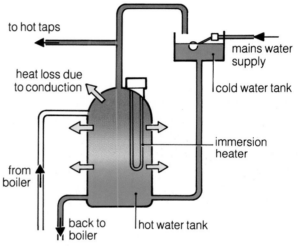

Domestic hot water system

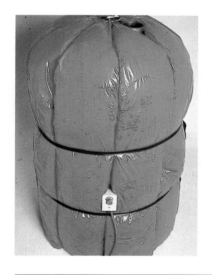

The cost of energy saving in the home

Double glazing and insulation materials cost money. However, with the savings made on heating bills, these products are eventually paid for. The 'pay-back' period for the different products however, varies from a few months to many years. With draught-proofing, the materials are paid for and you begin to make savings after just six months. Hot water tank insulation takes 1 year, loft insulation 2–4 years, cavity wall insulation 3–5 years and double glazing 30–40 years.

Questions

1 The modern jug kettle is tall and narrow (unlike the traditional kettle) and has its element set close to the bottom.

Explain how its design contributes to energy saving.

2 Showers are becoming very popular, and their use can save energy. Electric showers heat the water just before it is 'delivered'.

Explain why it is more economical to have a shower rather than a bath.

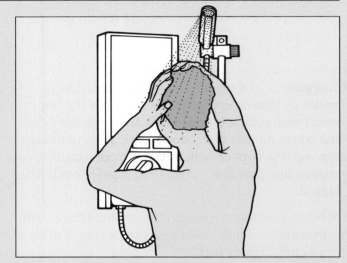

3 Modern washing machines have a 'half load' button. What is the purpose of this control, and how does its use save energy?

4 Thermostatic radiator valves (fitted to each radiator) can help to save energy.
  a Find out what a thermostat does.
  b Try to explain how the valves might operate and say how their use can save energy.

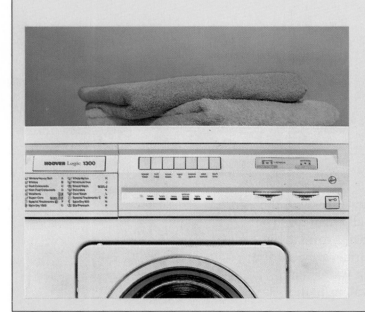

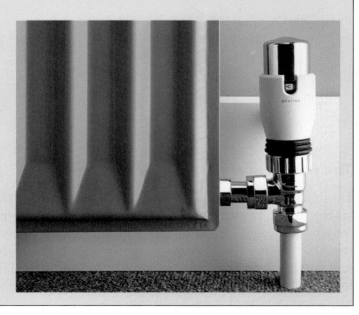

Using energy in transport

About 25% of the total energy we use in Britain is used to run our transport system. This includes motorcycles, cars, lorries, aeroplanes, ships and trains. Unfortunately these are almost entirely dependent on oil and use around 59% of the total volume of oil we consume.

Oil is a complex mixture of chemicals from which numerous products can be made in addition to petrol and diesel fuel. Oil can be processed to provide fertilizers, medical drugs, detergents, plastics – indeed, many of the products which we regard as essential to our modern way of life.

Energy saving in transport

Clearly, oil is a very versatile and valuable material. If the present industrial growth rate continues however, it is estimated that supplies of oil could begin to run out within the next 30–40 years. It is essential therefore, that we reduce the use of oil in the transport sector. This can be achieved by developing a more efficient system, which includes the use of vehicles which are propelled by energy sources other than oil.

The transport system

There are two basic classes of vehicle: those which carry their fuel with them, and those which 'pick up' energy (electrical energy) as they go along.

Most road vehicles at present use the internal combustion engine and carry their fuel (petrol or diesel) with them. This type of vehicle is popular because it has lots of advantages. There is no limit to the distance which the vehicle can travel and there are no restrictions of access on the normal road network. These vehicles are convenient to use because they can be parked at home and driven off at any time. The disadvantages however, include the cost in terms of energy usage, atmospheric pollution, noise, congestion, road maintenance costs and not least, injury and loss of life through accidents.

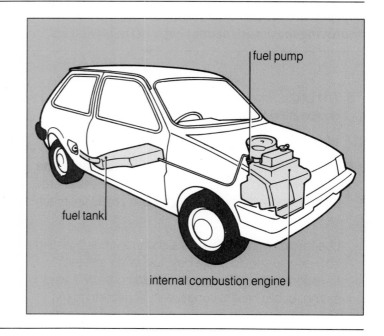

Vehicles which pick up their energy as they go along include trams, monorail vehicles, underground trains and some main line trains. Railways are particularly suited to 'electrification' and a great deal of investment is being made in this direction. Electrically propelled vehicles have the advantages of being pollution free, quiet in operation and more economical. However, there is evidence to suggest that the magnetic field produced by the electric current in overhead wires can be harmful to people and animals.

The major disadvantage of electric **road** vehicles at present is their limited range (the distance they can travel using their stored energy). However, improvements in battery technology are expected to double this range in the next few years. For vehicles which pick up electricity from overhead wires or from the railway track, the disadvantages include their restriction to definite routes, and the visual pollution caused by the wires and gantries.

Improving efficiency

Energy can neither be created nor destroyed, but in use is changed (or transferred) into other forms of energy. No machine however, can completely transfer all the available energy into useful work. In other words, no machine is 100% efficient. **Friction** exists in every moving system, and the effect of friction is to convert mechanical energy into **heat** energy which is usually lost to the surrounding air.

Vehicle manufacturers are constantly striving to improve the efficiency of their engines, as well as improving the aerodynamic shape of their vehicles.

Rover CCV – drag coefficient 0.27

Questions

5 The photograph shows a lorry with an energy saving device fitted to its cab.

What is it, and how does it help to save energy?

6 **500 people** can travel in **125 cars** or ten **buses** or **one train**. Travelling by bus or train uses much less energy per person than travelling by car, and produces much less pollution.

Use this information to write a short report suggesting how people should make best use of our present transport system. The report should consider energy saving, public health, congestion, convenience etc.

Using energy in industry

About 34% of the total energy we use in Britain is used by industry.

Energy is needed to make every single product, and is used at every stage of manufacture. Take for example, a product made from metal. The metal-bearing ore is first extracted from the ground. The machines which do this use energy. The ore is then transported – this uses energy. Energy is used to melt the ore, and again to prepare the metal for rolling into sheets and bars. Energy is used to cut the metal and to machine it into its final form. The finished product may then be packaged, which also uses energy.

Steel foundry

80% of the energy used in industry is used by the machines and processes which **make** the products. The remainder is used to heat and light the buildings and to provide hot water and other facilities for the work force.

Each time we throw away an empty drinks can therefore, discard an unwanted household appliance, throw away a cardboard box, or indeed throw away anything, we are wasting valuable resources. Not only are we wasting materials, but we are wasting energy, because more energy must be used to replace the articles which we discard.

Refuse tip

Energy saving in industry – a time for change

Today's society is based on **inbuilt obsolescence**. In other words we design things to be thrown away. Clearly this cannot continue. To help save energy and materials, every product should be made to last much longer. However, people like having new things regularly, and industry has become used to a large turnover. Further, millions of people earn a living by making things. You might like to think about this problem and try to work out a solution.

Consumerism – How long can our planet support it?

Energy saving in production

About 70% of the energy used in industry is used to generate heat for industrial processes. This includes furnaces, boilers, heat baths, etc. Much of this equipment is old and inefficient. Large energy savings could be made here by upgrading the equipment, by installing better insulating materials and controls.

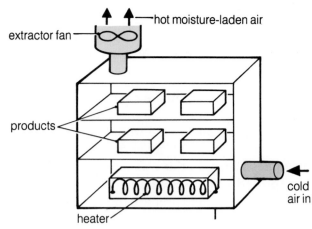

Traditional oven

1 Replacing old equipment

Some equipment uses outdated methods, and should ideally be replaced. An energy saving of up to 80% can be made, for example, by replacing the traditional drying oven with a modern type.

In the traditional oven, products for drying are placed in the oven and the air surrounding them is heated. The moisture-laden air is then extracted. Unfortunately, this process removes hot air in addition to the moisture – thus wasting energy.

In the modern equipment, the moisture-laden air is passed through a **de-humidifier** which removes the moisture. The hot air is then passed back into the oven. Not only does this process save energy, but it also saves **time**, since the air does not have to be heated up from cold each time the oven is re-filled.

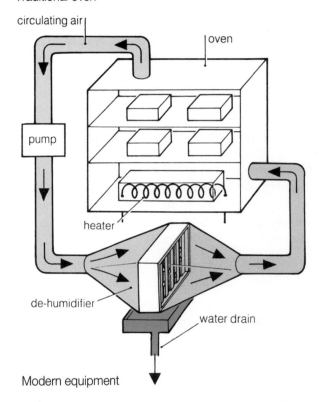

Modern equipment

2 Improving insulation

As with domestic housing, industry can reduce heat loss from its buildings by installing suitable insulation. Unfortunately, many factory buildings are very old and in a poor state of repair. This can include damaged roofs, walls and windows, which result in heat loss by convection. The cost of energy saving for some business people therefore, can be very high and have a long 'payback' period.

Industrial buildings in poor state of repair

3 Low cost energy saving

As in the home, a lot of energy saving can be made by following a few simple rules. In addition, some low cost equipment and controls may be needed. For example, machines should always be switched off when not in use – this includes office equipment such as electric typewriters and desk lamps. Lights shouldn't be left on unnecessarily – these can be controlled with a simple time delay switch in areas where safety permits – and doors shouldn't be left open unnecessarily – these can be fitted with a spring return mechanism, and so on.

4 Energy manager

These energy saving measures are fine, but unless someone takes responsibility for ensuring that they are carried out, the savings can be small. Many businesses today employ an **energy manager**, whose job it is to examine the use of energy in a factory or industry, and to find ways of reducing it. This will include all forms of energy saving from heating and lighting, through to processing and machining.

Questions

8 A local company manufactures 100 watt light bulbs which sell for 50p each.

Describe some of the advantages, and disadvantages, of producing a similar bulb which would last for twice as many hours, and sell for 70p.

9 An old factory premises with a 12 metre high ceiling was taken over by a small electronics firm. To reduce costs, the management decided to install a 3 metre high false ceiling.

Explain fully how this would this help to save the firm money.

10 A newly appointed energy manager told the company manager that energy savings could be made immediately by simply cleaning the 'very dirty' windows in the factory.

Explain this, and say what form(s) of energy would be saved.

11 People often forget to switch off lights when they are not in use.

Which of the following rooms in a factory could usefully have the lights controlled with a 5 minute delay time switch:
a canteen,
b washroom,
c machine shop?

Explain your answer.

Project

Energy is expensive. Looking for ways of using less energy is therefore very important. Think of a situation in the home, office, industry, transport or your own school where energy is wasted.

Describe the situation and follow the design process (outlined in Chapter 1) to find a solution to reduce the energy usage.

Electricity

Of all the forms of energy we use today, electrical energy is the most versatile and convenient. The electric current is carried easily along wires to where it is needed. It is clean, pollution-free (in use) and can be switched on and off at will. Most importantly however, it can be readily **transferred** into other forms of energy. The hairdryer is shown here as an example. Electrical energy is transferred into heat energy by the element, and into rotary kinetic energy by the motor, to drive the fan. A flow diagram can be drawn to show this energy transfer.

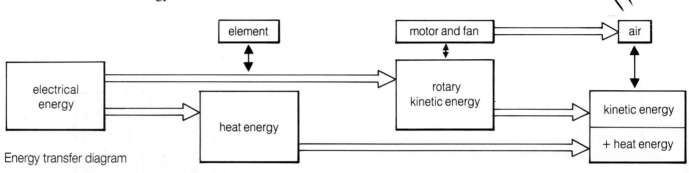

Energy transfer diagram

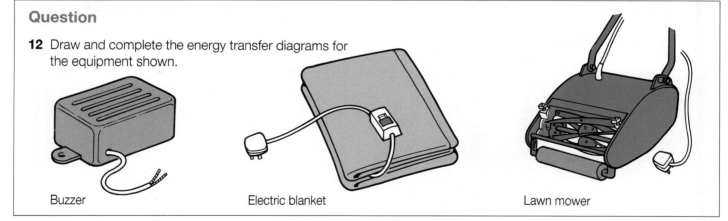

Question

12 Draw and complete the energy transfer diagrams for the equipment shown.

Buzzer   Electric blanket   Lawn mower

How electricity is made

Electricity is made by rotating a coil of wire in a magnetic field.

A simple generator can be made in the school science laboratory. The 'finger-powered' generator shown will produce enough electricity to 'flicker the needle' on a galvanometer.

In a power station, huge generators are rotated by turbines driven by high pressure steam.

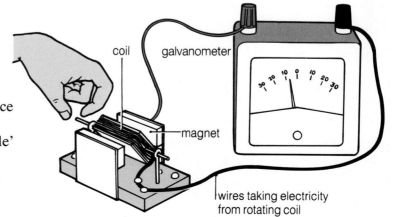

The power station

In Britain over 75% of our electricity is generated in **coal**-burning power stations. A further 19% comes from **nuclear** power stations, about 4% from **oil**-burning stations, and less than 2% from **hydro-electric** schemes. However, demands do change. During the 1984–85 miners strike, for example, 50% of Britain's electricity was produced using oil.

Ratcliffe power station

Generating equipment

Power stations burn coal or oil, or use nuclear fuel to produce **heat**. The heat is used at the boiler to turn water into high pressure steam, which then passes into a turbine. The expanding steam gives up its energy to the turbine blades as it 'presses' against them, causing them to rotate. The steam then enters a condenser where it condenses back into water before returning to the boiler to restart the cycle.

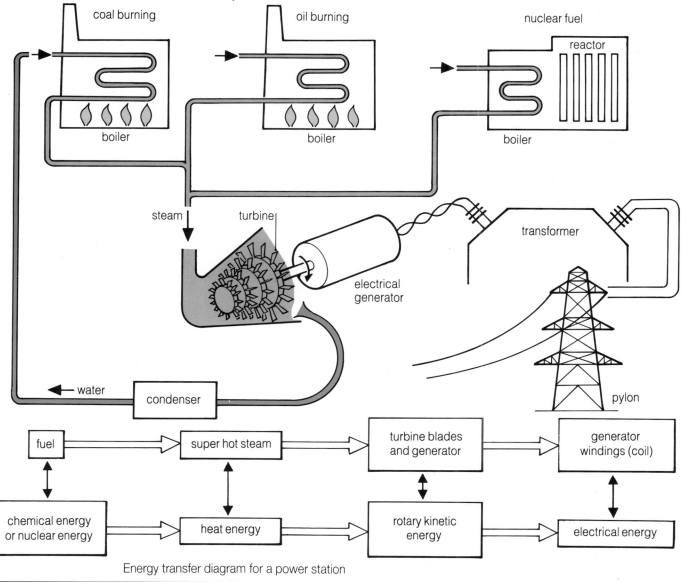

Energy transfer diagram for a power station

289

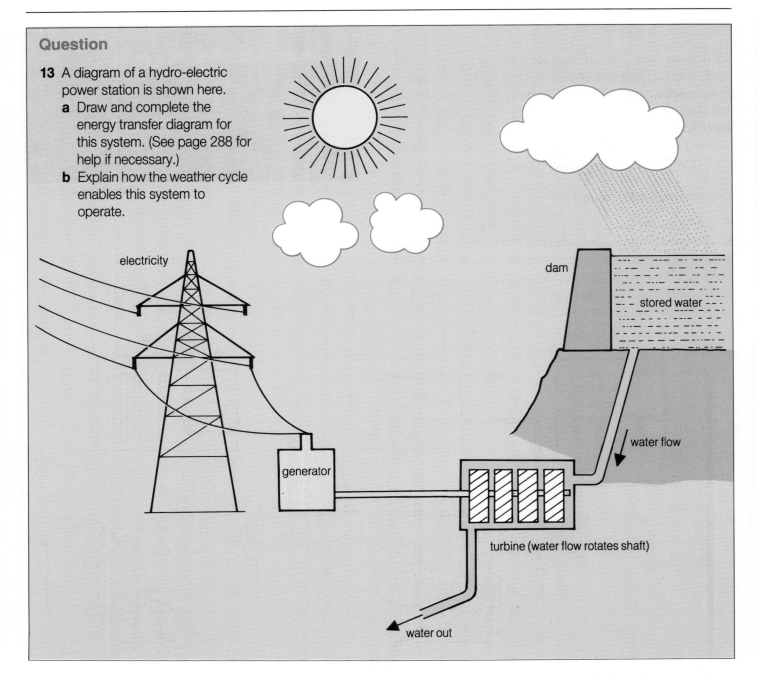

Question

13 A diagram of a hydro-electric power station is shown here.
  a Draw and complete the energy transfer diagram for this system. (See page 288 for help if necessary.)
  b Explain how the weather cycle enables this system to operate.

electricity

dam

stored water

water flow

generator

turbine (water flow rotates shaft)

water out

The fuels

Coal, oil and uranium are the main sources of energy used in the generation of electricity today. However, for many years technologists have been experimenting with **alternative sources** of energy, some of which will be discussed later in this chapter. The need for alternative energy sources arises for a number of reasons. Three important reasons are:

1 The fossil fuels – coal, oil and natural gas – are **non-renewable**. In other words, there is a limited amount which will eventually run out.
2 Coal and oil have additional important uses other than for burning as fuel.
3 The extraction, transportation and use of these fuels can have serious social and environmental consequences.

Some factors associated with this list are summarised in the diagram opposite.

Fuels

| Coal | Oil | Uranium |

Supplies

| two or three centuries | 30–40 years | limited |

Alternative uses

Coal
When coal is burnt as a fuel, many useful products are wasted. If properly processed, coal can provide the raw materials for the production of plastics, fertilizers, manufactured fibres, insecticides and so on. All these are available when coal is heated to make **coke** and gas, as well as producing road tar and creosote.

Oil
Oil is a complex mixture of chemicals from which numerous products can be manufactured. Separation of these chemicals takes place in a distillation tower. Some of the oils which are normally burnt as a fuel can be converted (by a process known as **cracking**) into materials suitable for making plastics and other useful materials.

Social and environmental impact of using coal, oil and nuclear fuel

Coal
Mining can be a very unsightly operation and the waste products (slag) are an additional eyesore. The unlimited **burning** of coal however, creates the major problems. Sulphur dioxide, produced when coal is burned makes acid rain. Acid rain from British power stations is blamed for environmental damage in parts of Europe. Forest trees are dying and fish have been killed in polluted rivers and lakes. However, an even greater threat to the environment is carbon dioxide produced when coal is burned. Adding carbon dioxide to the atmosphere raises the earth's temperature by slowing down the escape of the sun's heat back into space – the **greenhouse effect**. Some people believe that this could turn the present major food-producing areas of the world into deserts, and cause the ice caps to melt, producing major flooding in some parts of the world.

Oil
Whilst in-land drilling can be unsightly, the damage to the land is less severe than in coal mining. However, off-shore drilling can cause serious problems if an oil spillage occurs. Similarly, a major spillage from an oil tanker can result in severe pollution causing injury and death to marine life and birds, and damage to beaches and harbours. The major pollutants from oil, however, are lead, carbon monoxide and acid gases. These are produced when petrol is burnt in the internal combustion engine. Lead, which is **added** to petrol to make engines run more smoothly and efficiently, is known to affect the development of the brain in young children and even unborn babies. Carbon monoxide affects respiration. It combines readily with the haemoglobin in the blood preventing the uptake of oxygen. Acid gases help to make acid rain.

Nuclear fuel
Natural uranium is safe to handle. However, the safe disposal of radioactive waste presents a serious problem. Some of the waste products are highly radioactive and will remain so for hundreds of years. During the fission process (in the nuclear reactor) dangerous radiation is released. Under normal operating conditions this radiation is contained within the core. However, if an accident should occur – as at Chernobyl in the Soviet Union, 1986, – the effects can be devastating. Whilst only a small number of people were killed at Chernobyl, many were seriously injured and thousands have been made homeless as cities and farmland have been made unsafe for human habitation. Further, it is estimated that millions of people across Europe, whose atmosphere was contaminated by the massive radiactive cloud, are now at a greater risk of developing cancer.

Making electricity in the future

In recent years the public interest in how electricity is made has grown, and the 'anti-nuclear energy' campaign has strengthened. Further, energy policy is now a major political concern. If a future government decided to phase out nuclear power, our dependence on coal would increase, and the need to develop alternative energy sources would become paramount. The next section investigates some of these possible alternatives.

Alternative energy sources

Unlike the fossil fuels which will eventually run out, some energy sources are **renewable**. A renewable energy source is one which can be used over and over again. These sources can be harnessed to produce electrical energy and include:

- Energy from the **sun**. (Heat and light energy)
- Energy from the **wind**. (Kinetic energy)
- Energy from the **waves** and **tides**. (Kinetic energy)
- Energy from the **earth's core**. (Heat energy)

Solar energy – energy from the sun

Solar cells

A **photovoltaic cell** is a device which converts light energy directly into electrical energy. When first developed these were rather inefficient and very expensive. They were used mainly on satellites to power on-board electronics equipment. Today however, they are much more efficient and less expensive. Even so, their economic use for the generation of electricity relies on their exposure to intense and continuous sunlight. California can offer these climatic conditions and is in fact the world leader in the use of solar energy systems.

For the large scale generation of electricity on earth however, huge 'solar farms' (acres of solar panels) would be needed to compete with conventional power stations. Unlike the United States, Britain does not have huge cloudless desert regions on which to construct solar farms. The prospect of generating electricity in this way therefore, is unrealistic for Britain.

Kirkpatrick Centre, Oklahoma City

Solar furnace

A solar furnace collects heat energy from the sun and concentrates it into a small area by reflection, using a hugh parabolic mirror. The intense heat can then be used to change water into high pressure steam. This in turn can be used to drive a turbine generator to produce electricity.

In Britain however, this energy supply is limited and variable, especially in winter when our energy needs are greatest. The use of solar furnace power stations in Britain therefore, is at present unrealistic.

Water heating

The large scale generation of electricity using solar energy in Britain is clearly impractical at present. However, we could usefully harness the sun's energy **now** to help with the heating of our domestic hot water using **solar panels**.

One of the simplest forms of solar panel is constructed from metal pipes through which water is circulated. When the sun shines onto the pipes, heat energy is transferred from the metal to the water, raising its temperature. The warm water then 'gives up' its energy at the heat exchanger in the water storage tank.

Solar panels work best, of course, in hot weather. Even so, providing the air temperature is not too low, water heating is still possible in Britain on cloudy days. In fact, a well-designed system could be expected to supply up to 40% of the hot water needs of an average family in Britain, for a year.

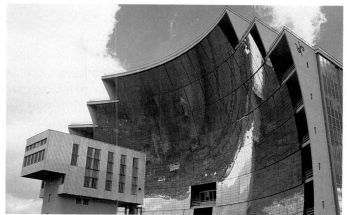

Parabolic reflector at Odeillo-Font-Romeau solar power station

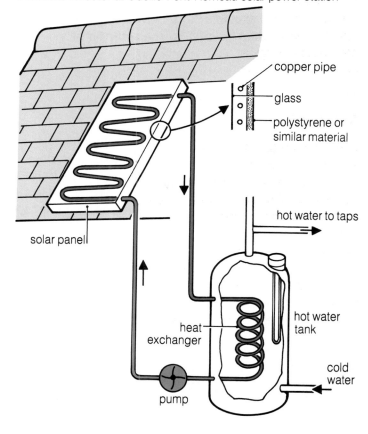

Question

14 Most solar panels use copper piping at present, although special synthetic rubbers and plastics may eventually replace copper.
   a What property makes copper particularly suitable for solar panels?
   b What is the best colour to paint a solar panel unit? Explain your answer.
   c To make the panel more efficient (waste less energy) a transparent cover is fitted to retain heat in the manner of a greenhouse. How does the use of polystyrene (fitted at the back of the unit) help to improve the efficiency of the panel?

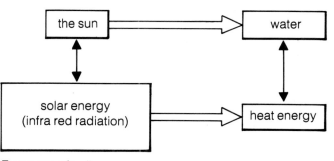

Energy transfer diagram

Wind power

The British Isles is one of the windiest regions of the earth. By harnessing just a small percentage of the available wind, we could meet most of our electrical energy needs. However, to do this we would need to use vast numbers of wind-powered generators – **aerogenerators**.

Unlike the traditional windmill, with its slow moving machinery and gentle sounds, the aerogenerator is a huge machine operating at high speeds.

Aerogenerators transfer the kinetic energy of the wind into electrical energy, by the rotation of a generator.

British test site

Britain has a test site at Burgar Hill in the Orkney Islands (Scotland). The latest machine to be tested is a 3 megawatt (3 000 000 watt) aerogenerator. It is twin-bladed, 60 metres from tip to tip, and drives a 100 ton gearbox and generator mounted on top of a 45 metre high concrete tower. To generate the same power as an average conventional power station however, hundreds of aerogenerators of this generating power would be required. Clearly, the amount of land required for one 'wind farm' would be very large. Further, it is important to remember that unlike a normal power station, a wind power station will only produce electricity when the wind is blowing. Further, aerogenerators would have to be shut down in severe weather conditions. At the other extreme, they require a minimum 'cut in' wind speed to operate at all. For these reasons, aerogenerators will only have a low availability. In other words, they could only be used alongside conventional power stations, to supply electricity when weather conditions were favourable.

Aerogenerator, Orkney Islands

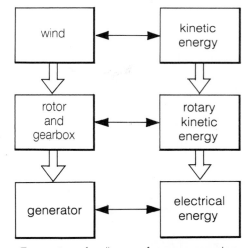

Energy transfer diagram for aerogenerator

The social and environmental impact of wind power schemes in Britain

Wind power is one of the most promising renewable energy sources for the large scale production of electricity in Britain. However, because of the physical size of aerogenerators and the numbers required, **visual pollution** would be a major problem. Further, the noise generated by large numbers of aerogenerators could be a nuisance. One important benefit of wind power of course, is that it would produce no atmospheric pollution.

Wave power

Wave power is really another kind of wind power, since the waves are produced by the wind blowing across the sea. Strong winds blow conveniently towards the British Isles across the North Atlantic ocean. These winds produce a deep ocean **swell** which contains a vast amount of motion energy or **kinetic energy**. For more than a century, technologists have experimented with devices for harnessing this 'free' energy source.

A variety of different systems are under investigation. The **Salter's duck** (and similar systems) produces a turning motion between the 'float' and a central spine. The motion produced however, is too slow to drive an electrical generator directly – an additional energy transfer system is required. This can be a pump, for example, which forces fluid through a turbine which rotates an electrical generator.

A less complex system is the **oscillating water column**. This relies on a rising and falling water column to force air through a turbine which rotates an electrical generator.

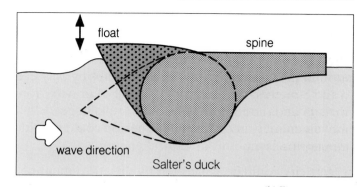

Salter's duck

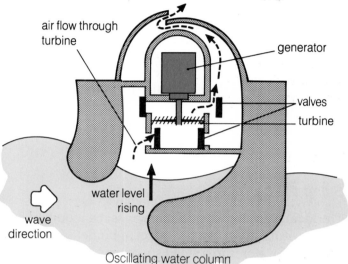

Oscillating water column

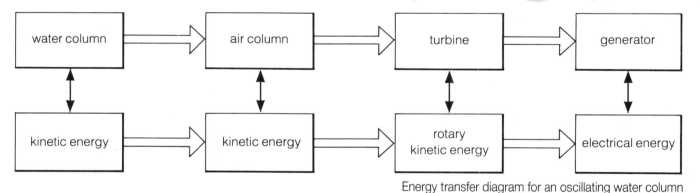

Energy transfer diagram for an oscillating water column

The social and environmental impact of wave power systems in Britain

The seas around the coast of Britain are at their roughest during the winter when our demand for energy is highest. Further, being an island, the availability of sites for wave-powered electricity generation is large. However, to build just one wave power station with an output equal to a conventional power station, would require several miles of generating equipment. The most obvious objection therefore, would be visual pollution. In addition, it is likely that many of the local coastal amenities (sailing, fishing, water sports etc.) would have to be restricted – depending on location.

Tidal power

With the ebbing and flowing of the tide, the **sea level** around the coast of Britain rises and falls by between **3** and **8 metres**, twice a day. The pull of gravity from the sun and moon is responsible for this huge movement of water, which if harnessed could provide an enormous amount of natural energy.

Electricity could be generated by this movement of water by the use of a special type of dam called a **barrage**. The sea would be allowed to flood through sluice gates in the barrage whilst the tide was rising. At high tide the gates would be closed. Then at a convenient time when the tide was ebbing, the water would be released through **water turbines** to generate electricity.

Harbour wall, St Ives, illustrating change of sea level

Siting the barrage

The ideal place for a barrage is across the mouth of an estuary. An estuary has the effect of funnelling a huge volume of water into a small space each time the tide rises. One of the most suitable sites in Britain is the Severn Estuary near Bristol. This estuary funnels down rapidly from several miles wide to a narrow river.

The simplest scheme would involve the construction of a single barrage across the Severn Estuary between Wales and England. Using this barrage, electricity could be generated for two six-hour periods each day whilst the tide was ebbing. Unfortunately, the time of the ebb of the tide changes by just under an hour each day. The generating period for electricity therefore would also change, and it would be difficult to absorb this irregular supply of electricity into the national grid. However, by using a more complex system, which included some facility for water storage, electricity could be made available when required, and not just when the tide provided it.

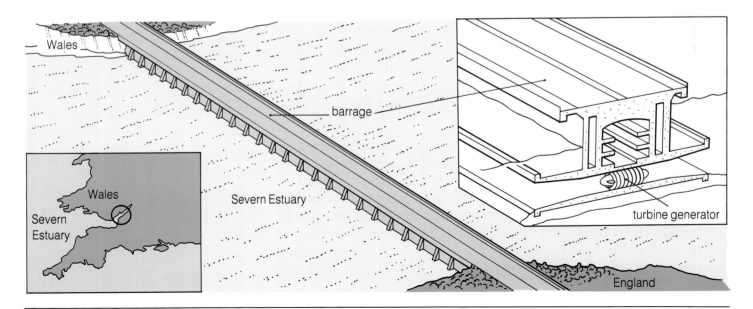

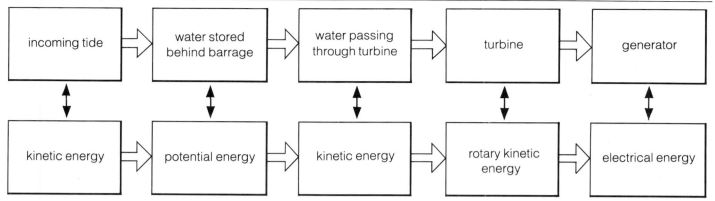

Energy transfer diagram for a tidal barrage

Possible developments

Throughout Britain, eight possible sites have been identified for tidal barrage schemes. If three of the most economical sites were developed, it is estimated that they could provide up to 4% of Britain's electrical energy requirements by the year 2020.

The cost of building a barrage however, would be enormous. Further, it could take up to fifteen years to complete. In this respect, it is not a very tempting project for a developer, since no return on the investment would be received during this period.

The social and environmental impact of tidal power in Britain

The siting of a tidal barrage would cause widespread changes to the natural environment of an estuary. For example, by retaining water behind a barrage for extended periods, the habitat of wading birds and wildfowl would be significantly affected. Further, the long term effects of silting could permanently change the characteristics of some habitats.

The effects upon people however, are less predictable. Some might consider a barrage to be unsightly, whilst for others it could provide useful amenities – not least a roadway which could improve access and reduce congestion. Further, the project could provide employment for many local people. However, during the long construction period, a great deal of inconvenience could be caused to the local communities, although it could be expected that a fair amount of haulage of materials would be made via the estuary.

Geothermal energy

The earth is a massive reservoir of natural heat energy. At its 'birth' it was a molten mass at a temperature of around 6000°C. The earth has been cooling down ever since, and will continue to do so for millions of years.

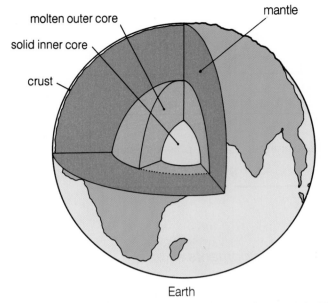

Earth

In some places on the earth, this natural heat energy reaches close to the surface. Occasionally, molten material from the earth's core escapes to form volcanoes. In Iceland and New Zealand, water trapped below ground in cavities becomes heated and escapes under pressure as hot water geysers. Even in Britain, hot water springs occur. The Romans took advantage of 'geothermal energy' at the now famous Roman baths in Bath.

If geothermal energy could be harnessed at temperatures around 250°C or higher, it could be used to make electricity, the heat being used to turn water into high pressure steam to drive turbine generators. To achieve these temperatures however, it would be necessary to drill deep into the earth's surface to reach the so-called 'hot rocks'. In Britain it would be necessary to drill as deep as 6000 metres (about four miles) to reach temperatures useful for the generation of electricity.

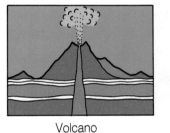

Volcano

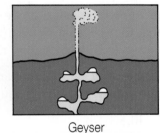

Geyser

A geothermal power station

One method of 'collecting' geothermal energy for conversion into electricity is shown here.

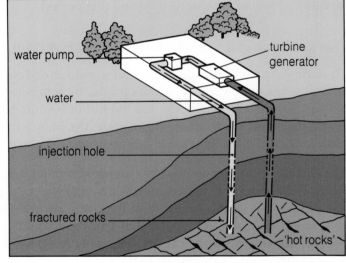

The system consists of two boreholes which penetrate the earth's crust into a region of hot rocks. During construction an explosive charge would be detonated at the bottom of the injection hole to fracture the rocks. When operating, water would be forced down the injection hole under pressure. It would then penetrate the hot rocks, pick up heat, and return to the surface via the second borehole. At the surface, steam would be released from the pressurised system to drive turbine generators.

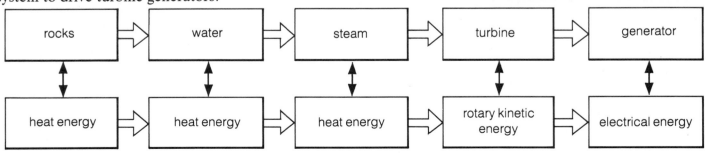

Energy transfer diagram for a geothermal power station

Problems with geothermal energy

At one of the world's prime test sites at Los Alamos in New Mexico, the thermal gradient averages 100°C per kilometre. In other words, for each kilometre depth of borehole, the temperature rises by an average of 100°C. In Cornwall however (at one of Britain's prime sites), the thermal gradient averages only 30°C. The cost of developing a site in Britain therefore would be very high, since the cost of drilling rises rapidly with increasing depth. Further, whilst experiments are being carried out into techniques for fracturing the rocks for water penetration, a great deal still has to be learnt, especially at the depths required in Britain.

The production of electricity from geothermal energy in Britain is unlikely within the foreseeable future. However, the use of this abundant free energy source to provide **district heating** is much more likely. The much lower temperature required here could be reached with cheaper boreholes, and the water pumped directly into people's homes.

Svatsengi, Iceland

The social and environmental impact of geothermal energy

The drilling of boreholes is a noisy operation which could take many months during the preparation of the site. Once complete however, the intrusion upon the landscape would be similar to a conventional power station in terms of its buildings, transformer equipment and distribution pylons. However, unlike a coal-fired station, there would be no need for railway or road connections for the transportation of fuel. Neither would large fuel storage areas be required. In the case of district heating systems, only a relatively small building would be needed to house the heat exchanger and pumping equipment.

Surprisingly, geothermal systems are likely to create some atmospheric pollution during their operation. This could take the form of the release of noxious gases such as hydrogen sulphide, and even radioactive materials such as radon gas. Finally, a less predictable consequence of geothermal energy could be the risk of earth movements due to changes in underground fluid pressures.

Energy storage

A serious problem with most alternative energy sources is that they are unable to provide a constant supply of energy. The wind for example, doesn't always blow, and the sun doesn't always shine. An **energy storage** system is likely to be needed therefore, to supply electricity when the equipment is not operating.

Battery

Batteries are one method of storing electricity. Those available today however, have a low storage capacity, and therefore huge numbers would be required. Further, batteries store direct current electricity (DC), whilst the electricity received in our homes is AC – alternating current.

Flywheel

The flywheel is another means of storing energy. When the generating equipment is producing electricity, some could be used to drive a motor which would in turn rotate a huge mass – a flywheel. When electricity is no longer being produced, the rotary kinetic energy stored in the flywheel could 'take over' and drive a generator to produce electricity.

Hydrogen gas

One of the more futuristic energy storage systems uses electricity to produce hydrogen gas. The gas is produced by the electrolysis of water and is stored under pressure in liquid form. It can then be converted back into electricity when required using a **fuel cell**. A fair amount of development is still required however, before the fuel cell can be used for the large scale production of electricity.

In addition to using hydrogen for the production of electricity, the gas could be used for domestic heating, fuel for industry, and fuel to power road transport and aircraft. The latter could prove particularly important as oil reserves begin to run out. The great advantage of using hydrogen as a fuel is that it causes no pollution. The only by-product is water.

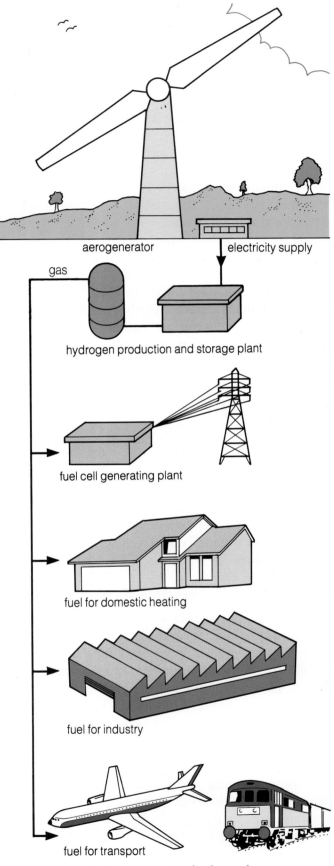

aerogenerator   electricity supply

gas

hydrogen production and storage plant

fuel cell generating plant

fuel for domestic heating

fuel for industry

fuel for transport

Hydrogen gas – production and usage

Water storage

Another system which could be adopted is the tried and tested water storage method. When the generating equipment is producing electricity but demand is low, the unwanted supply could be used to drive pumps to pump water into a reservoir. The water could then be released when required to drive turbine generators. The problem with this approach however, is the necessity for suitable reservoir sites.

The Dinorwig pumped-storage power station in North Wales is an example of the use of stored water to provide electricity on demand.

Dinorwig pumped-storage power station

The demand for electricity in the home and in industry changes throughout the day and night. For example, at night when most people are in bed, demand is low. At around 7 o'clock in the morning however, demand suddenly rises, and so on.

Electricity cannot be stored in large quantities, but the CEGB (Central Electricity Generating Board) must have a large, quickly available reserve to meet these sudden increases in demand. In England and Wales the reserve is normally provided by operating coal-fired power stations at below full capacity, so that output can be increased to meet additional demands. However, pumped-storage stations can be brought into operation much more quickly. If required, Dinorwig can provide up to 1800 million watts of power in about 11 seconds.

A pumped-storage power station differs from a normal hydro-electric power station in that it has two reservoirs, and uses the same water over and over again. During the night, surplus electricity provided by conventional power stations is used to pump water from the lower to the upper reservoir. Here the water is stored until it is needed to provide electricity during peak demand times throughout the following day.

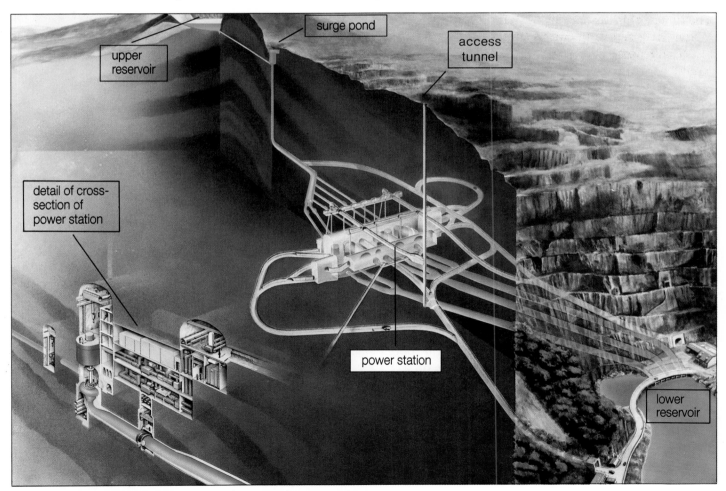

Artist impression of cross-section of Dinorwig pumped-storage scheme

Measuring energy

When energy is used, it is transferred from one form into another. When this happens we say that **work** has been done. If you learn how to measure work therefore, you will be able to measure energy, since work is the transfer of energy.

In the pictures, Sarju and Sarah are at work in a warehouse. The work involves lifting boxes onto shelves. In doing this work, **chemical energy** from their bodies is **transferred** into **potential energy** in the boxes.

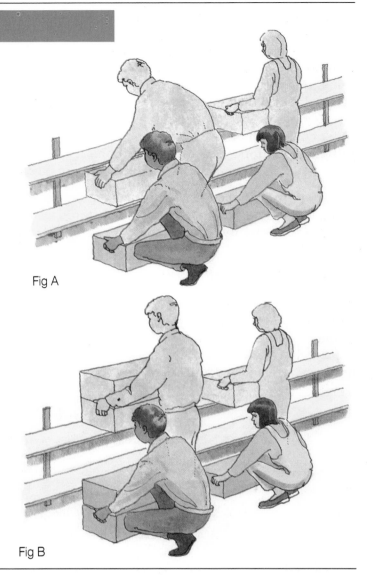

Fig A

Now, if all the boxes are the same weight, who has done the most work in Fig. A? Sarah, because she has lifted the box through a greater distance than Sarju. And in Fig. B? Sarju, because he has lifted two boxes which required him to exert more force.

From the above you should be able to see that **distance** moved, and **force** exerted are the important factors involved in measuring **energy transferred** or **work** done. The equations to use are

Energy transferred = force × distance moved

Work done = force × distance moved

Note   When using these equations, force must be measured in **newtons (N)** and distance must be measured in **metres (m)**. The energy transferred or work done will then be measured in **joules (J)**.

Fig B

Useful information

Before trying to use the above equations, it is important that you understand the meaning of **force**, **mass** and **weight**.

If you hold a 1 kg **mass** in your outstretched arm, you will very quickly become aware of the **force** which the mass exerts on your hand. This downward force of course, is caused by the pull of gravity. If you repeat the experiment, but this time hang the mass on a spring balance, you will be able to measure this force. The force is measured in **newtons (N)**.

Notice that gravity exerts a force of 10 newtons on a mass of 1 kg.

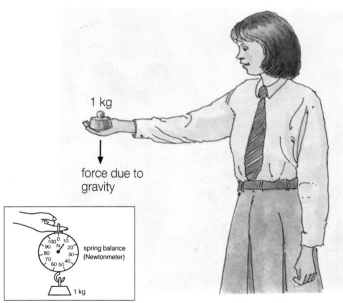

1 kg

force due to gravity

spring balance (Newtonmeter)

1 kg

If you experiment with a 2 kg mass, you will discover that gravity exerts a force of 20 newtons upon it. 3 kg, 30 newtons, and so on. In conclusion therefore, we can say that gravity exerts a force of 10 newtons on every kilogram mass (10 N/kg). Further, the pull of gravity on an object, measured in newtons, is called **weight**.

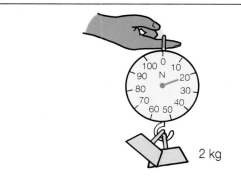

2 kg

Example of work calculation

The motor shown lifts a load of 500 g over a distance of 75 cm. In doing this, how much work is done by the motor? The equation we need is:

work done = force × distance moved

Remember, gravity exerts a downwards force of 10 N on each kilogram. To raise a mass against gravity therefore, the motor must exert an upward force of 10 N on each kilogram.

Therefore,

500 g = 0.5 kg = 5 n

work done = 5.0 × 0.75

= 3.75 J

75 cm = 0.75 m

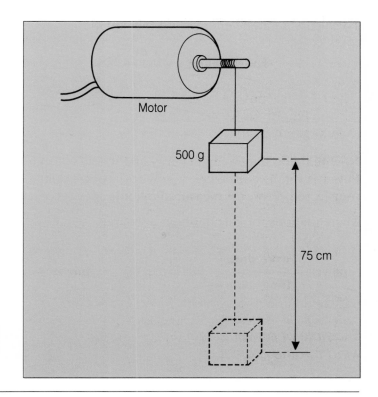

Motor

500 g

75 cm

Question

15 How much work would the motor in the previous example do in lifting a load of 1.5 kg over a distance of 150 cm?

More about potential energy

Potential energy is the energy which something has due to its **position** or **state**. For example, the water behind a dam has potential energy because of its position. The water can fall from this position and exert a force over a distance and therefore do work, in this case, drive a turbine to generate electricity. Because **gravity** provides the force which makes the water fall, the energy stored in the water is called **gravitational potential energy**.

To measure gravitational potential energy, use the equation,

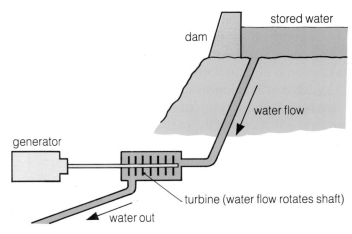

stored water

dam

water flow

generator

water out

turbine (water flow rotates shaft)

$$\mathbf{PE} = m \times g \times h$$

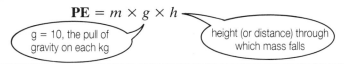

g = 10, the pull of gravity on each kg

height (or distance) through which mass falls

Measuring kinetic energy

Kinetic energy is the energy which something has because it is **moving**. Moving water for example, has the energy to turn a water wheel. By exerting a force over a distance the water transfers its energy to the water wheel and therefore does work.

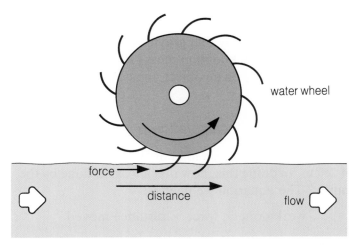

water wheel

force

distance

flow

The amount of kinetic energy which something has depends upon the **mass** of the substance on the move (*m*) and the speed or **velocity** at which the mass travels (*v*).

To calculate kinetic energy, use the equation,

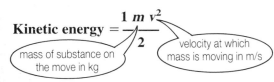

$$\textbf{Kinetic energy} = \frac{1\ m\ v^2}{2}$$

mass of substance on the move in kg

velocity at which mass is moving in m/s

Power

Now that you understand energy and work, you can learn about power. **Power** is simply a measure of how fast work is done, or how fast energy is transferred. Power is measured in joules per second or watts (W).

The equations for calculating power are

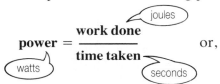

joules

$$\textbf{power} = \frac{\textbf{work done}}{\textbf{time taken}} \quad \text{or,}$$

watts

seconds

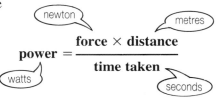

newton

metres

$$\textbf{power} = \frac{\textbf{force} \times \textbf{distance}}{\textbf{time taken}}$$

watts

seconds

Example of power calculation – wind turbine project

The wind turbine shown was made by a 4th year pupil in a technology 'challenge'. The brief was to design a machine which would transfer the kinetic energy of the wind into gravitational potential energy in a 0.5 kg mass at maximum speed. When tested, the turbine raised the load over a distance of 0.5 m in 40 s. The power calculation for this machine is shown below.

$$\text{Power} = \frac{\text{force} \times \text{distance}}{\text{time}}$$

$$= \frac{5 \times 0.5}{40}$$

$$= 0.0625 \text{ watts}$$

Question

Before any building or structure can be safely erected, a **geological** survey is carried out to determine whether the **ground**, under the foundations, would be strong enough to carry the load.

The bridge in diagram 1 could **not** be safely constructed as shown, for obvious reasons. However, to overcome the problem the abutments could be supported on **piles**. These are steel tubes which are driven down through the soft ground to the hard rock, and then into it. The machine which does this is called a **pile driver**.

One type of pile driver is illustrated here. It is basically a crane which raises and then drops a solid steel cylinder – a drop hammer. The drop hammer is released inside the pile case where it falls until it hits the bottom of the pile which is sealed with a base plate welded across it. Repeated drops of the hammer gradually drive the pile to the required position.

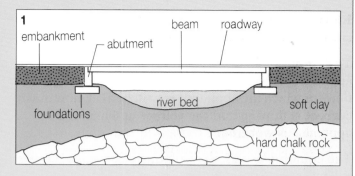

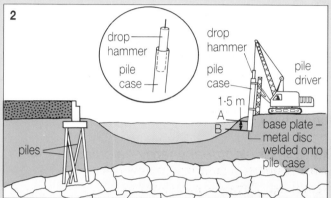

16 Before work can begin, the drop hammer must be lowered to a position about 1.5 m above the base plate. Drops from much above this height would 'knock out' the base plate.

  a Describe the energy transfer which occurs as the drop hammer falls between A and just above B.

  b If the drop hammer had a mass of 4000 kg, how much potential energy would it possess at position A?

  c If the velocity of the drop hammer was 5.477 m/s just before it reached position B, how much kinetic energy would it possess?

Pile driver working at Chatham Marina, Kent

Electrical energy

Electrical energy is the energy carried by an electric current.

The amount of electrical energy used by an appliance depends upon three factors: the length of **time** for which the appliance is switched on, how much **current** is flowing and the **voltage** at which the appliance is working.

The equation used for calculating electrical energy is shown. Like all other forms of energy, electrical energy is measured in joules.

Electrical energy = volts × current × time

$$= V \times I \times t$$

Notice that I is used to represent current.

Example of electrical energy calculation

The energy used by a 240 V fan heater, taking a current of 12.5 A for 2 hours can be calculated thus,

$$\text{electrical energy} = V \times I \times t$$

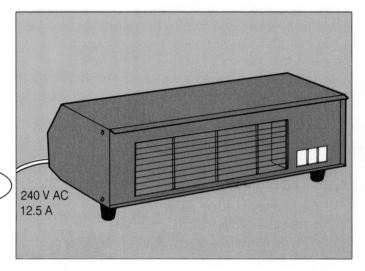

240 V AC
12.5 A

(2 hours = 2 × 60 × 60 = 7200 secs)

$$= 240 \times 12.5 \times 7200$$

$$= 21\ 600\ 000 \text{ joules}$$

Electrical power

Electrical power is a measure of how fast electrical energy is transferred into other forms of energy. It is measured in **watts**.

To measure electrical power, use the equation,

$$\text{Power} = \frac{\text{energy transferred}}{\text{time}}$$

or

$$\text{Power} = \frac{V \times I \times t}{t}$$

which gives

$$\textbf{Power} = V \times I$$

Example of power calculation

What is the power of a 240 V fan heater taking a current of 12.5A?

$$\text{Power} = V \times I$$

$$= 240 \times 12.5$$

$$= 3000 \text{ watts or 3 kW.}$$

Note   1000 watts = 1 kilowatt (1 kW)

The electricity bill

The **kilowatt hour (kWh)** is the unit of electricity used by the electricity board. The cost of each kilowatt hour is printed on the electricity bill. You can use this information to work out the cost of using any appliance.

Example

The cost of running a 3 kW fan heater for 2 hours can be calculated as follows:

$$\text{cost} = \text{power} \times \text{time} \times \text{cost per unit}$$

p   kw   h   p/kwh

$$= 3 \times 2 \times 5.5$$

$$= 33\text{p}$$

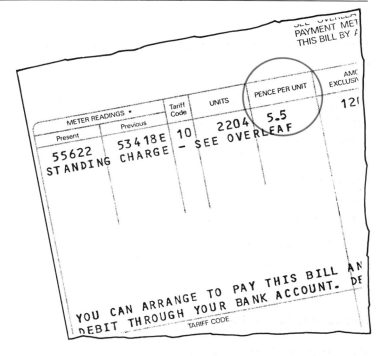

The efficiency of energy transfer

In any energy transfer system, the amount of useful energy we get out is always less than the energy we put in. Some energy is always converted into forms which we cannot use, usually heat. The device shown is 50% efficient.

The equation for calculating efficiency is,

$$\textbf{Efficiency} = \frac{\textbf{work or energy output}}{\textbf{work or energy input}} \times \textbf{100}$$

For the device shown in the block diagram:

$$\text{Efficiency} = \frac{100}{200} \times 100$$

$$= 50\%$$

The importance of energy saving has been discussed in this chapter. You will realize therefore, that the **inefficiency** of energy transfer is a problem which must be tackled. Indeed, it is an important area of research today.

The most common cause of inefficiency in a machine is **friction**. This can be reduced by lubrication. The study of friction forces and lubrication is called **tribology**.

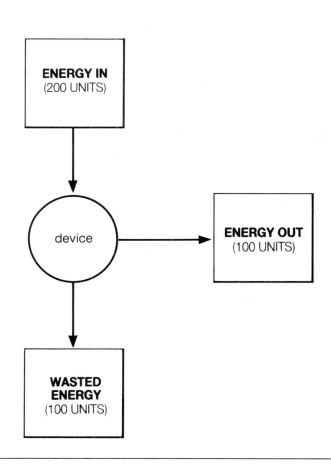

Questions

17 A 2.5 kW electric hot-plate and a 2.5 kW electric kettle are used to boil the same quantity of water to make tea. The cost of electricity is 5.5 pence per unit.
  a Why is it much quicker, and therefore uses less energy, to use the electric kettle?
  b If it takes 2 minutes to boil the water in the electric kettle, how much does it cost?

18 A 240 V hairdryer draws 5 A of current. Electricity costs 5.5 pence per kWh.
  a What is the hairdryer's wattage?
  b How much does it cost to run the hairdryer for 15 minutes?

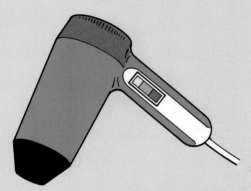

19 The diagram shows an experiment to find the efficiency of a small motor and home-made gearbox.

When lifting a load of 1 kg, the voltage across the motor was 11 volts, and the current flowing through it was 0.3 amps. It took the motor 18 seconds to lift the load through a distance of 75 cm.

What is the efficiency of the system?

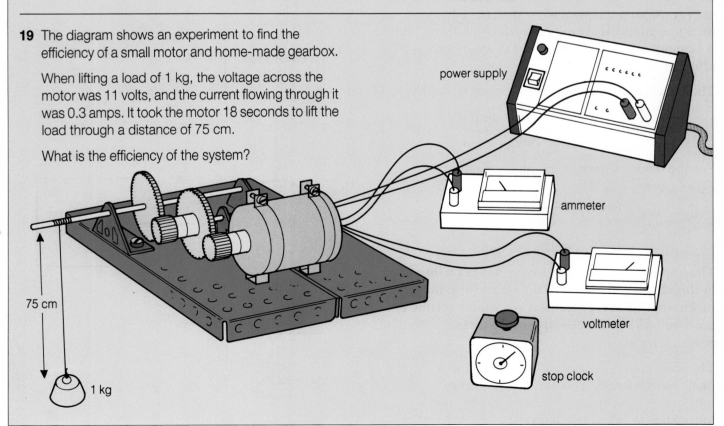

power supply

ammeter

voltmeter

stop clock

75 cm

1 kg

Numerical answers

Structures

11 **a** 250 N
    c 25 N

12 **a** 50 000 N

13 **a** 1000 Nm
    b 750 Nm

Mechanisms

1 **a** 2.5:1
  b 120 rpm

2 **b** 1120 rpm
  c 400 rpm

4 **a** 0.4:1
  b 161.25 metres per minute

5 **a** 40 teeth
  b 2:1
  c 30 rpm

6 **b** 9:1
  c 4

7 **a** 3:1

9 5 s

10 6 cm

11 120 rpm

13 200 N

14 **a** 125 N
    b 100 N

15 **b** 333.3 N

Control electrics and electronics

1 **a** 120 Ω
  b 0.05 A

2 **a** 0.12 A
  b 0.24 A

3 **a** 10 V
  b 0.02 A

4 **a** 0.16 A
  b 0.16 A
  c 0.16 A
  d 75 Ω

5 5 Ω

Pneumatics

3 94.2 N

5 502.6 N

6 457.4 N

Energy

15 22.5 J

16 **b** 60 000 J
    c 59 995 J

17 **b** 0.458p

18 **a** 1200 W
    b 1.65p

19 12.6%

List of suppliers

RS Components
PO Box 99
Corby
Northants
NN17 9RS

Rapid Electronics
Heckworth Close
Severalls Industrial Estate
Colchester
Essex
CO4 4TB

Technology Supplies
Phoenix Bank
Market Drayton
Shropshire
TF9 1JS

Technology Teaching Systems
Penmore House
Hasland Road
Hasland
Chesterfield

Economatics (Education) Ltd
Epic House
Orgreave Road
Handsworth
Sheffield
S13 9LQ

Testbed Technology Ltd
PO Box 70
The Science Park
Hutton Street
Blackburn
Lancashire
BB1 3BY

EMA Model Supplies Ltd
58–60 The Centre
Feltham
S41 0SJ

Commotion
241 Green Street
Enfield
EN3 7TD

Your local S.A.T.R.O.

Project Index

Pupil's note

More than 80 projects have been included in this book. Nearly half are project briefs which identify needs or opportunities for design and technological activities. These could be used as a starting point for your own design and making activities, or as a stimulus for identifying needs and opportunities yourself. The others are examples of completed projects which may also serve to stimulate your own ideas.

The text which follows the project index gives further guidance on how to begin to identify needs and opportunities for design and technological activities yourself.

Briefs

alternative energy vehicle   102
automatic box sorter   162
automatic door   193
automatic porch light   150
builder's lift   102
burglar alarm   159
cantilever grandstand   67
car park barrier   192
car park exit barrier   143
clay extruder   192
coin sorter   103
damp detector   161
electronic ruler   161

energy saving project   287
'fast reaction' game   123
footbridge   67
fun park cable car   103
goods transporter   160
mechanical toy   102
motor car courtesy light   159
noughts and crosses   160
personal alarm   162
personal safe   161
playframe activity centre   66
pop group's mobile stage   66
rapid assembly shelter   67

reaction comparitor   139
reaction trainer   139
self-balancing crane   160
shop window display   103
'steady hand' game   126
structures mini-project – bridge   63
structures mini-project – cantilever   65
touch-sensitive switch   138
transistor tester   159
walking machine   192
water storage tank   66

Further ideas for projects   67, 103, 162, 193

Examples of completed projects

advertising board   185
automatic stamping machine   194
bath water level alarm   129
belt strap manufacturing machine   194
burglar deterrent   167
bus step aid   195
cantilever   68
car park barrier   107, 194
conveyor belt   77
cot mobile   80
crazy snake   97
dispensing machine (gobstopper dispenser)   167
dockside crane   85

electronic weighing machine   144
energy converters   104, 105
factory lift   164
fairground ride   69
fork lift truck   165
fun robot   164
'game of chance'   128
horse jump   89
IN/OUT cat flap   166
lightweight pushchair   68
log sorting machine   105
plant care system   163
pneumatic grab   176
printing machine   82
railway level crossing barrier   107

remote-controlled hoist   195
road bridge   69
robot arm   106
shop window display   73
Simon's money box   126
sliding door   87
sorting device   106
stair lift   163
stamping machine   170, 172
tourist information map   166
warehouse lift   165
water pollution indicator   134
wind turbine   304

Identifying needs and opportunities for design and technological activities – further guidance

Situation analysis

Situation analysis was described briefly on page 10. It is likely that within the area around your school and home there will be many places where this kind of study can take place, including shops, parks, banks, car parks, schools, factories and so on.

Observing peoples' actions and reactions in a given situation is an excellent way of identifying needs and opportunities for design and technological activities. If possible, talk to people in the given situation, ask them questions and ask for their opinions; but don't forget to explain 'what you are doing' and why you need the information.

Safety note – It is advisable never to talk to strangers if you are alone.

Design analysis

Design analysis, in which you study existing designs, is another useful way of identifying needs and opportunities. This involves examining designs and asking questions about them, such as

What is it?
What is its function?
Does it do its job well?
Is it easy to use?
Does it look attractive?
Is it value for money?
In what ways could it be improved?

A close examination of this kind often reveals weaknesses in a design. Using this information you could possibly improve on the design or even produce a new design to perform the required function.

Questionnaires

When designing for people it is important to take account of their differing needs, tastes and opinions. To find out what people 'think', therefore, you need to ask them questions. One way of doing this **for a large group of people** is to use a questionnaire. A questionnaire is simply a list of questions designed to obtain the information you require quickly and efficiently.

Writing a questionnaire

1 Use a spider diagram to help you 'think up' questions.
2 Give your questionnaire a title.
3 Write some questions with 'yes' or 'no' answers or multi-choice answers. (Use boxes for these 'tick' answers.)
4 Include questions which ask people for their opinions. (Leave space for these answers.)
5 Check your questionnaire carefully to make sure that it will provide the information you require.

Keywords

One very effective way of identifying needs and opportunities for design and technological activity is shown here. This method relies solely on your imagination and creativity.

Begin by writing down a **keyword** or words (shown here in red). Then build up a spider diagram by adding **link words** – words which relate to the keyword/s (shown here in blue). Finally, use the link words to identify needs or opportunities. (Some examples are shown here in black.)

Almost any word can be used, but obviously words like 'it', 'the', 'big', 'down' etc., should be avoided. You could choose, for example, words related to **activities** (e.g. swimming, sitting, laughing, etc.), **objects** (e.g. chair, shirt, pencil, etc.), **people** (e.g. child, pensioner, tourist, etc.), **environments** (e.g. kitchen, bus shelter, classroom, etc.) and so on.

Note – This activity can be performed in a slightly different way with a number of people sitting together and spontaneously stating their thoughts and ideas about 'something'. The starting point can be specific (as above) or can begin with the first word which someone says. Everything should be recorded, however silly it might sound using a spider diagram or notes. This approach is called brainstorming.

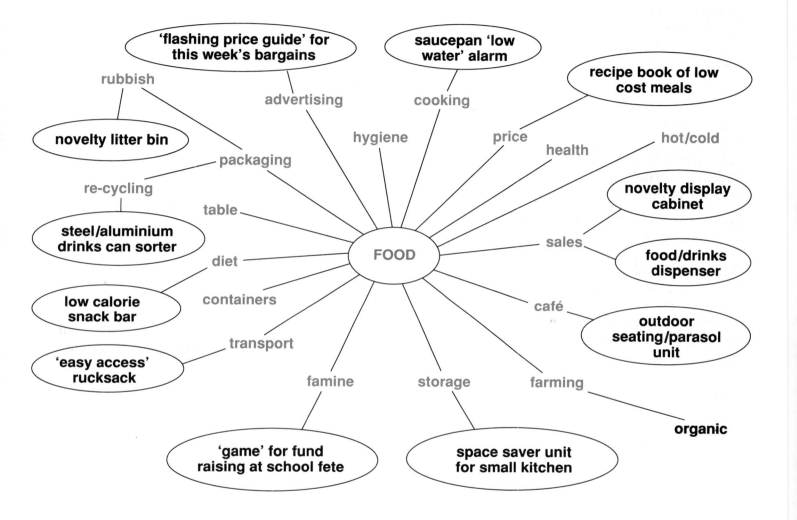

Index

abrafiles, 258
acid rain, 291
acrylic, 245
adhesives, *see* gluing
aerogenerators, 294
aesthetic judgement, 37
aesthetics, 11, 20
air bleed circuits, 182
alloys
    aluminium, 211
    brass, 212
    carbon steels, 207
    stainless steel, 209
aluminium, 206, 211
ammeters, 114
amplifiers
    Darlington pair, 136
    operational, 140
amps, 110
AND gate, 154
annealing, 208
anthropometrics, 40
appearance, 21
ash, 228
atoms, 240, 241
automatic control
    electrical, 121, 124, 125, 153, 154
    pneumatic, 185, 186
automatic sliding door, 125

bakelite, 247
balance
    of human body, 42; *see also* visual
        balance
    principle of moments, 59
basic electrics, 110
batteries, 300
    in parallel, 110
    in series, 110
beams
    cantilever, 62
    design of, 57
    reinforced concrete, 58
    stiffness of, 56
    strength to weight ratio of, 57
beech, 228
belts, drive, 72
bench hooks, 260
bending
    acrylic, 262
    metal, 259
bending forces, 53

bistable multivibrator, 166
blanking, 213
body, in balance, 42
body dimensions, 41
body fatigue, 42
body movement, 41, 42
body proportion, 40, 41
brakes
    disc, 190
    drum, 190
    hydraulic, 190
brass, 212
brazing, 265
brittleness, 199
building blocks, in electronic systems,
    131
bulbs
    in parallel, 111
    in series, 111
buzzers, 122, 129

cams, 92, 93
cantilever, 62, 65
capacitors, 145
cast iron, 210
casting
    die, 216
    sand, 216
catalysts, 241
cells, in wood, 223
centre of gravity, 49, 50
centre punches, 257
centre squares, 257
chain and sprocket systems, 76
    applications of, 77
Chernobyl, 291
chipboard, 231
chips, 140
chisels
    bevel edged, 261
    firmer, 261
chlorofluorocarbon (CFC) gases, 255
circuit construction techniques, 156–7
circuit design information, 135
circuits, electrical
    automatic, 121, 124, 125, 153, 154
    bistable, 139
    integrated, 140
    latch, 125, 126
    light sensing, 134, 137, 143
    modelling of, 156
    moisture sensing, 129

parallel, 110, 111
reversing, motor, 120, 124
series, 110,111
temperature sensing, 135
time delay, 145–50
tone generator, 151
touch sensing, 138
weight sensing, 144
circuits, hydraulic
    brake, 190
    pump driven, 191
circuits, pneumatic
    air bleed, 182
    automatic control, 185, 186
    dual control, 173
    piston position sensing, 182, 183
    sequential control, 186, 187
    time delay, 184
closed loop systems, 133
CNC lathe, 217
cold heading, 214
colour, 26–31
    association, 31
    and emotions, 30
    harmony and contrast, 28, 29
    and reflection, 204
    and size, 30
    tone, 28
    and weight, 30
colour wheel, 26, 27
colours
    cold, 30
    primary, 26
    secondary, 27
    tertiary, 27
    warm, 30
comfort and safety, 38–44
communication, by visual elements, 44
compressed air, 169
compression forces, 53, 63
compression moulding, 250
compressors, air, 169
construction work, 15–17
control
    in electrics, 117
    in electronics, 127
control components, 132
control logic, 152
control systems, 109
    closed loop, 133
    open loop, 133
contruction kits, 268

conversion of timber, 225
copper, 212
crank mechanisms, 90
cross linking, 243
current, 110
    measurement of, 114
cylinders
    double acting, 175, 176
    single acting, 170, 172, 174

deal (pine), 226
density, 200
design exercise, 45
design limits, 12
design process, 6–19
    brief, 6, 10
    construction work, 15–17
    evaluating, 9, 17
    flow chart, 9
    modifications, 17
    planning 8, 14
    prototypes, 8, 15
    realisation, 8
    reports, 18, 19
    research, 7, 11
    situations, analysis of, 6, 10
    solutions, 7, 8, 13
    specifications, 7, 12
    testing, 9, 17
    timetable, 14
    working drawings, 8, 14
die casting, 216
diode
    light emitting (LED), 127
    silicon, 127, 128, 135
disc sanders (linishers), 236
dislocations, 207
dividers, 257
double glazing, 280
drilling, 16, 259
drills
    hand, 259
    multi-head, 218
    pillar, 16, 72
drive belts, 72
drop forging, 214
ductility, 199

efficiency, 284, 307
effort, 94
electric trains, 284
electrical power, 306
electricity bill, 307
electricity generating equipment, 289
    making of, 288

electromagnets, 203
electronic systems, 131
emergency STOP buttons, 16, 126
energy, 273
    measurement of, 302–3
    storage of, 300
    transfer of, 71, 302
energy forms
    chemical, 274
    electrical, 275; measurement of, 306
    heat, 274
    kinetic, 275; measurement of, 304
    light, 274
    potential, 275, 303; measurement of, 303
    sound, 275
energy management, 287
energy saving
    in the home, 278–81
    in industry, 285–7
    in transport, 283–4
energy sources
    coal, 291
    geothermal, 298
    nuclear, 275, 291
    oil, 291
    renewable, 292
    solar, 276–7, 292, 293
    tides, 296
    wave, 295
    wind, 294
energy use, 276
    in the home 278–81
    in industry, 285–7
    in transport, 283–4
environmental impact of energy sources
    coal, 291
    geothermal, 299
    nuclear, 291
    oil, 291
    tidal, 297
    wave, 295
    wind, 294
environmental issues, 11, 285, 291, 294, 295, 297, 299
ergonomics, 38–44
ethene, 240, 241
evaluating, 9, 17
extrusion
    metal, 215
    plastic, 249

fabrication techniques, 263
feedback
    electronic systems, 133
    nervous system, 39

files and their uses, 258
filing, 258
finishing
    of metals, 270
    of plastics, 272
    of wood, 271
finishing materials, 236, 270–2
555 timer, 149
flow chart, for design process, 9
flow regulator, 176, 178, 179
folding bars, 259
force, transmission of, 100
forces
    bending, 53
    compression, 53, 63
    dynamic, 47
    in frame structures, 53
    in pneumatics, 174
    shear, 53
    static, 47
    tension, 53, 63
    torsion, 53, 198
forging, 214
form, 22, 43
fractures
    brittle, 199
    ductile, 199
frame structures
    forces in, 53
    non-rigid, 48
    rigid, 48
friction, 284, 307
fuel cells, 300
fuels, 290, 291
fulcrum, 94
function, 21

gear systems, 79
gear train
    compound, 80
    simple, 79
gears
    applications of, 82
    idler, 81
    spur, 79
geothermal power, 298
glass reinforced plastic (GRP), 248
global warming, 291
glue gun, 264
gluing
    of metal, 267
    of plastic, 267
    of wood, 264
golden mean, 33
greenhouse effect, 291
gusset plates, 48

hacksaws, 91, 259
hardboard, 232
hardness, 200
hardwoods, 222, 228–9
health and safety, 39
heartwood, 223
heat
    absorption, 205
    radiation 205
heat sink, 157
human body
    in balance, 42
    dimensions, 41
    fatigue, 42
    movement, 41, 42
    proportion, 40, 41
hydraulic systems, pump driven, 190, 191
hydraulics, 188–90
hydroelectric power, 290

impact extrusion, 215
industrial manufacturing
    with metals, 213
    with plastic, 249
    with wood, 233
information, where to obtain it, 12
injection moulding, 250
input components, 132
insulation
    cavity wall, 280
    roof, 279
    of tank, 281
integrated circuits, 140
interface, 135
iron, 207
    cast, 210

jacks
    hydraulic, 189
    scissor, 71
joint cutting machinery, 235
joints
    bridle, 263
    butt, 263
    comb, 263
    dovetail, 235, 263
    halving, 263
    housing, 263
    lap, 263
    in metal, 265, 267
    mitre, 263
    mortice and tenon, 235, 263
    moveable, 269
    in plastic, 267
    temporary, 268

in wood, 263, 264
joules, 273, 302

lacquer, 270
laminated forms, 230
latching relay, 125, 126
lathework, 217
levers, 94
    classes of, 96
    linkages, 97, 98
    mechanical advantage of, 95, 96
light emitting diode (LED), 127
lines, 22
linkages, 97, 98
load, 94
logic, 152
lubrication, 307

machines, 71
machining
    drilling, 16, 218, 259
    grinding, 218
    lathework, 217
    milling, 218
magnetism, 203
mahogany, 229
mallets, 259, 261
marking gauge, 256
marking out, 256–7
mass, 302
materials, 196
    manufacturing with, *see* industrial
        manufacturing
    metals, 206–12
    plastics, 240–8
    properties of, 198–205
    selecting, 196, 197
    wood, 222–32
    working with, at school, 256–72
matrix board, 156
mechanical advantage, of levers, 95, 96
mechanical power, measurement of, 302
mechanisms, 70
melamine formaldehyde, 248
metals
    ferrous, 206–10
    non-ferrous, 206, 211, 212
microswitches, 117, 118, 119, 121
    cam operated, 93
modelling of circuits, 156
molecules, 240, 241
moments
    bending, 62
    principle of, 59, 60
monomers, 241
motifs, 35

motion
    linear, 86, 88
    reciprocating, 90
    rotary, 72
motors, electric, control of, 118, 120,
        124, 125
moulding
    compression, 251
    extrusion, 249
    extrusion blow, 249
    injection, 250
moulding machines (wood), 234
mouldings, 234
movement, of human body, 41

n-type semiconductor, 127
nails, 264
National Curriculum Attainment Targets,
        4, 5, 18, 19
neutral axis, 57
newtons, 50, 302
NOT gate, 155
nylon, 246

oak, 229
obsolescence, inbuilt, 285
odd-leg callipers, 256
Ohm's law, 113, 114, 115
ohms, 111
open loop systems, 133
operational amplifier, 140
optical properties
    reflection, 204
    transparency, 204
OR gate, 152
oscillating water column, 295
output components, 132

p-type semiconductor, 127
paint, 270, 271
parana pine, 227
particle board, 231
patterns, 35, 36
pedestal grinder, 218
perspex, 245
phenol formaldehyde, 247
pine, 226
pinion, 79
pistons, in pneumatics
    position sensor, 182–3
    speed control, 177–8
pitch, of thread, 88
planes
    jack, 260
    smoothing, 260
planing, 260

planing machines, 233
planning, 8, 14
plasticisers, 245
plastics, 240
    properties, 242, 243
    structure, 240–1
plywood, 230, 231
polyester resin, 248
polymerization
    addition, 242
    condensation, 242
polymers, 241
polypropylene, 244
polystyrene, 246
polythene, 240, 241
    high density, 243
    low density, 244
polyvinyl chloride (PVC), 245
position sensor, piston, 182–3
potential divider, 127, 128, 141
power stations, 289
    hydroelectric, 290
power supply, dual rail, 141
press forming, 213
pressure, 174
printed circuit board (PCB), 156, 157
proportion, 32, 33
prototypes, 8, 15
pulley systems, 72
    applications of, 72, 73, 75
    stepped cone, 75

questionnaire, 10, 18, 312

rack and pinion, 86
    applications of, 87
rainforests, 239
ram mechanism, 93
receivers, 169
redundant members, 58
relay, 121, 122, 123
    connections, 124
    latch, 125, 126
    use in motor control, 124
reports, how to present them, 18
research, 7, 11
reservoir
    air, 184
    water, 301
resistance, 111, 202
    measurement of, 114
resistor colour code, 115
resistors
    in series and parallel, 111, 112
    light dependent (LDR), 112, 132, 134
    temperature dependent (thermistors),

113, 132
    variable, 112, 132
reversing circuits, motor, 120, 121, 124,
    125, 160, 165
rigidity, 48
riveting, 266, 267
rivets, 266
robots, 109
roll forming, 215
rotary to linear motion
    cam and follower, 92
    crank and slider, 90
    rack and pinion, 86
    screw and nut, 88
routing, 235

safety
    with buffing machines, 270
    when chiselling, 261
    when drilling, 16, 259
    emergency STOP buttons, 16, 126
    ergonomic, 39, 43
    with pneumatics, 180
    when shearing metal, 259
    when welding, 266
    in workshops, 15
safety guards, 119, 172
Salter's duck, 295
sand casting, 216
sanding, 236, 271
sapele, 229
sapwood, 223
sawing
    industrial, 233
    of metal, 258
    of plastic, 262
    of wood, 260
saws, 258, 260, 262
    band, 233
    circular, 233
    coping, 260
    hand, 260
    tenon, 260
    see also hacksaws
screw mechanisms, 88
    applications of, 89
screws, 264
scribers, 256
seasoning of timber, 225
semiconductors, 127, 129
sensing circuits
    light, 134, 137, 143, 164
    moisture, 129–30
    temperature, 135
    touch, 138
sensors, 112, 113

see also sensing circuits
sequential control, in pneumatics, 186–7
sewing machines, 91
shape, 22, 43
shaping
    of metals, 258
    of plastics, 262
    of wood, 260
shear forces, 53
shell structures, 47
silver soldering, 265
skeleton, human, 39
social impact of energy sources
    coal, 291
    geothermal, 299
    nuclear, 291
    oil, 291
    tidal, 297
    wave, 295
    wind, 294
social issues, 11, 285, 291, 294, 295, 297,
    299
softwoods, 222, 226–7
solar cells, 292
solar energy, 292
solar furnace, 293
solar panels, 293
solar power, 292, 293
soldering
    electrical, 157
    silver, 265
    soft, 265
solenoids, 203
sprockets, 76
spruce, 227
square thread, 88
stability, 49
steel
    high carbon, 209
    medium carbon, 208
    mild, 207
    stainless, 209
stencils, 35
stiffness, 199
strength
    compressive, 198, 224
    tensile, 198, 224
strip board, 156
structural analysis, 54
structural failure, 47
structural sections, 56
structural stability, 49
structures, frame
    forces in, 53
    non-rigid, 48
    rigid, 48

structures, shell, 47
struts, 54
surface finishes
    on metal, 270
    on wood, 271
surface grinders, 218
switches
    limit, 120, 121
    micro, 117
    push button, 117
    reed, 117
    rotary, 117
    slide, 117
    toggle, 117
symmetry, 33
systems
    electrical, 108–58
    mechanical, 70–101
    pneumatic, 168–91
systems control, 131–33

tactile qualities, 25
templates, 257
tension forces, 53, 63
tessellations, 35
testing, 9, 17
texture, 25
thermal conductivity, 201
thermal expansion, 201
thermistors, 113, 132
thermoplastics, 242, 243–6
thermosetting plastics, 242, 243, 247–8,
    251
thermostatic valves, 282
thermostats, 109
thread rolling, 215
threads, screw, 88
tidal barrage, 296
tidal power, 296
ties, 54
timber
    conversion, 225
    seasoning, 225
time constant, 148
time delays
    in electronics, 145–51
    in pneumatics, 184
timer 555
    astable operation, 151
    monostable operation, 149
timing circuits, in electronics, 145–50
tin snips, 259
tone generator, 151
torque, 72, 100
torque conversion, 100, 101
torsion forces, 53, 198

toughness, 200
transistors, 129–30, 134–6
    current gain, 136
    tester, 159
trees
    annual rings, 223
    cambium layer, 223
    coniferous, 222
    deciduous, 222
triangulation, 48
tribology, 307
truth tables, 153, 154, 155
try squares, 256

uPVC, 255
urea formaldehyde, 247

V thread, 88
vacuum forming, 252, 262
valves, pneumatic
    air operated, 180–1
    diaphragm operated, 181
    five port, 176–7
    pilot, 180
    shuttle, 173
    solenoid operated, 193
    three port, 170–1
varnish, 271
vehicles, electric, 284
velocity ratio
    chain and sprocket systems, 78
    gear systems, 79, 80
    levers, 94
    pulley systems, 74
    rack and pinion, 86
veneer, 230
vices
    hand, 259
    machine, 259
visual balance
    asymmetrical, 33
    radial, 34
    symmetrical, 33
visual contrast, 28, 34
visual design
    elements of, 22
    principles of, 32
visual harmony, 28, 34
voltage, 110
    measurement of, 114
voltmeters, 114
volts, 110

washing machines, 109
watts, 306
wave power, 295

weather cycle, 277
weight, 50, 302
welding
    arc, 266
    gas, 266
whitewood, 227
wind power, 294
wire
    connecting, 111
    resistance, 111
wood
    effects of water content on, 225
    properties, 223
    strength, 224
    structure, 223
work, 302
work hardening, 208
working drawings, 8, 14
worm and wormwheel, 84
    applications of, 85
    gear ratio, 84

Acknowledgements

Figures (by page)

4 (tractor) Massey Ferguson; (packaging) Shell; (truck) Sally & Richard Greenhill; (operating theatre) Malcolm Fielding, The BOC Group plc / Science Photo Library; **5** (car bodies) Science Photo Library; (power station) National Power; (jet) Austin J. Brown / APL; (records department) Hertfordshire Constabulary; **20** (pop concert) Elliot Landy / Redferns; (woodland) Spectrum Colour Library; (Asian family, children playing) Sally & Richard Greenhill; (restaurant) ZEFA; (western family) J. Bradbury / Spectrum Colour Library; **21** (garden) Spectrum Colour Library; (students) ZEFA Picture Library (UK) Ltd; **24** (guitar, relaxer bed, greenhouse, jack, cleaner) Littlewoods Organisation plc; (clock radio) Sony UK; (Concorde) ZEFA; **25** British Leather Confederation; **26** ICI Dulux; **29** (lawn edger, watch, kettle) Littlewoods Organisation plc; (bathroom) Crown Paints; **30** Crown Paints; **32** Maclaren; **33** (pool) W. F. Davidson / ZEFA; (Taj Mahal) W. R. Davis / Spectrum Colour Library; **34** (flower) J. Pfaff / ZEFA; (light fitting, lamp, table) Littlewoods Organisation plc; **35** (sweater) Patons & Baldwins Ltd; **36** (shoe, rack) Littlewoods Organisation plc; **37** (design exhibit) Design Council; (students) Sally & Richard Greenhill; (Taj Mahal) S. Martin / ZEFA; **38** (multiflash photo, toddler, lady on ladder) Littlewoods Organisation plc; (in kitchen) Sally & Richard Greenhill; (old lady in chair) Richard Nichalas / Science Photo Library; (man with machine) Sheila Terry / Science Photo Library; **39** (rucksack, skateboard, lady with TV) Littlewoods Organisation plc; **42** (dashboard) Ford; (ticket barriers) ZEFA Picture Library UK; (surfboard) Jon Nicholson / Allsport; **43** (mixer, camera) Littlewoods Organisation plc; (car seat) Volvo Car Corporation, Sweden; **44** (frying pan) Littlewoods Organisation plc; (Heathrow) W. R. Davis / Spectrum Colour Library; **46** (shopping centre) British Gas West Midlands; (jet) Austin J. Brown / APL; (Forth bridges) Scottish Tourist Board; **47** (Lloyd's building) Janet Gill; **59** Spectrum Colour Library; **67** Novosti / Frank Spooner Pictures; **70** (crane) Forestry Commission; (water wheel) Barnaby's Picture Library; (aerogenerator) North of Scotland Electricity Board / Charles Tait Photographic; (derrick) British Petroleum; (mixer & mechanism) LEGO UK Ltd; (tractor) Massey Ferguson; **71** (forklift) Sanderson (Forklifts); **73** (washing machine) LEGO UK Ltd; (car engine) Practical Motorist; **76** Havlicek / ZEFA; **92** (car engine) Ford; **108** (payphones) Mercury Communications; (aircraft exterior & autopilot) Austin J. Brown / APL; (vending machine interior & exterior) Sankey Vending; **109** (robots) Philippe Plailly / Science Photo Library; **117, 121, 124, 127** (diodes) Graham Portlock; **139** Allsport / Tony Duffy; **141, 145, 149, 153** Graham Portlock; **168** (bus) London Transport Museum; (tyre bay) Kwik-Fit; (compressor) Atlas Copco; **172, 173, 175, 178, 180** Parker Hannifin; **190** (undercarriage) Austin J. Brown / APL; **203** The Natural History Museum, London; **206** Australian Overseas Information Service, London; **218** Fredk. Pollard & Co. Ltd; **222** Barnaby's Picture Library; **223** Biophoto Associates; **225** Cubbage Bollmann Ltd; **226, 227, 228** (ash) Building Research Establishment; **228** (beech), **229** Timber Research & Development Association; **239** Hutchison Library; **240** ICI; **262** C. R. Clarke; **268** (Lego) James Galt & Co. Ltd; (Fisher technic) Economatics Education; (Meccano) Atlascraft; **274** (fireworks) ZEFA; (food) Graham Portlock; (car) Shell; **275** (pop singer) Frank Spooner Pictures; (clock) Carle Triberg / Hubert Herr GmbH; (explosion) DUP Photri / ZEFA; **278** (weightlifter) Gamma / Frank Spooner Pictures; (foods) Ian Cook; **280** ICI Polyurethanes; **281** Spectrum Colour Library; **282** (washing machine) Hoover plc; (radiator valve) Drayton; **283** G. Mabbs / ZEFA; **284** (train) British Rail; (Rover) Austin Rover; **285** (foundry) British Steel; (shopping centre) Spectrum Colour Library; **289** PowerGen; **292** Tom McHugh / Science Photo Library; **293** Alex Bartel / Science Photo Library; **294** North of Scotland Electricity Board / Charles Tait Photographic; **296** Spectrum Colour Library; **299** Simon Fraser / Science Photo Library; **301** National Grid Company; **305** Marcus Taylor Offshore Photography.